800
CLASSIC ORNAMENTS
AND
DESIGNS

Edited by
Ernst Günther

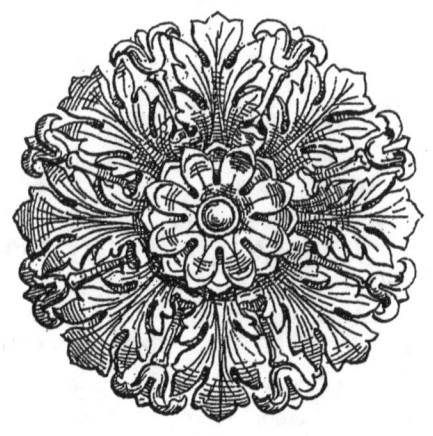

DOVER PUBLICATIONS, INC.
Mineola, New York

Copyright

Copyright © 1999 by Dover Publications, Inc.
All rights reserved.

Bibliographical Note

This Dover edition, first published in 1999, contains all of the plates in *Kleines Ornamenten-buch . . . ,* published by Lissa u. Gnesen, ca. 1843.

DOVER *Pictorial Archive* SERIES

Library of Congress Cataloging-in-Publication Data

Kleines Ornamentenbuch. English.
   800 classic ornaments and designs / edited by Ernst Gunther.
       p.   cm. — (Dover pictorial archive series)
   "Dover edition first published in 1999, contains all of the plates in Kleines Ornamentenbuch . . . published by Lissa u. Gnesen, ca. 1843"—T.p. verso.
   ISBN-13: 978-0-486-40261-1 (pbk.)
   ISBN-10: 0-486-40261-4 (pbk.)
   1. Decoration and ornament. I. Gunther, Ernst, fl. 1843–1874.   II. Title.   III. Title: Eight hundred classic ornaments and designs   IV. Series.
   NK1530.K5713   1999
   745.4—dc21
                                                                                  98–44432
                                                                                  CIP

www.doverpublications.com

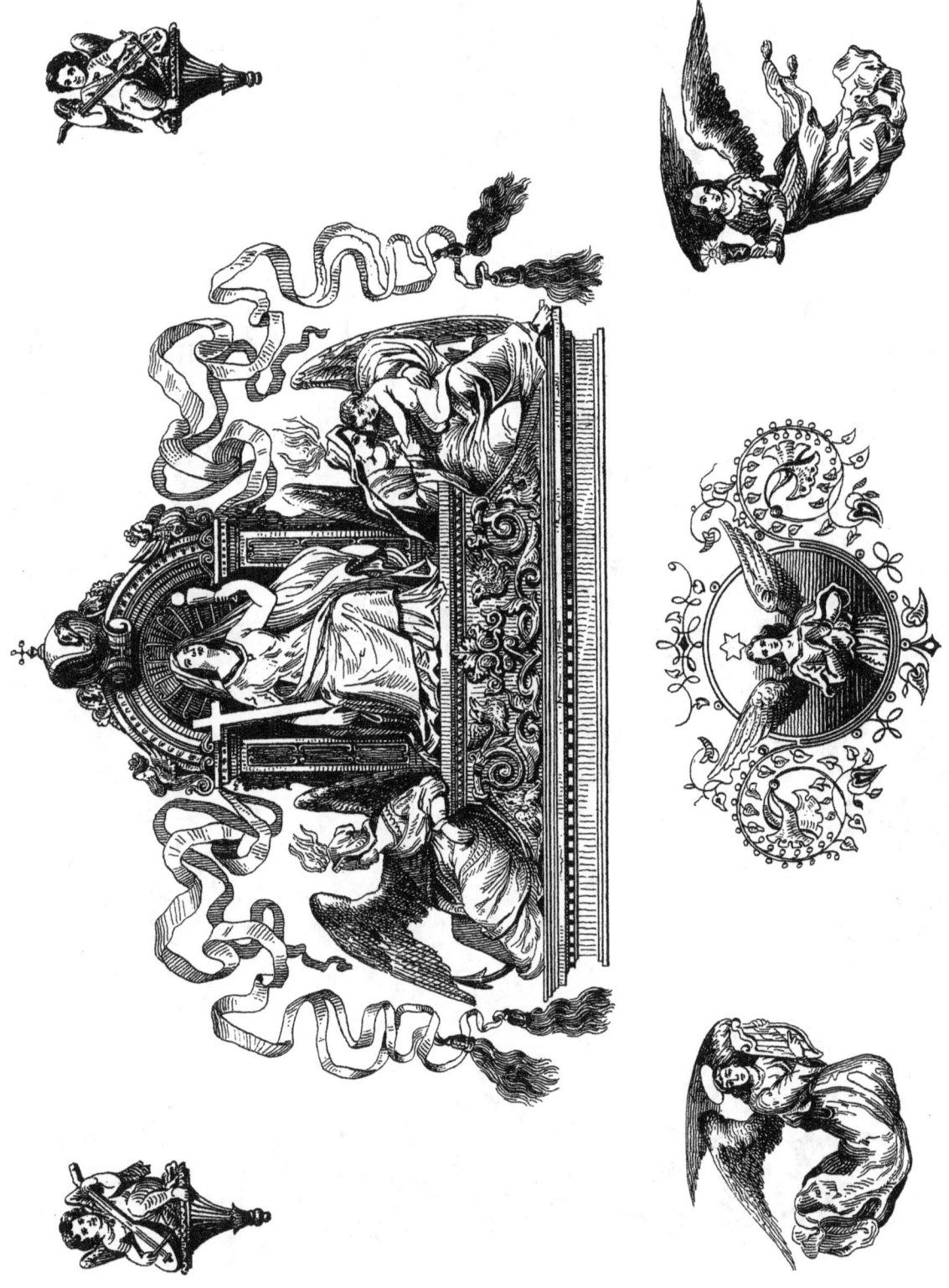

1

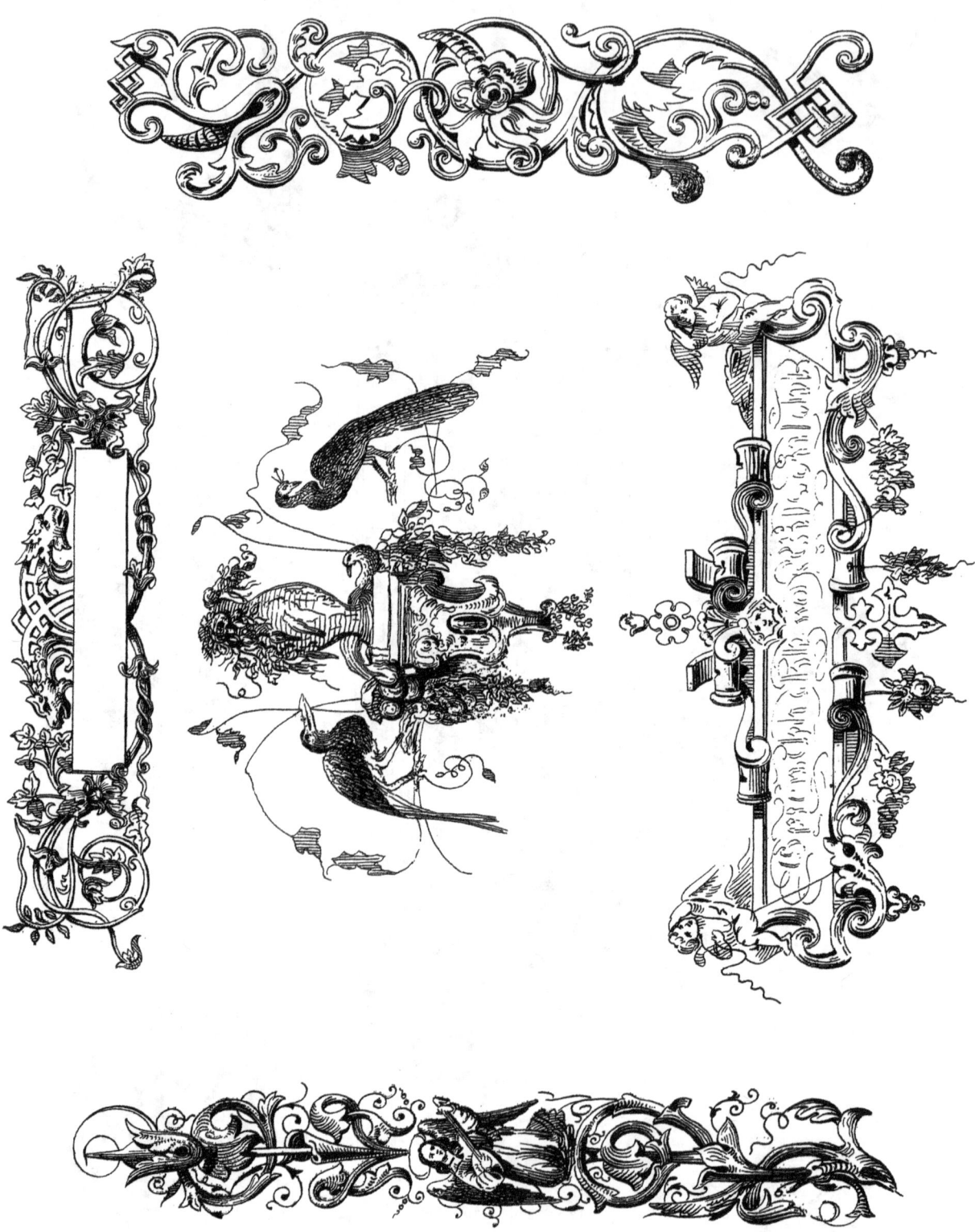

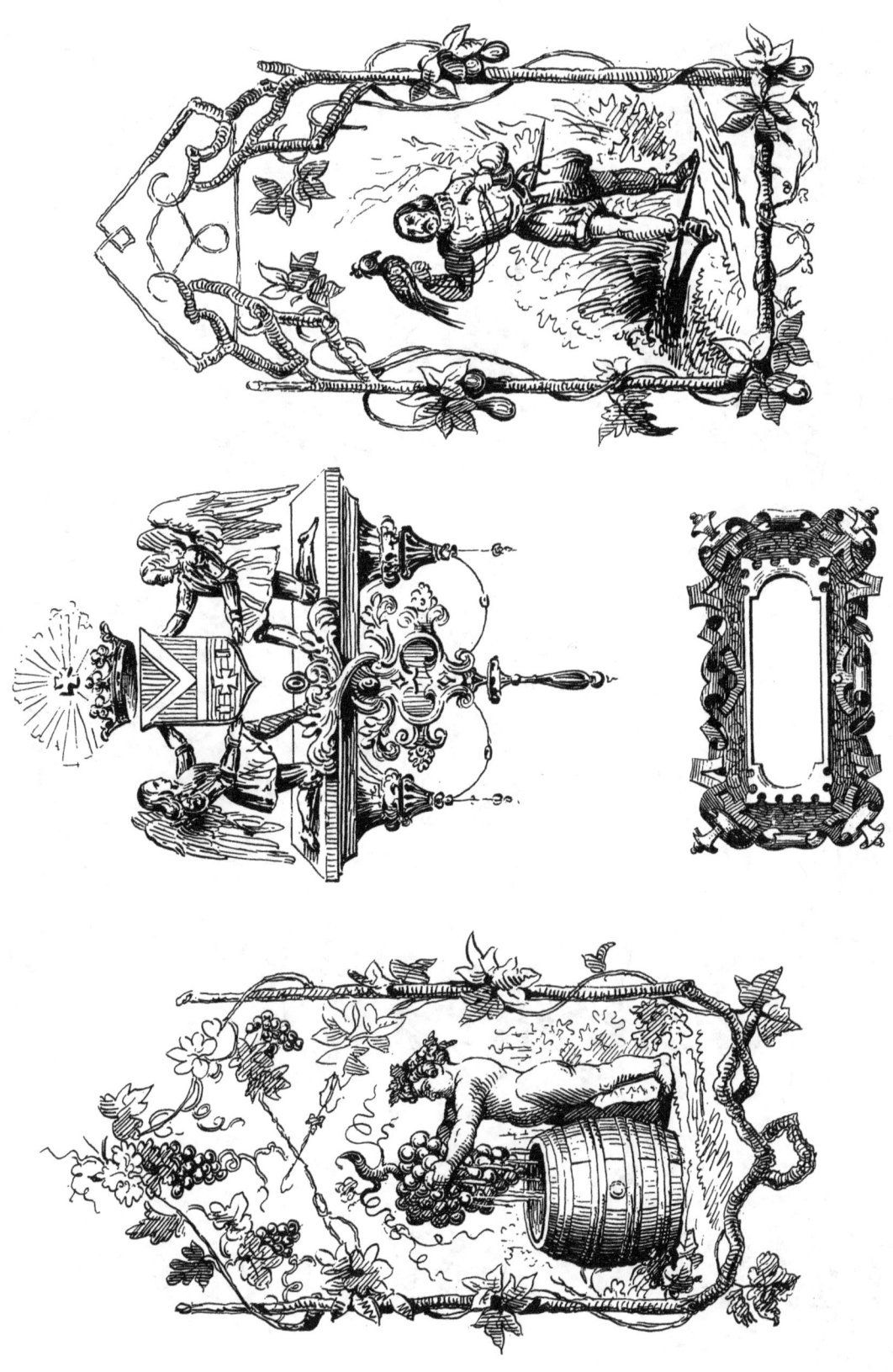

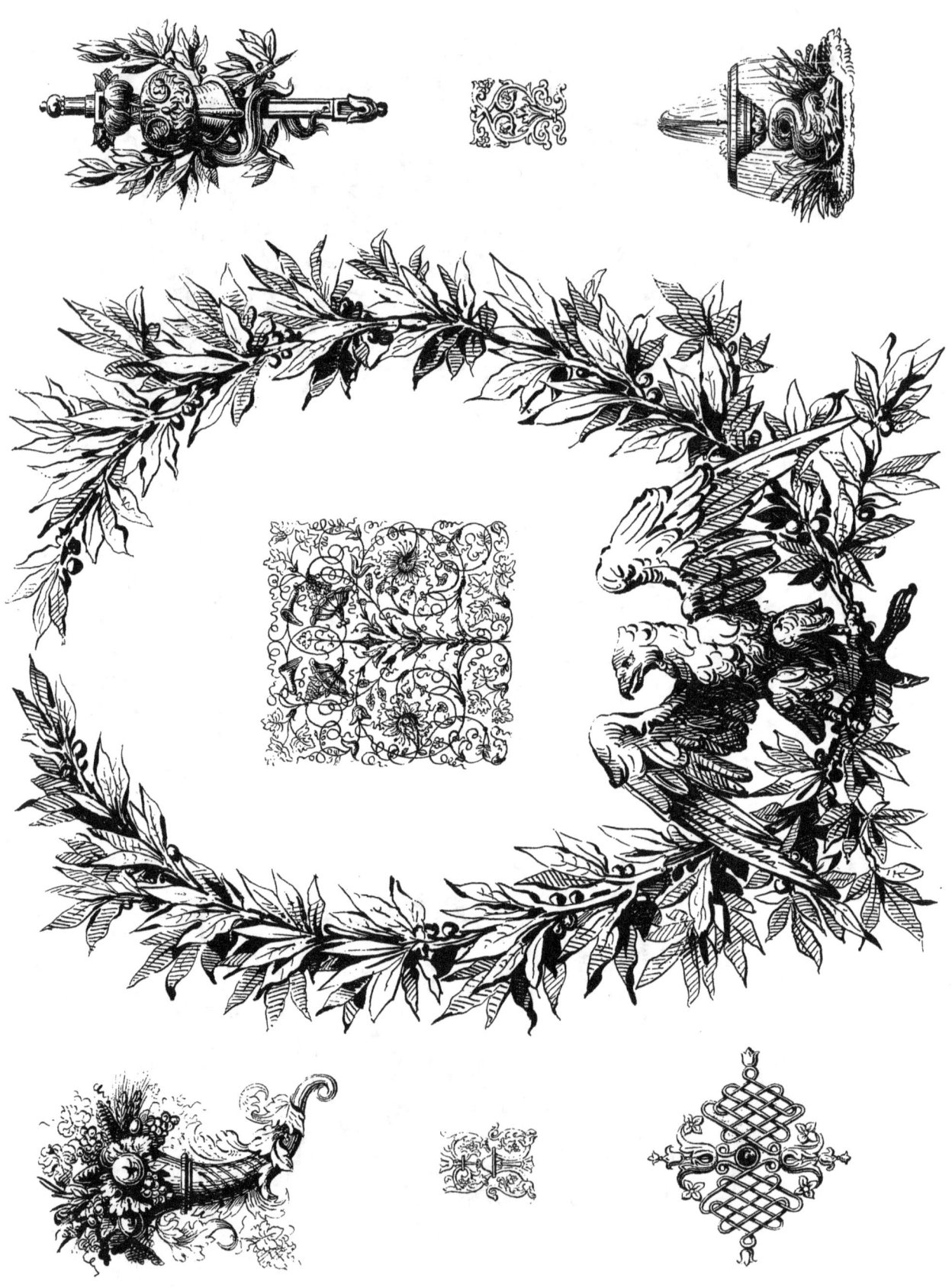

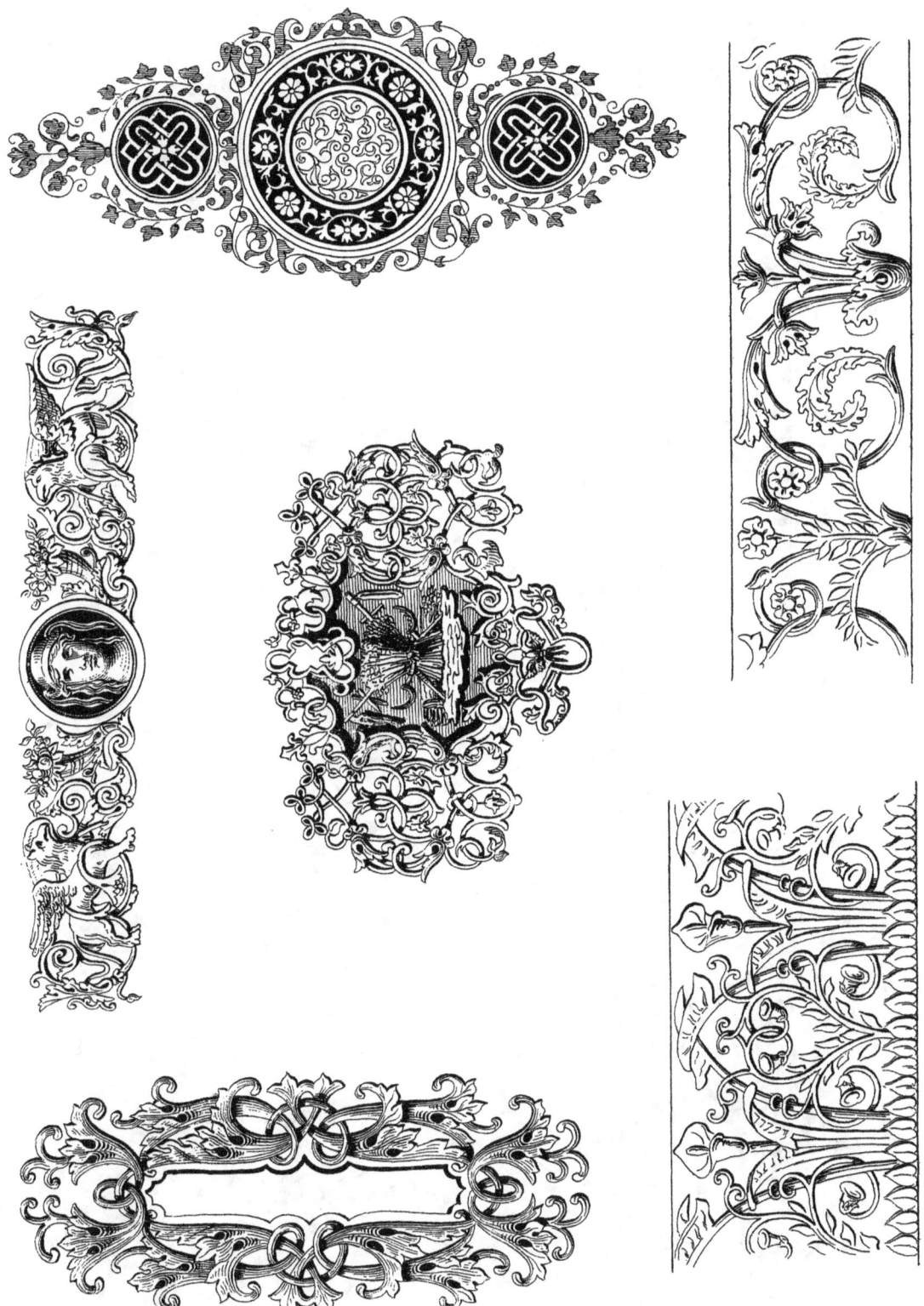

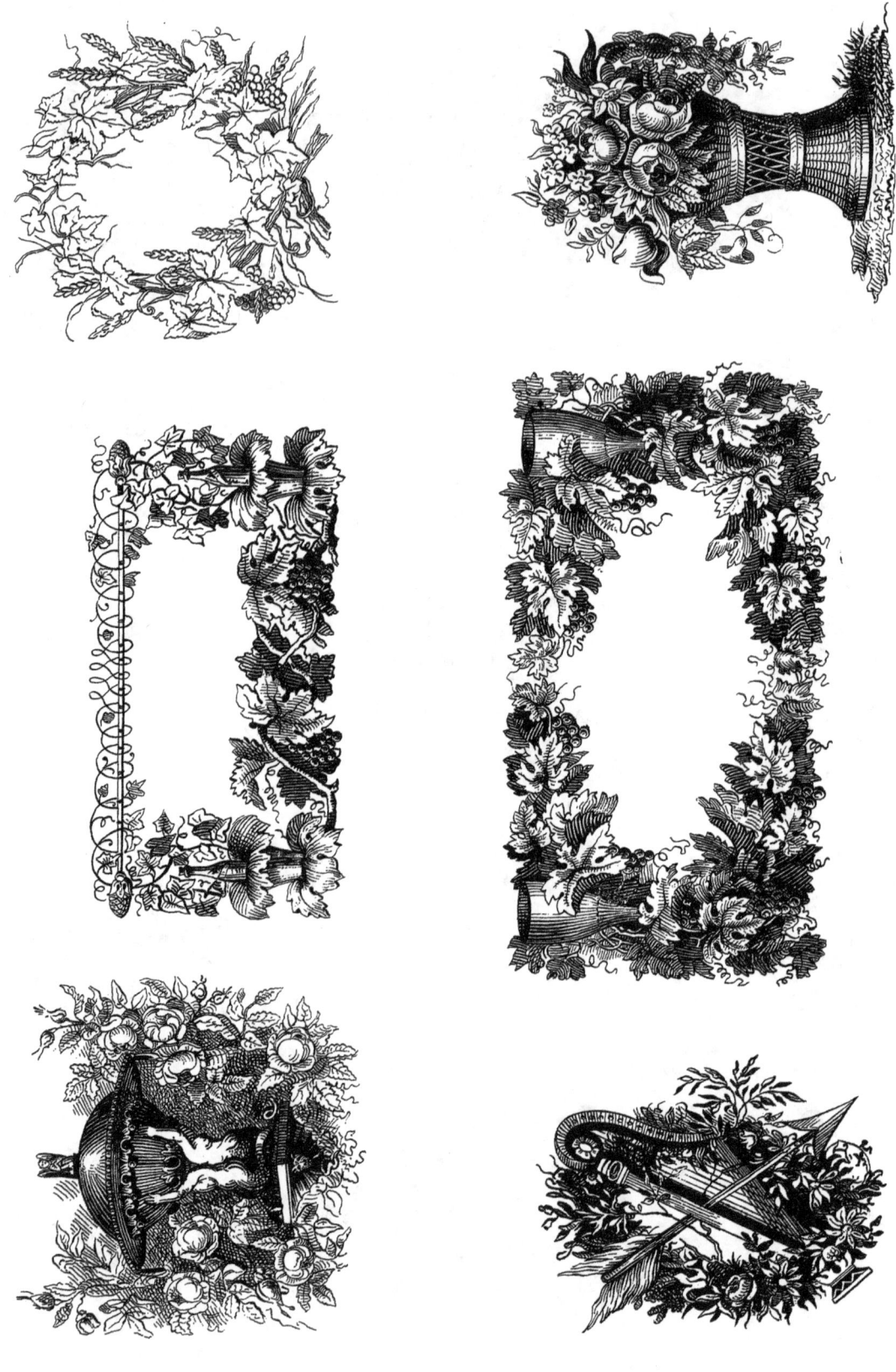

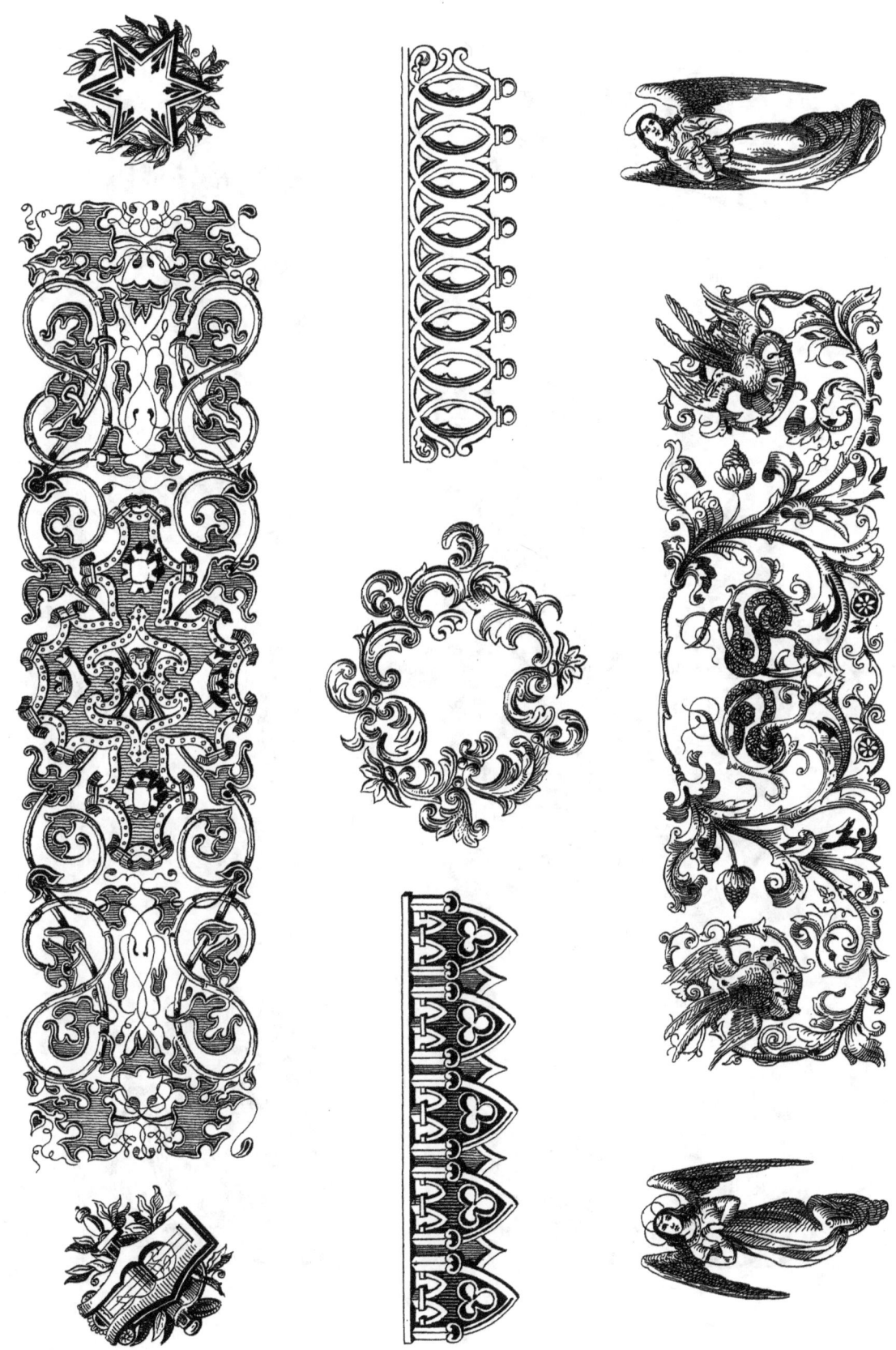

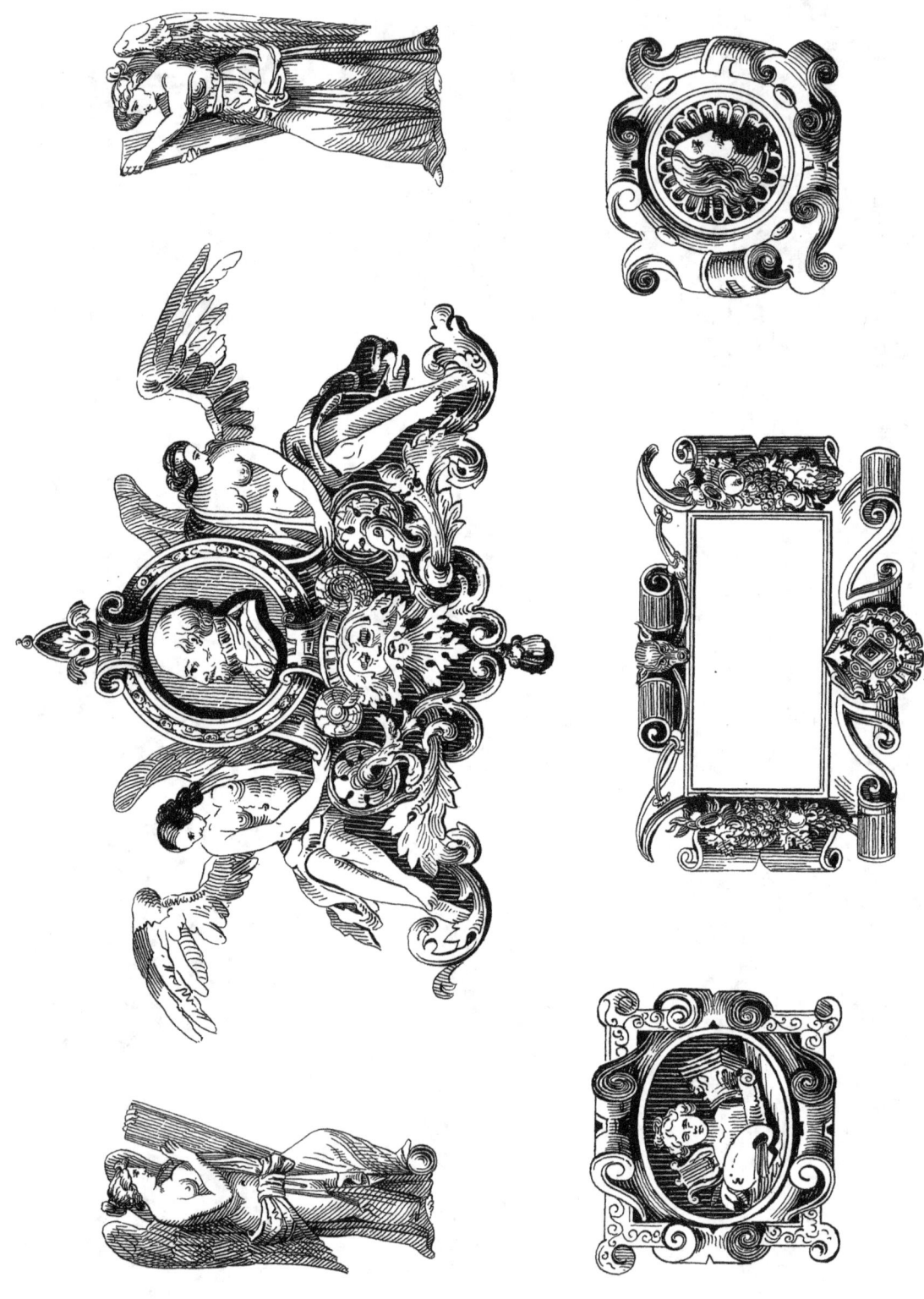

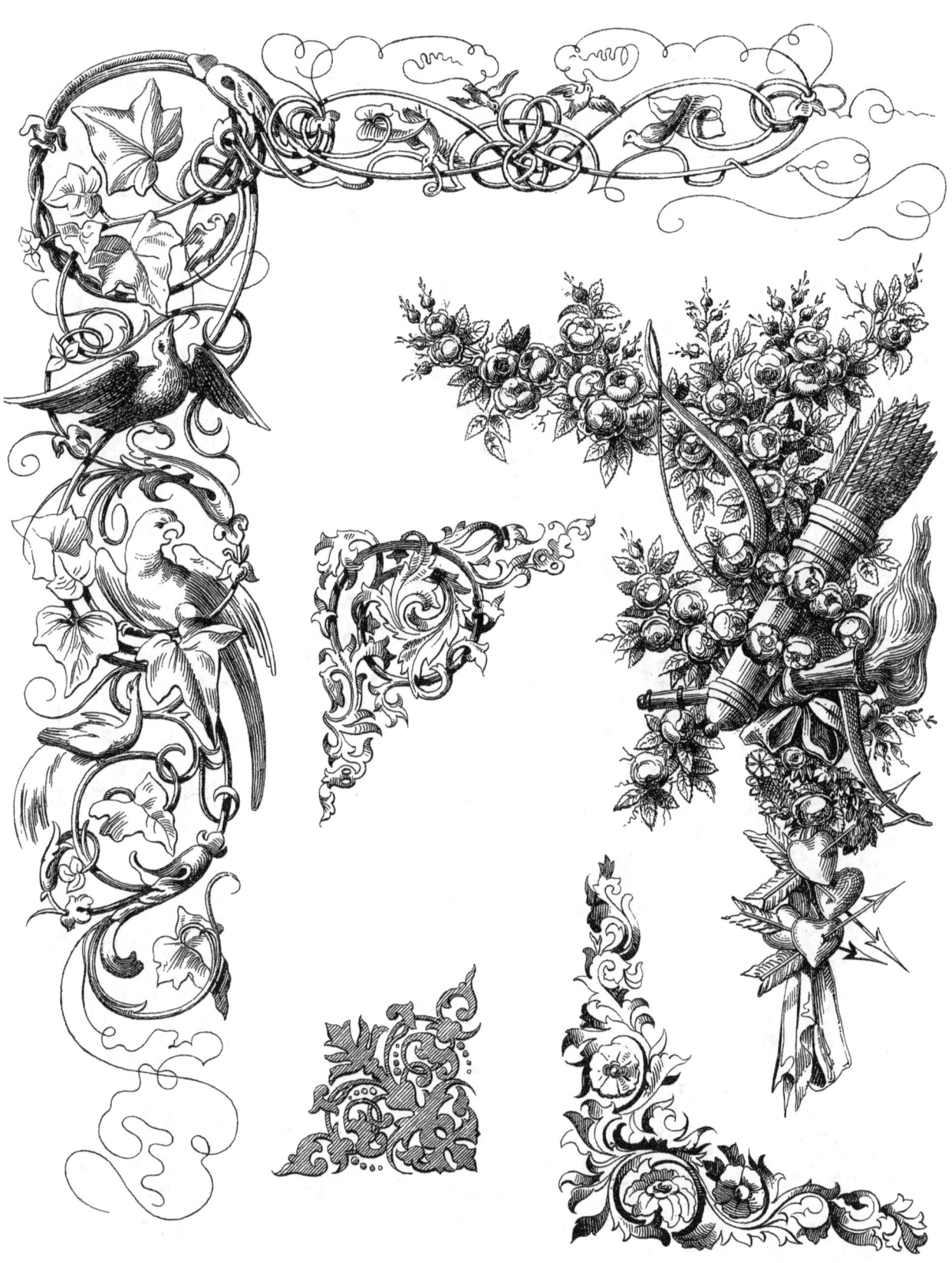

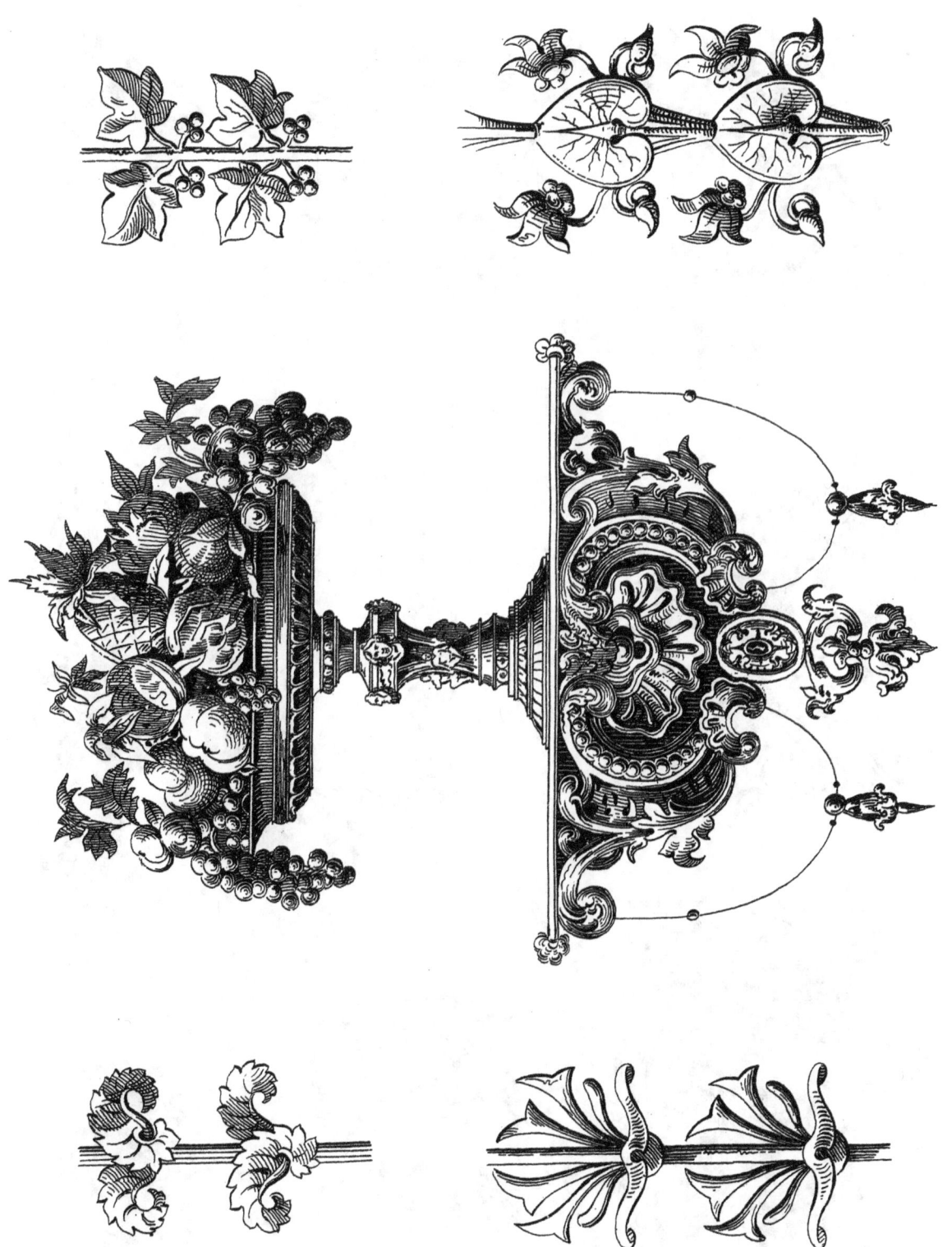

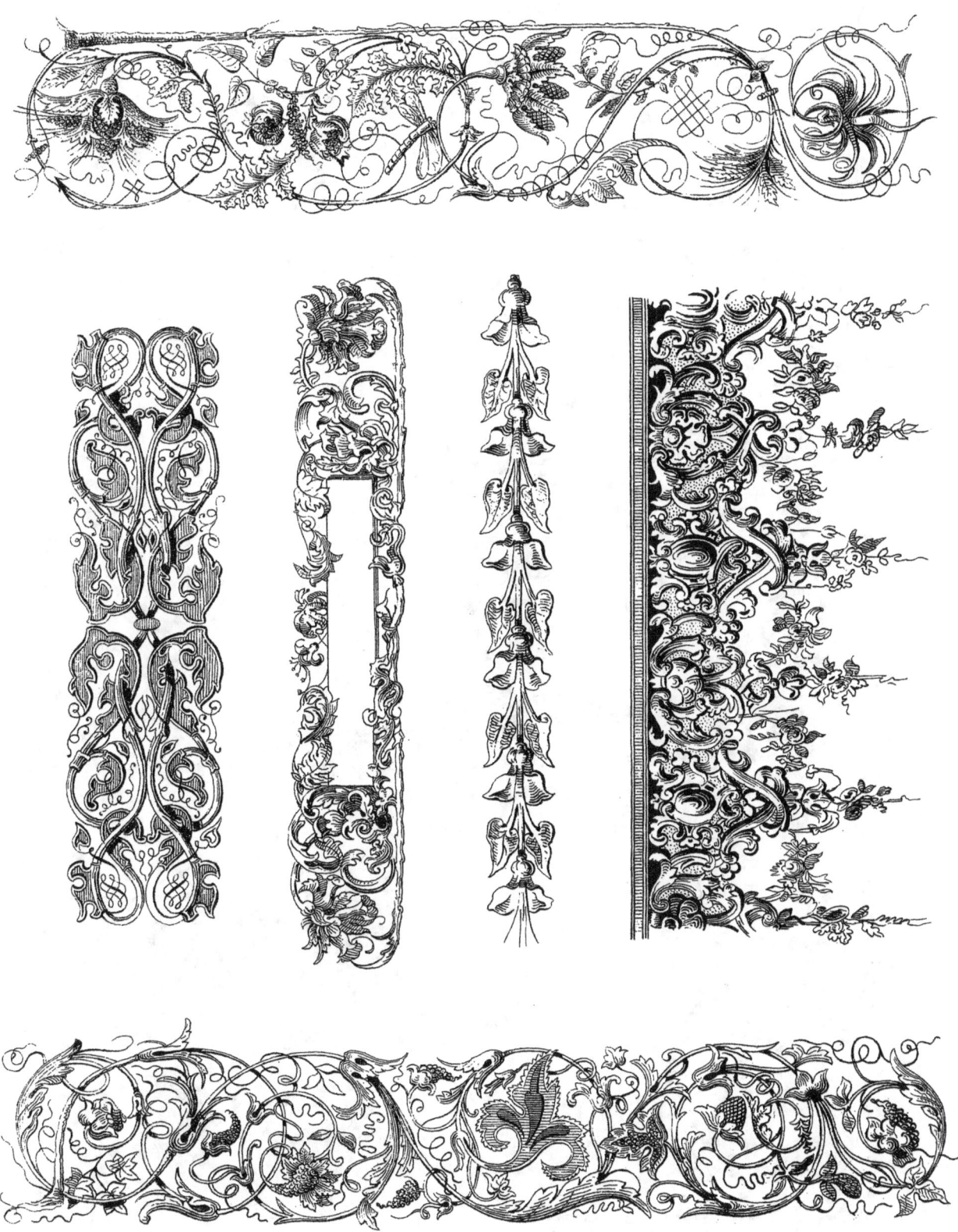

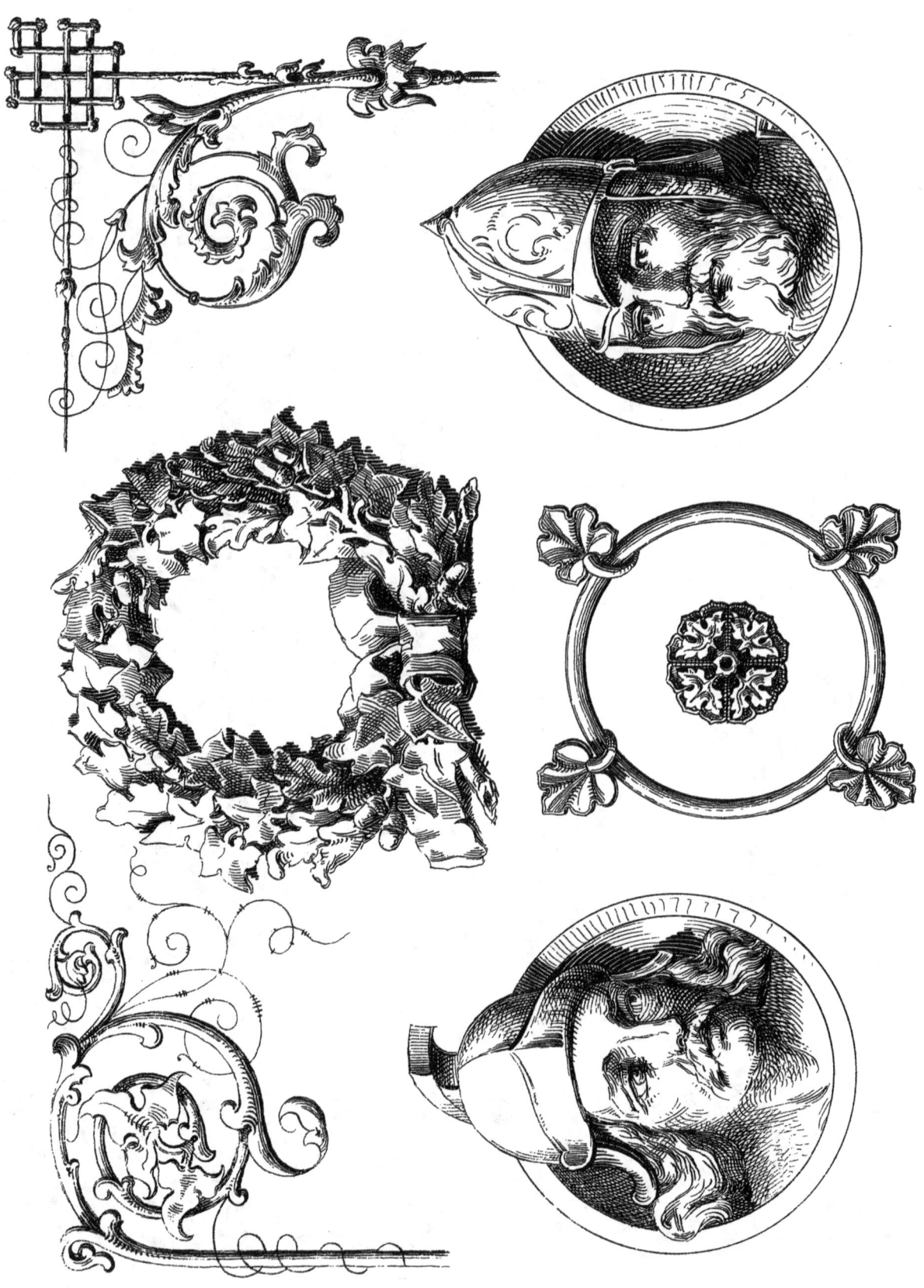

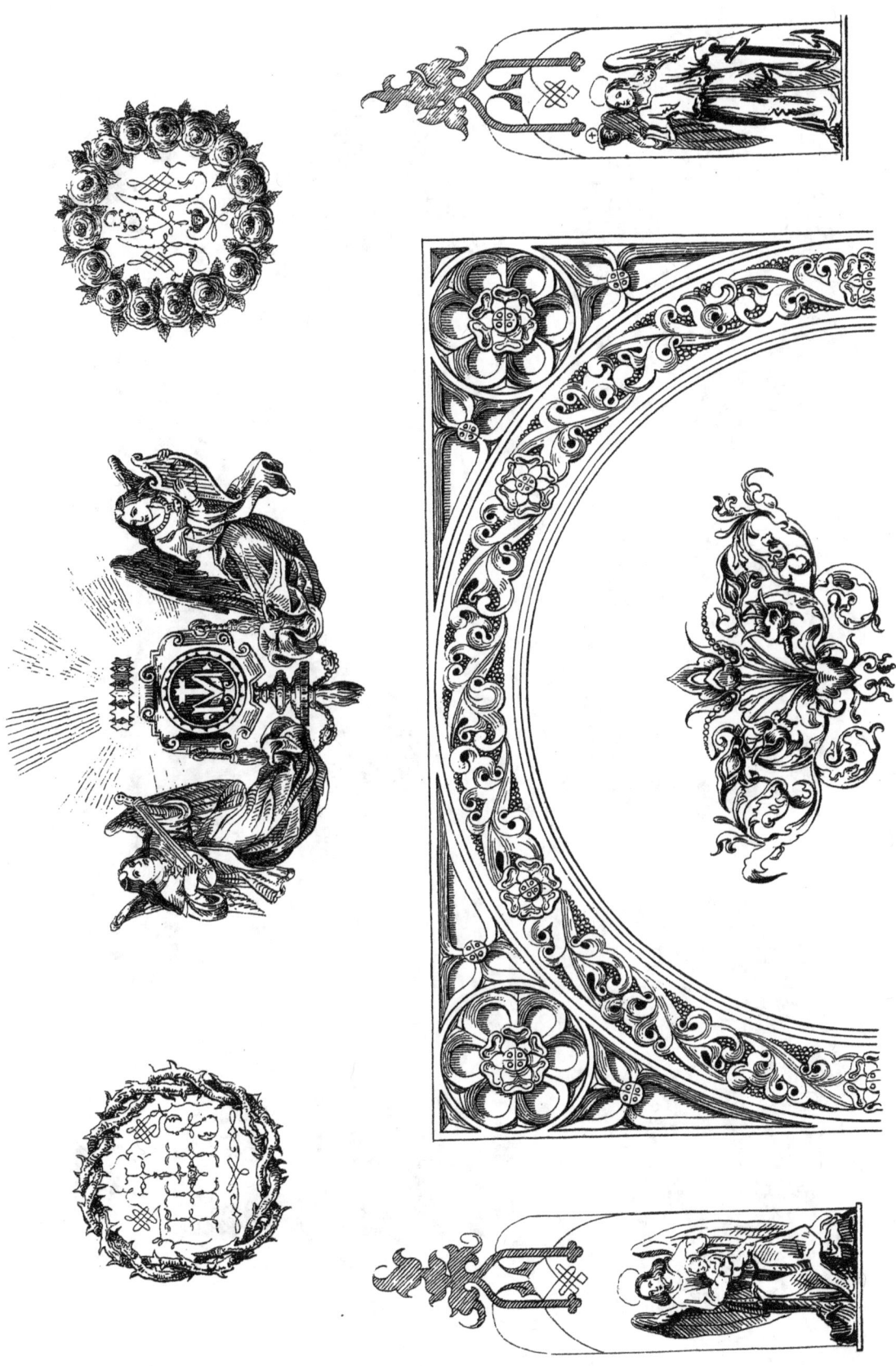

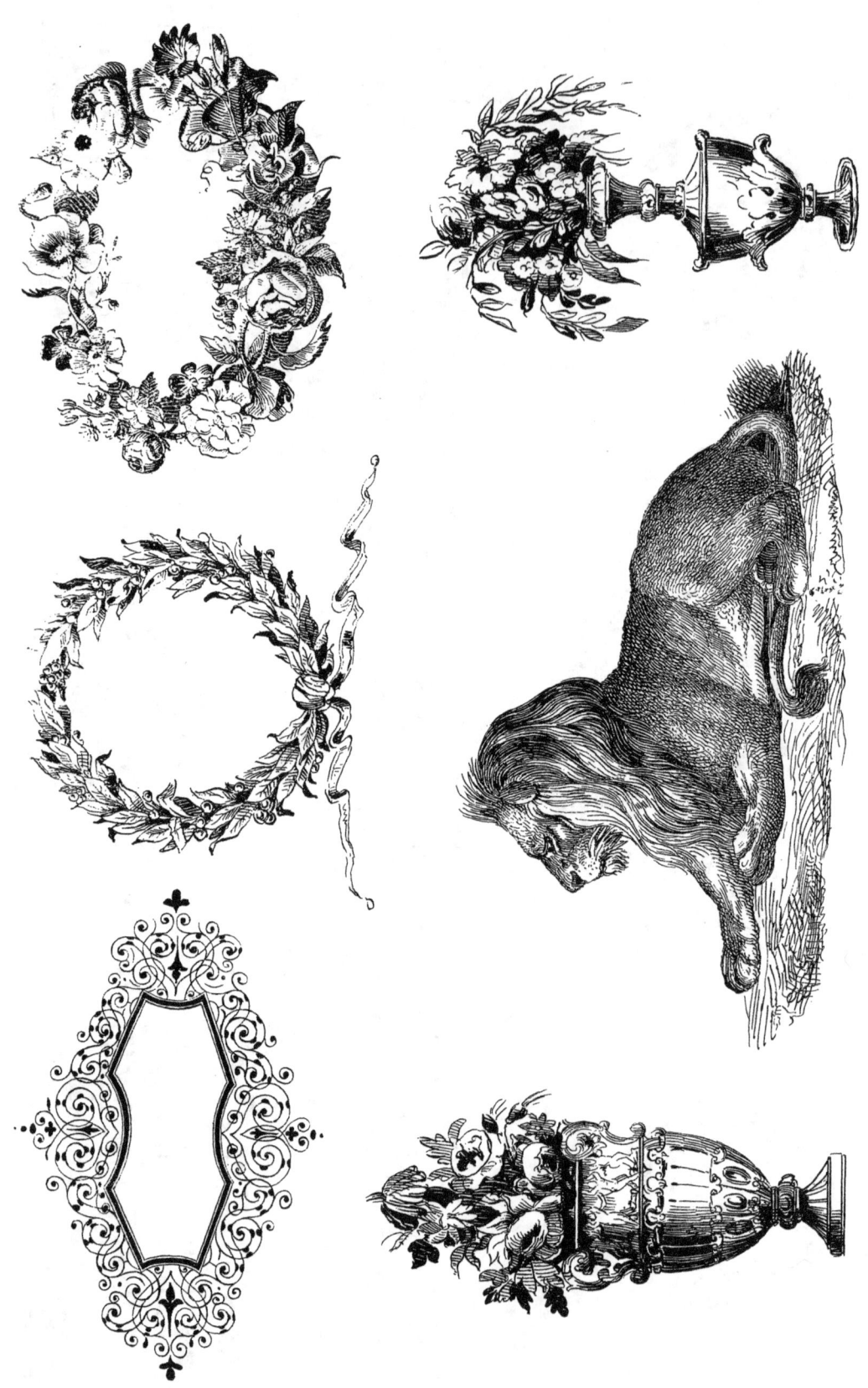

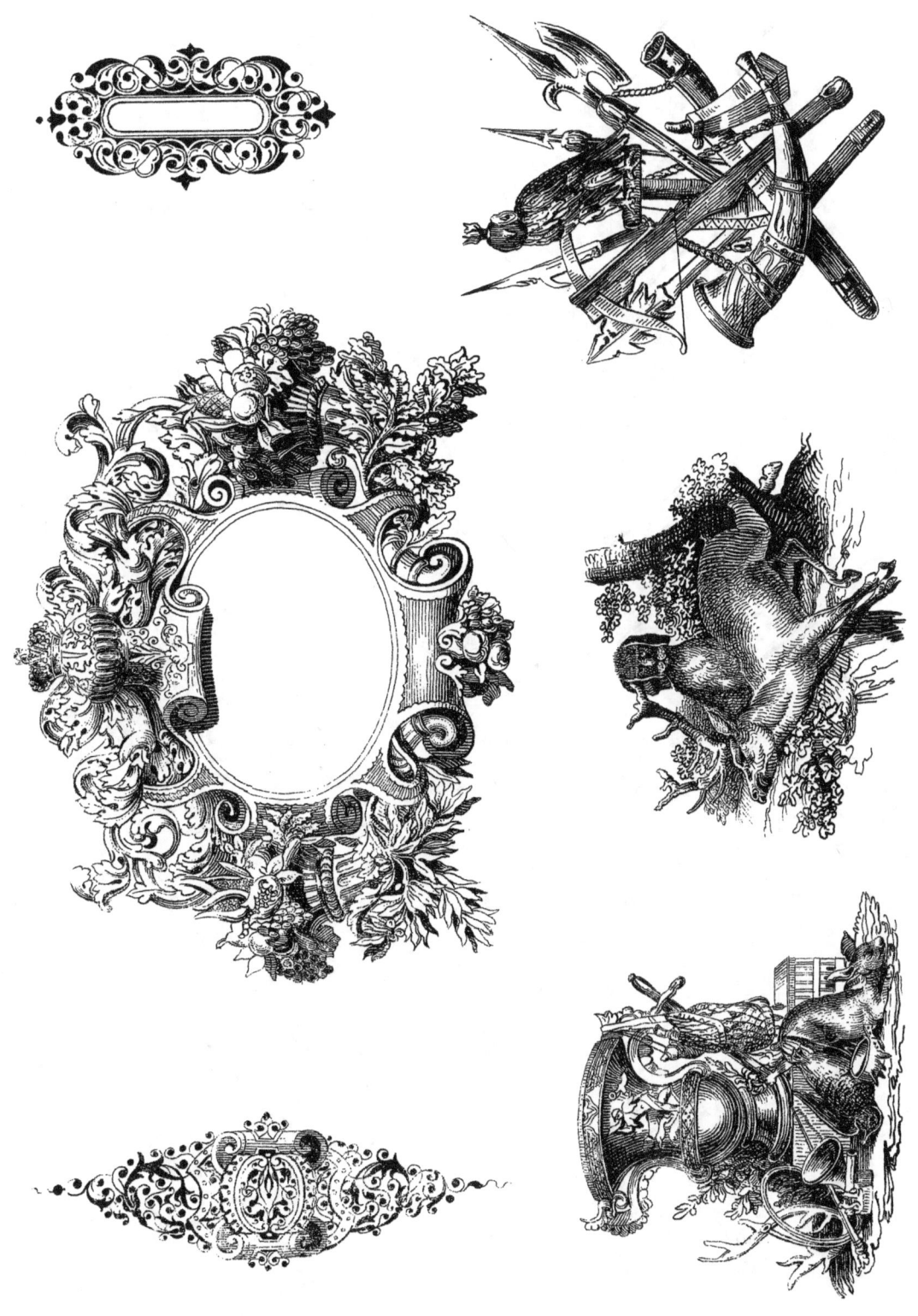

Aa Bb Cc Dd Ee Ff Gg Hh Ii Kk Ll
Mm Nn Oo Pp Qq Rr Ss Tt Uu Vv Ww
Xx Yy Zz 1 2 3 4 5 6 7 8 9 0

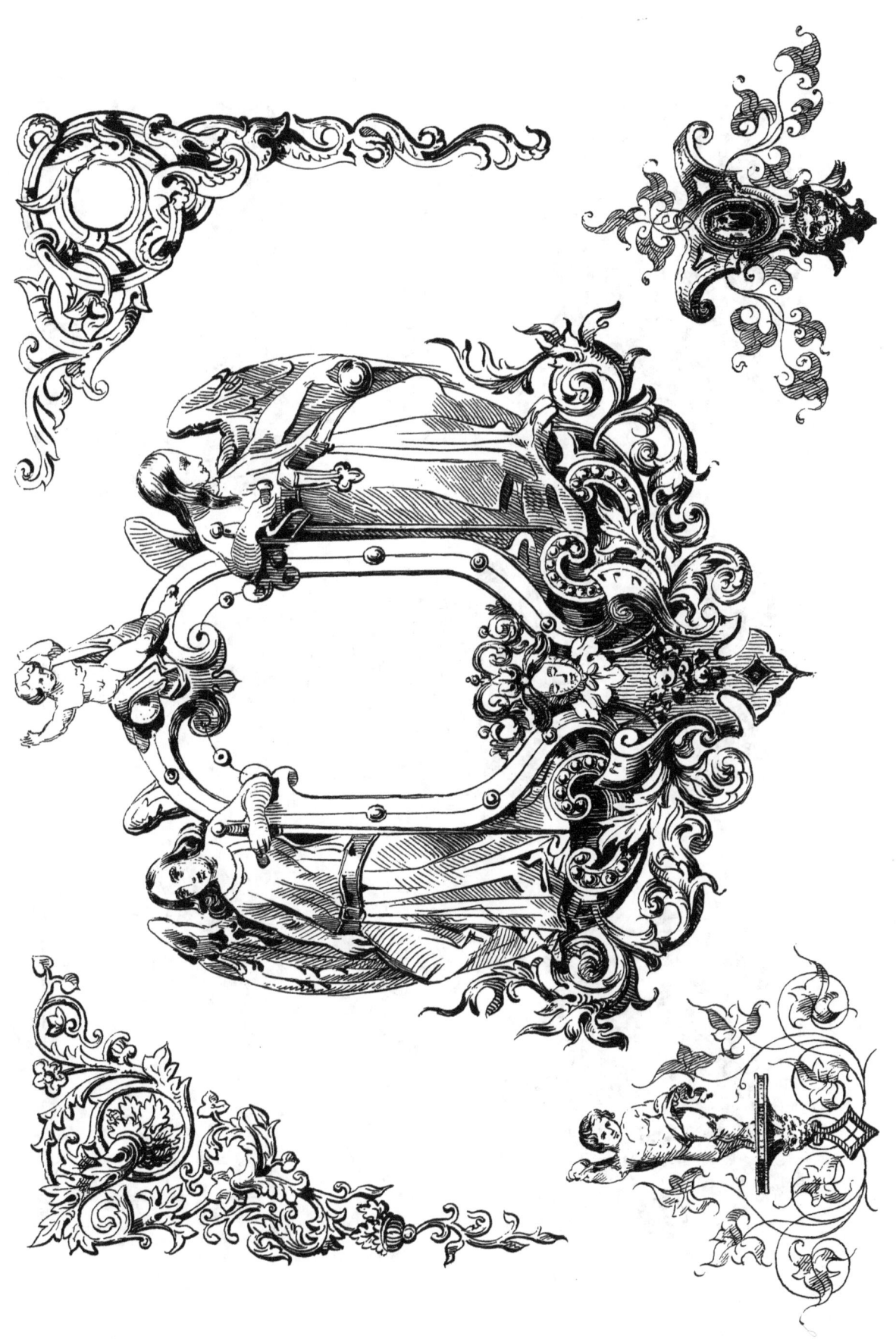

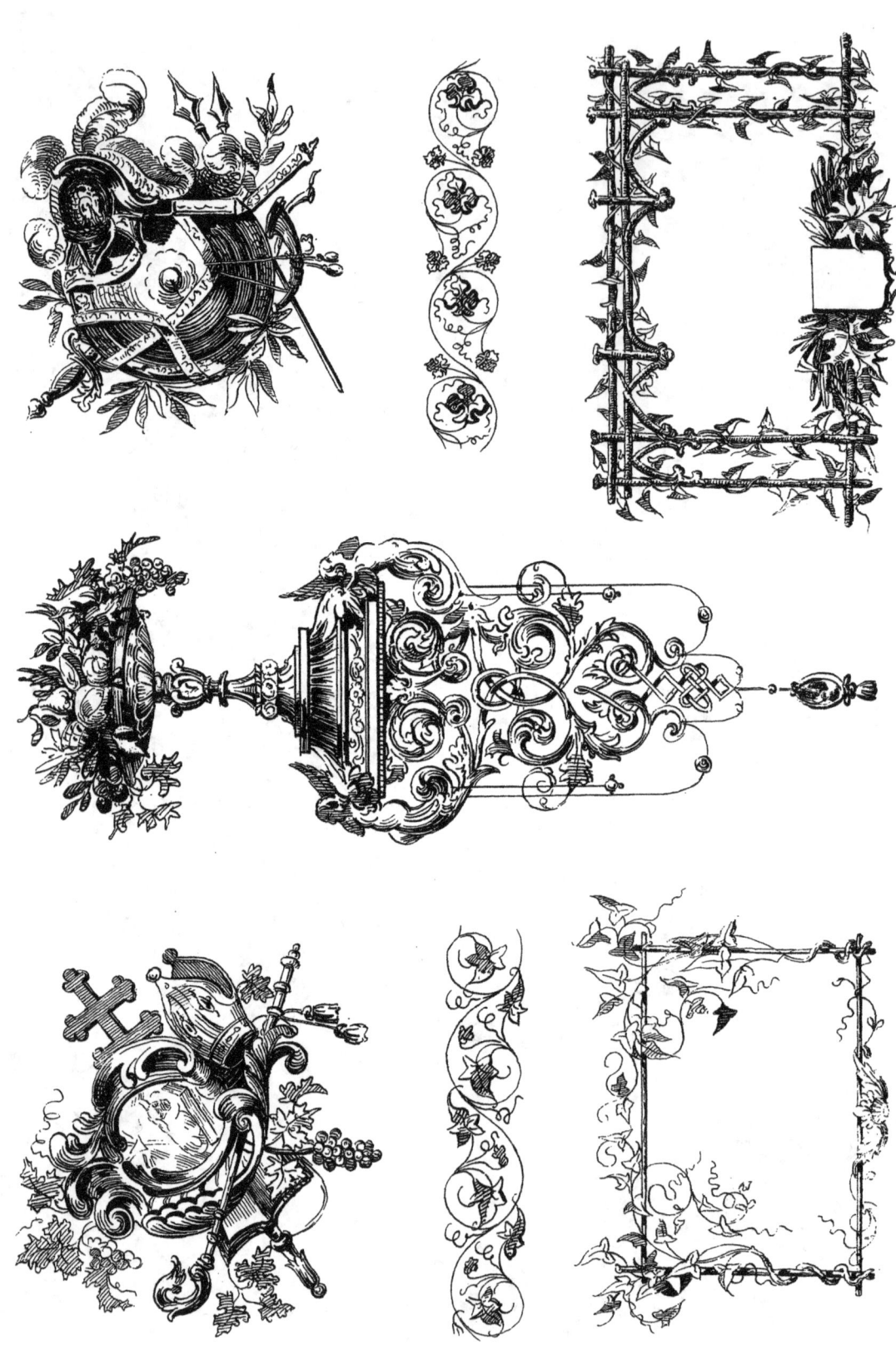

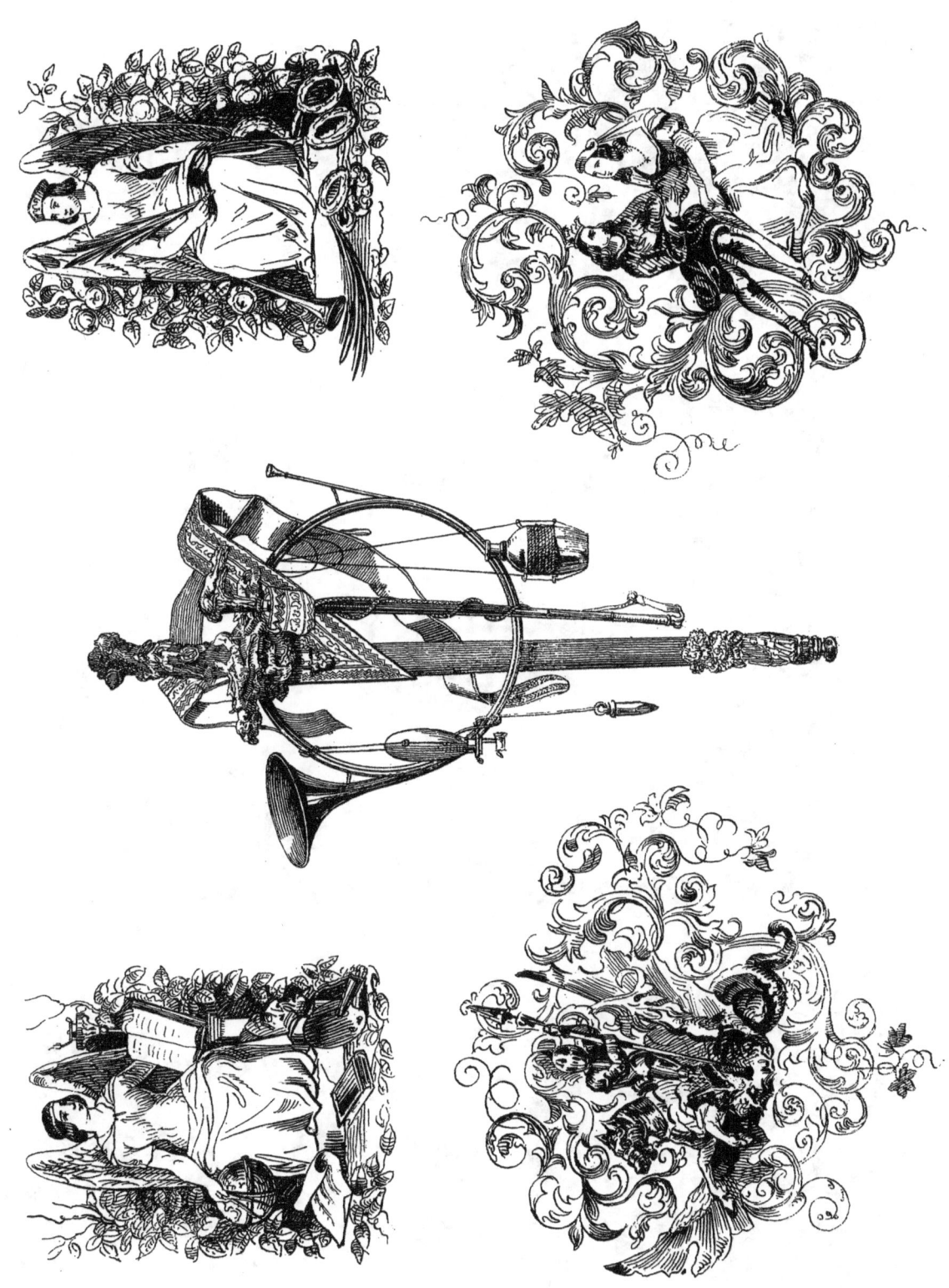

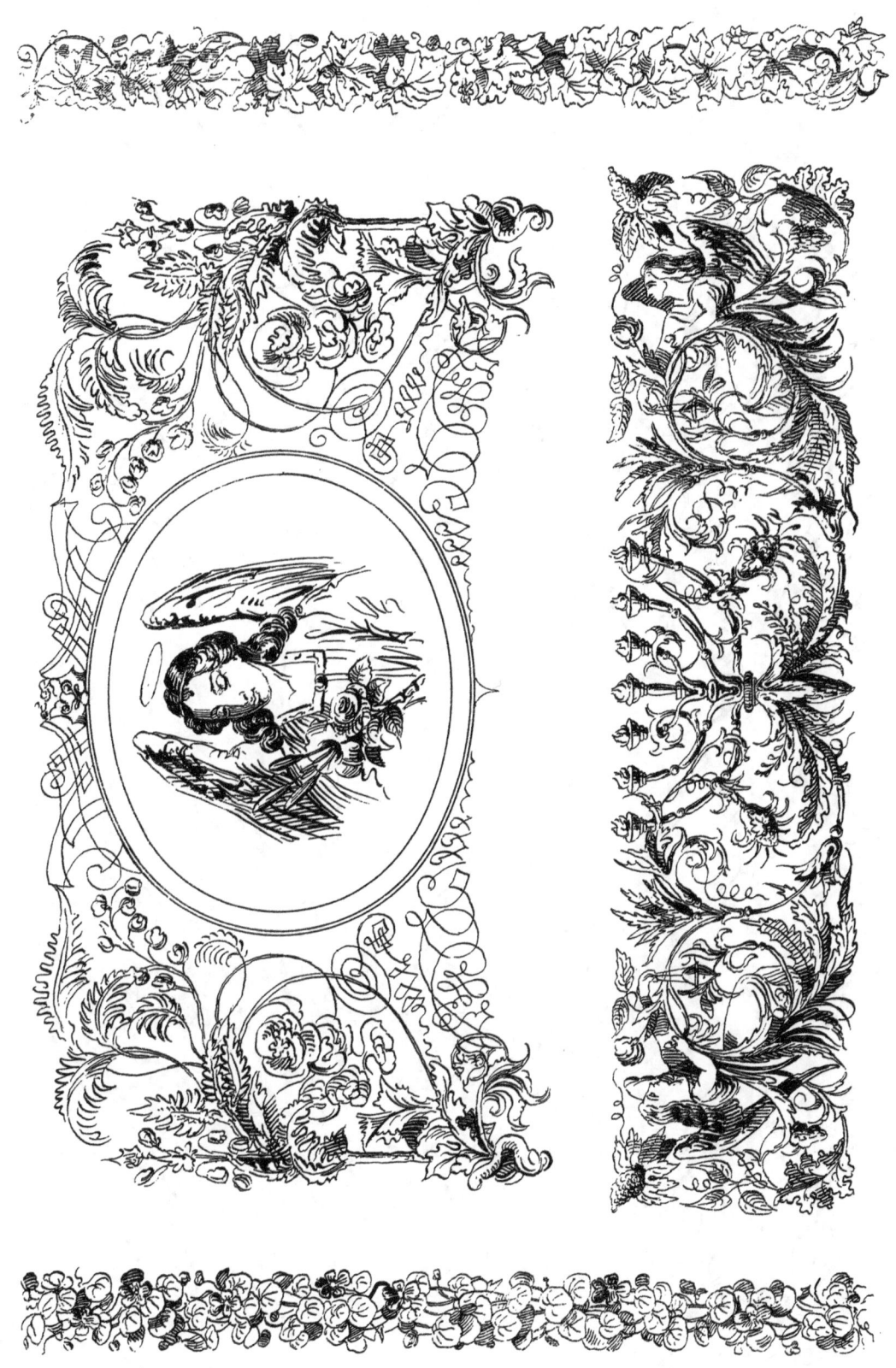

Italienische Alphabete.

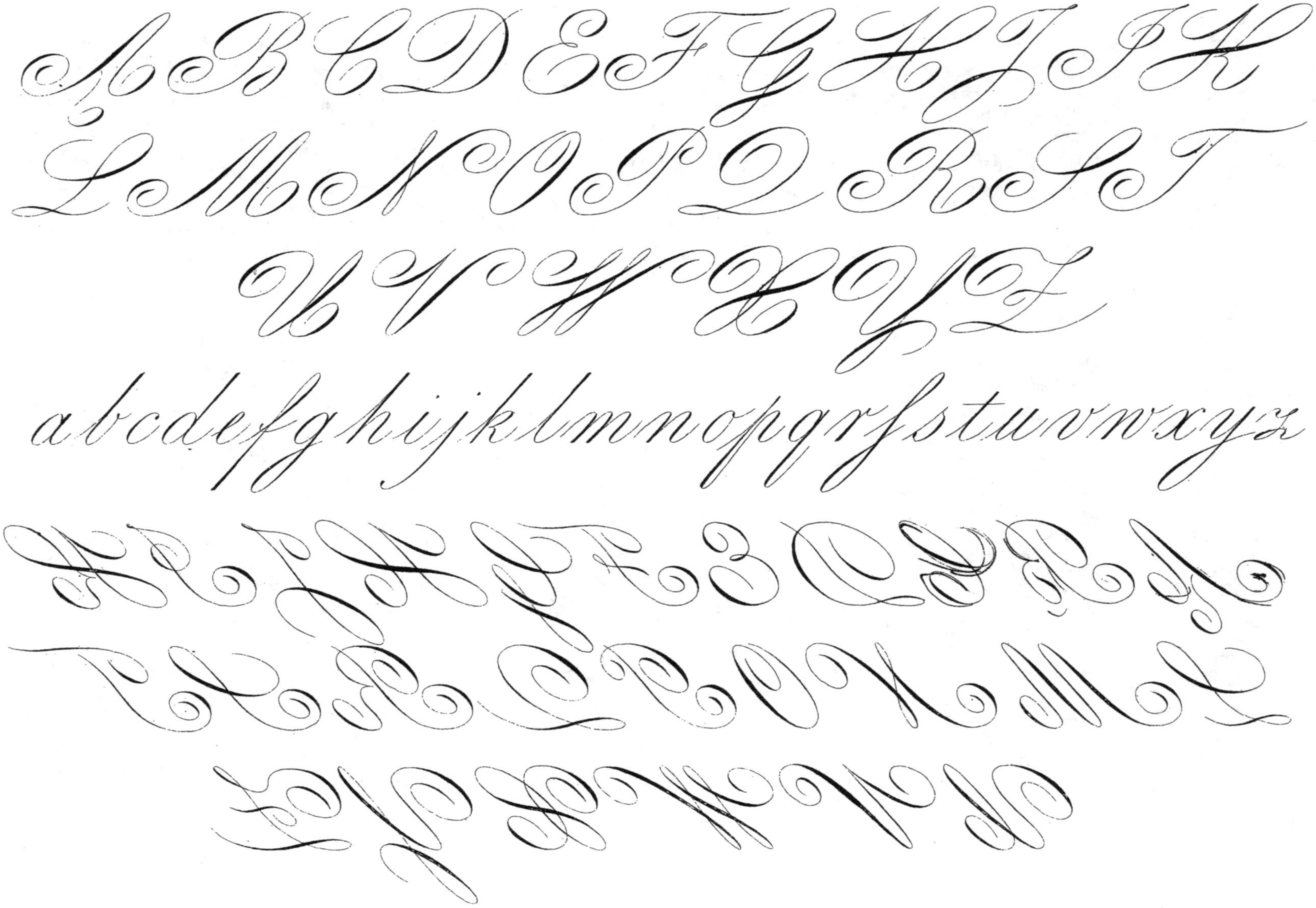

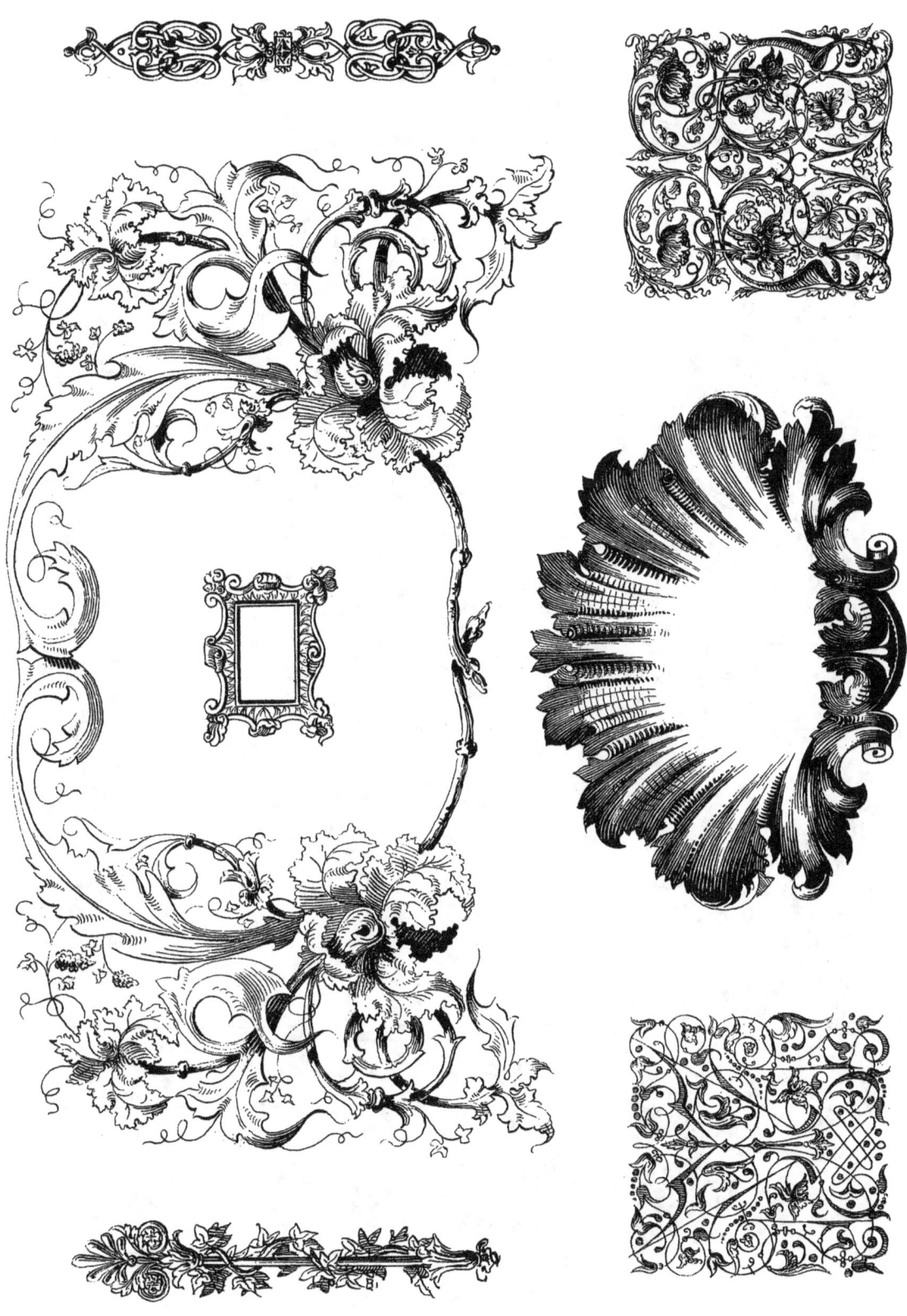

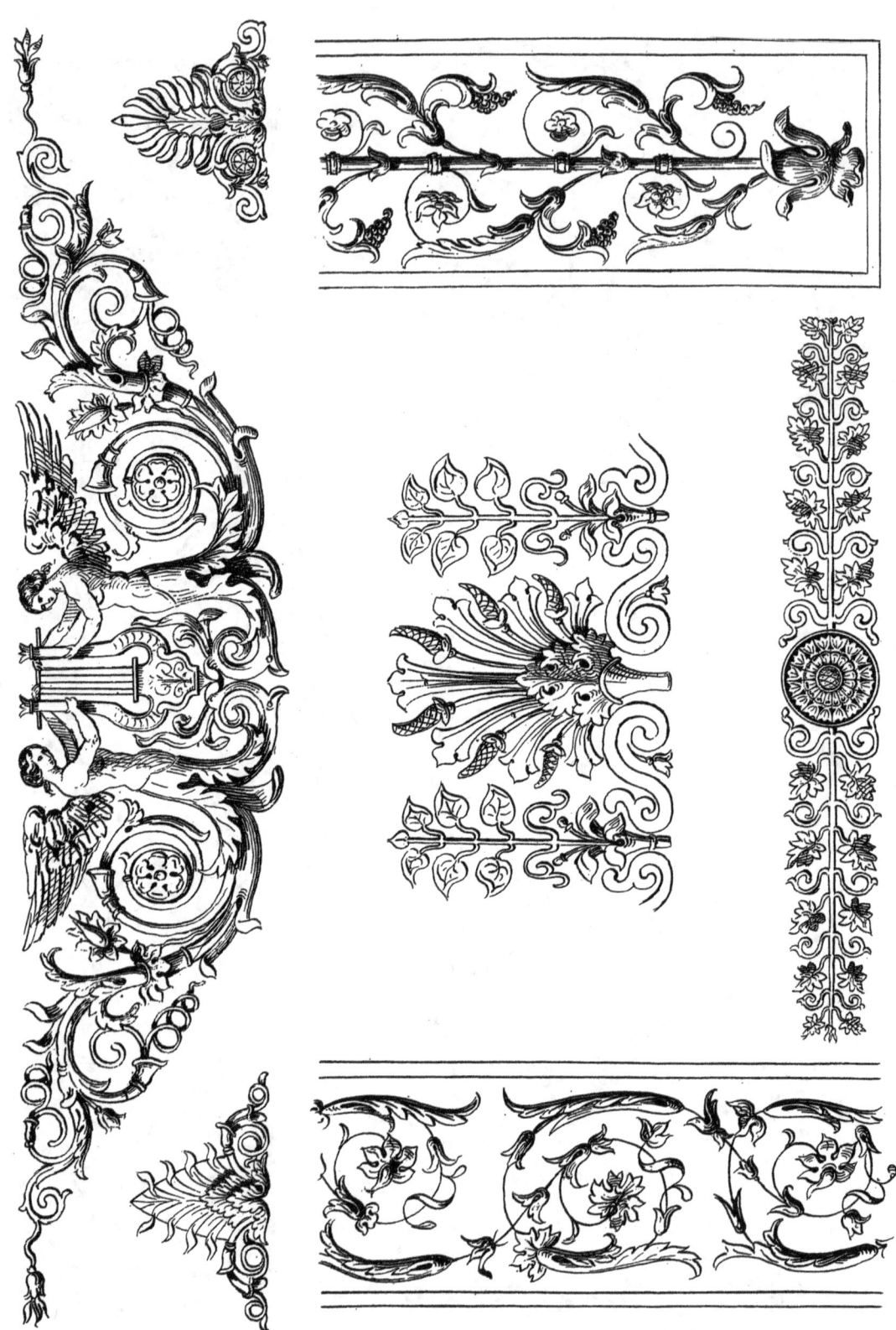

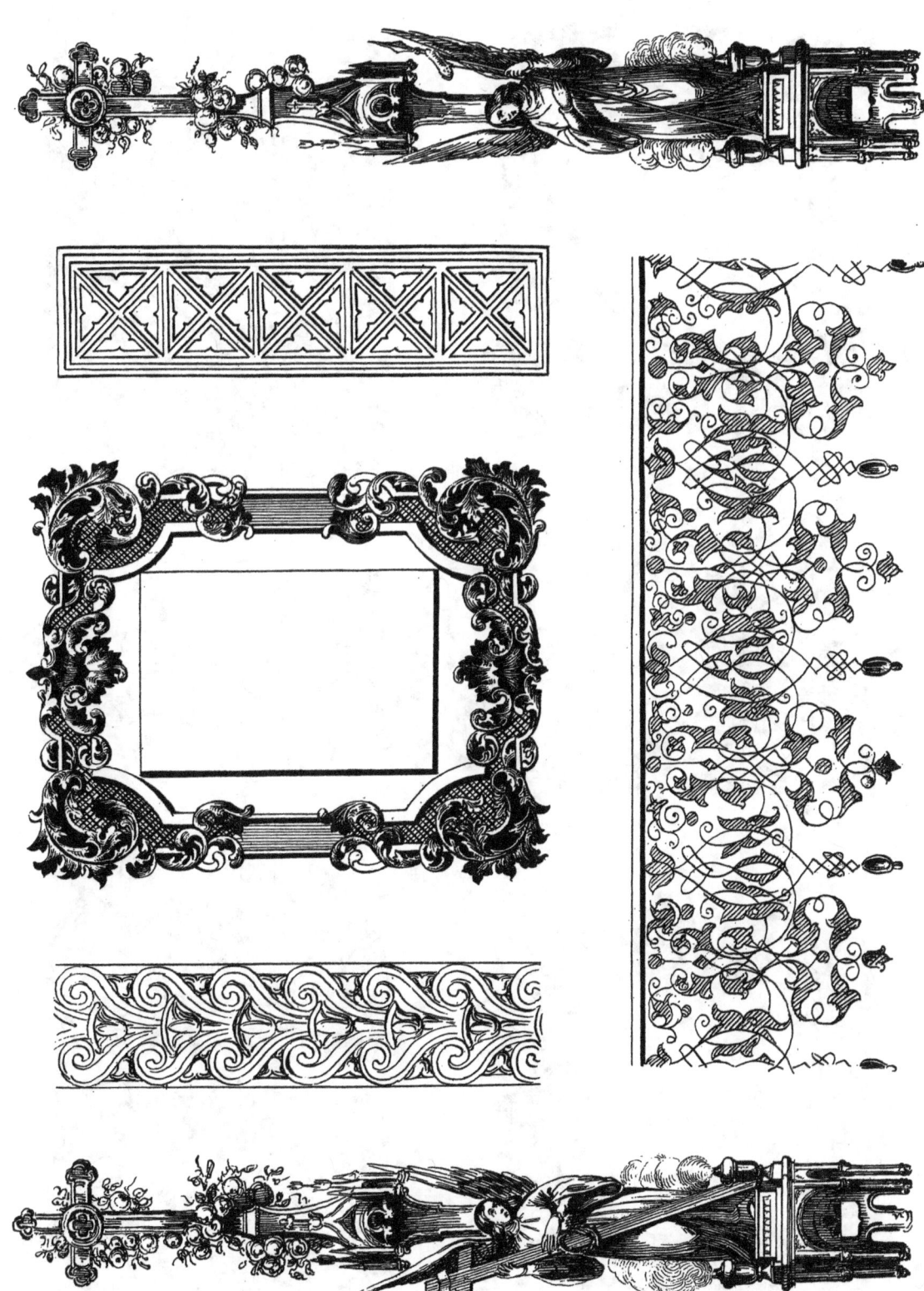

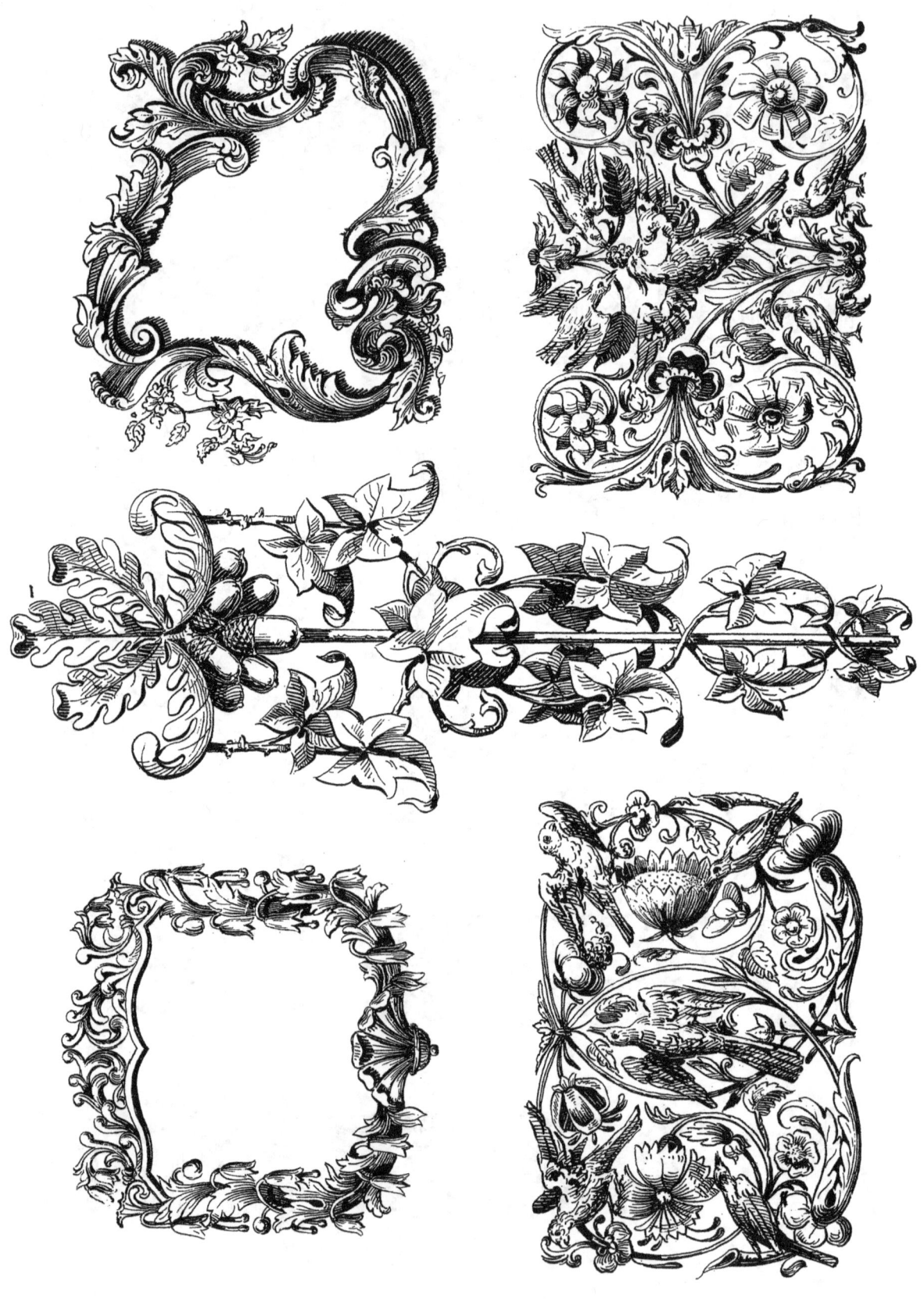

28

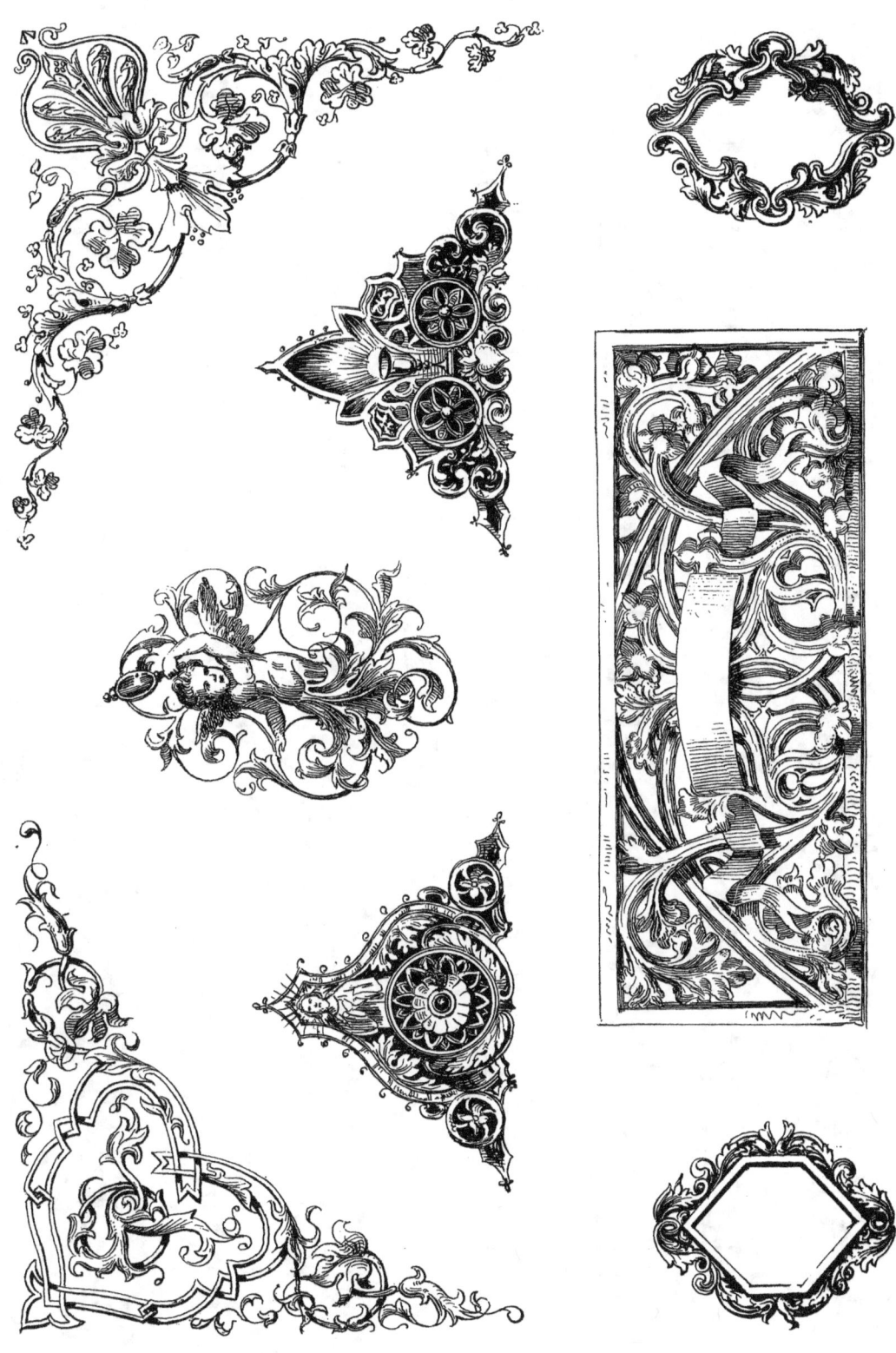

Gothische Schrift.

ABCDEFG HIK LMN OPQRSTUW
abcdefghijklmn OO XYZ opqrstuvwxyz.

Fractur-Schrift.

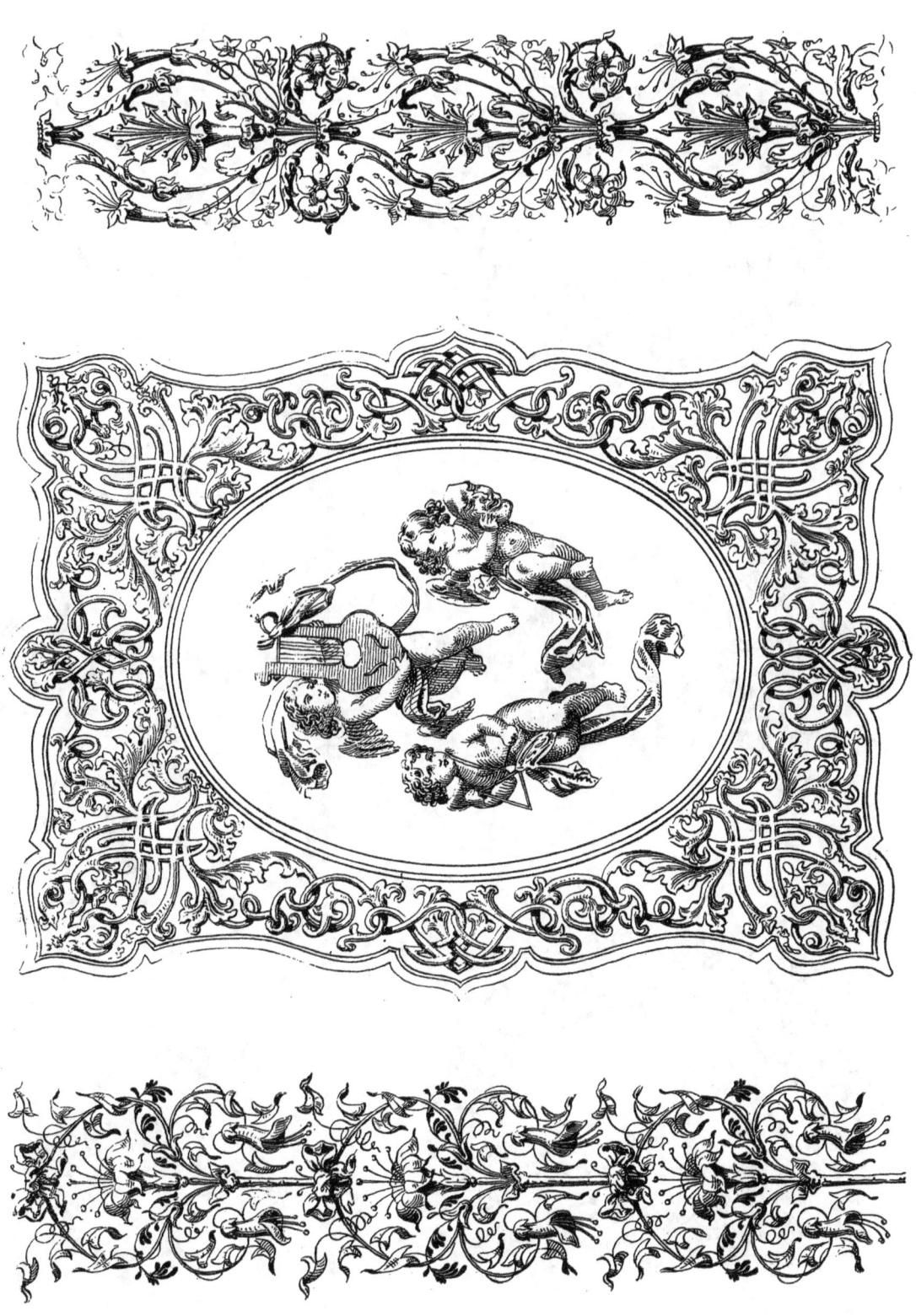

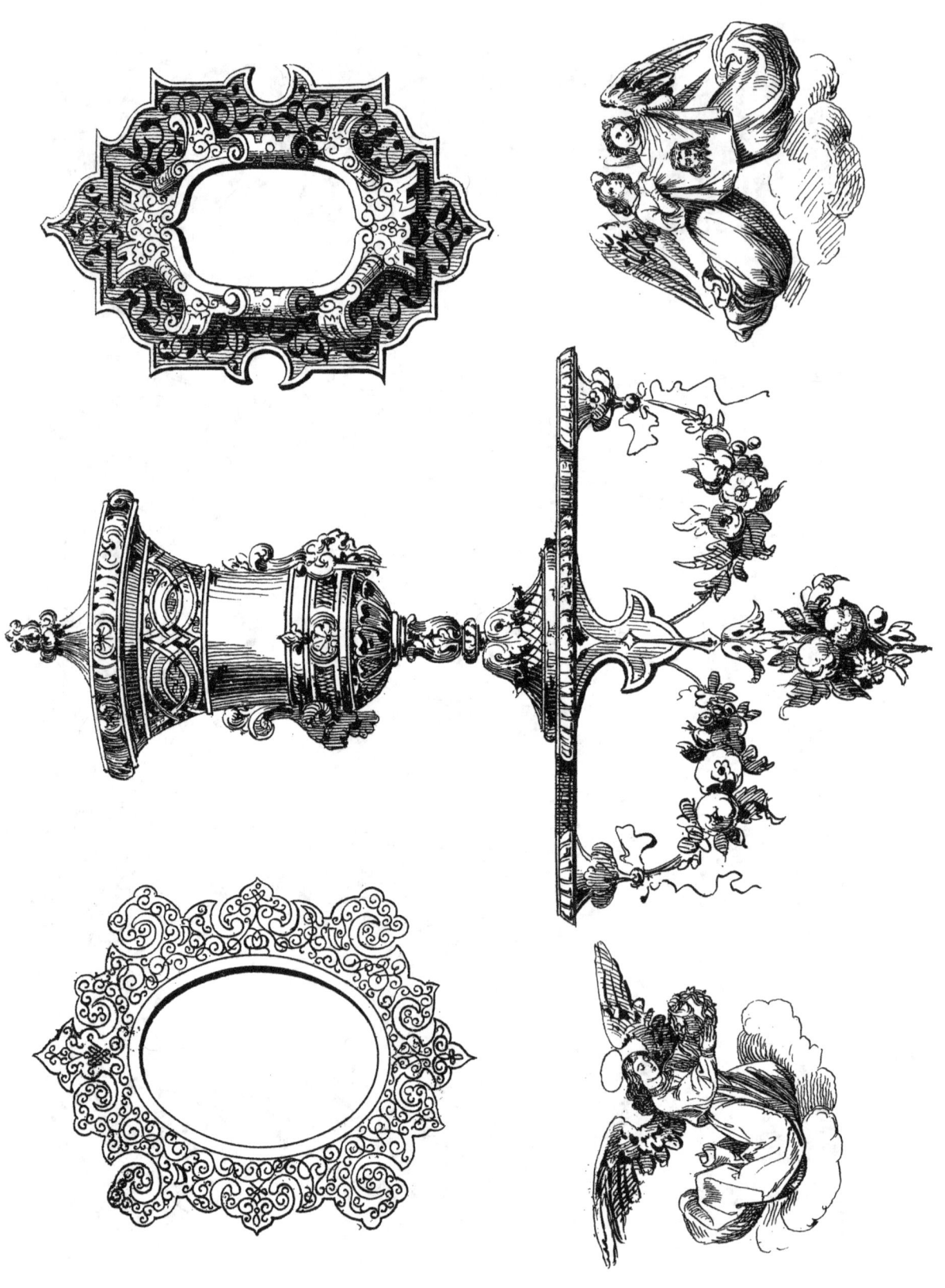

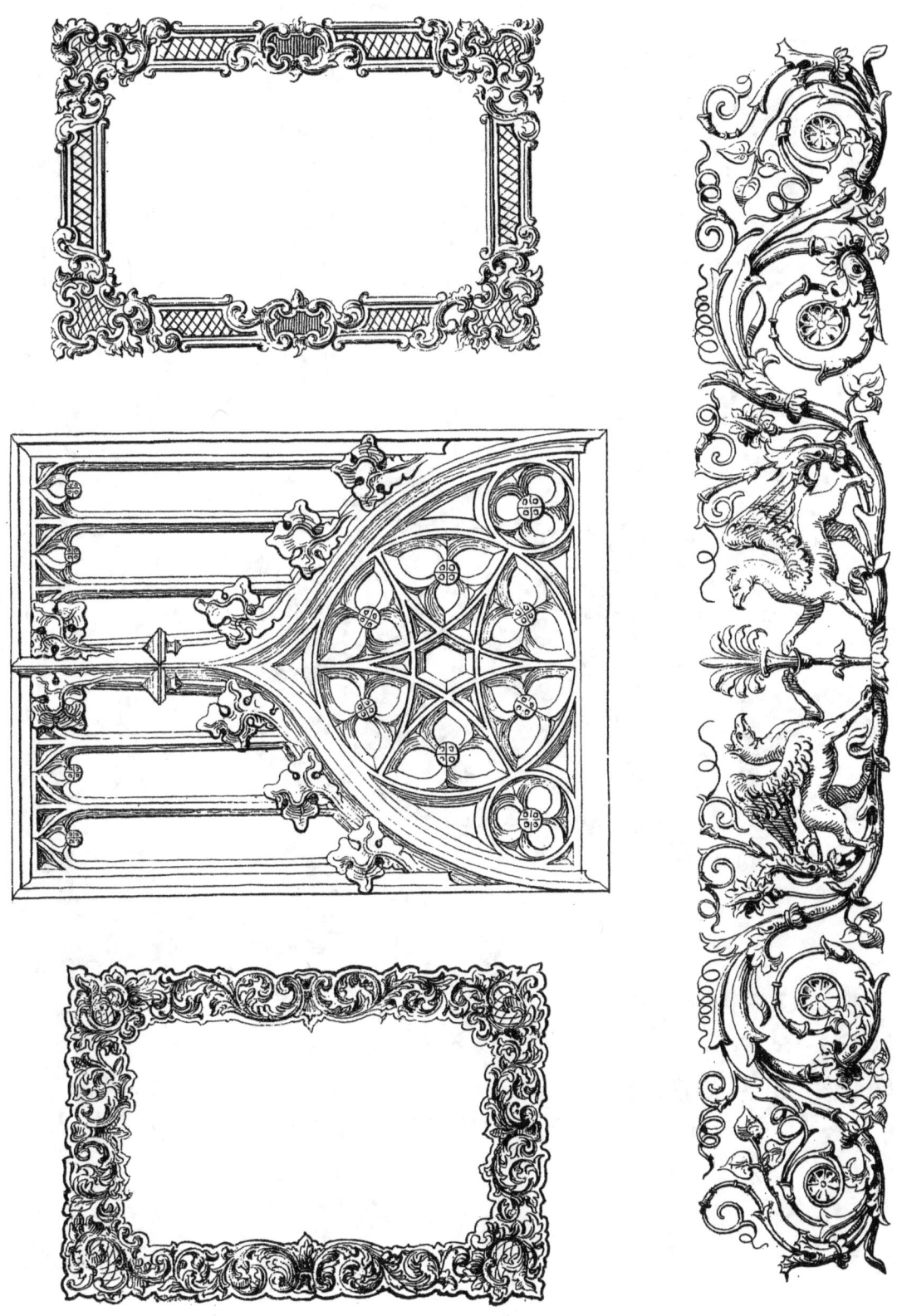

33

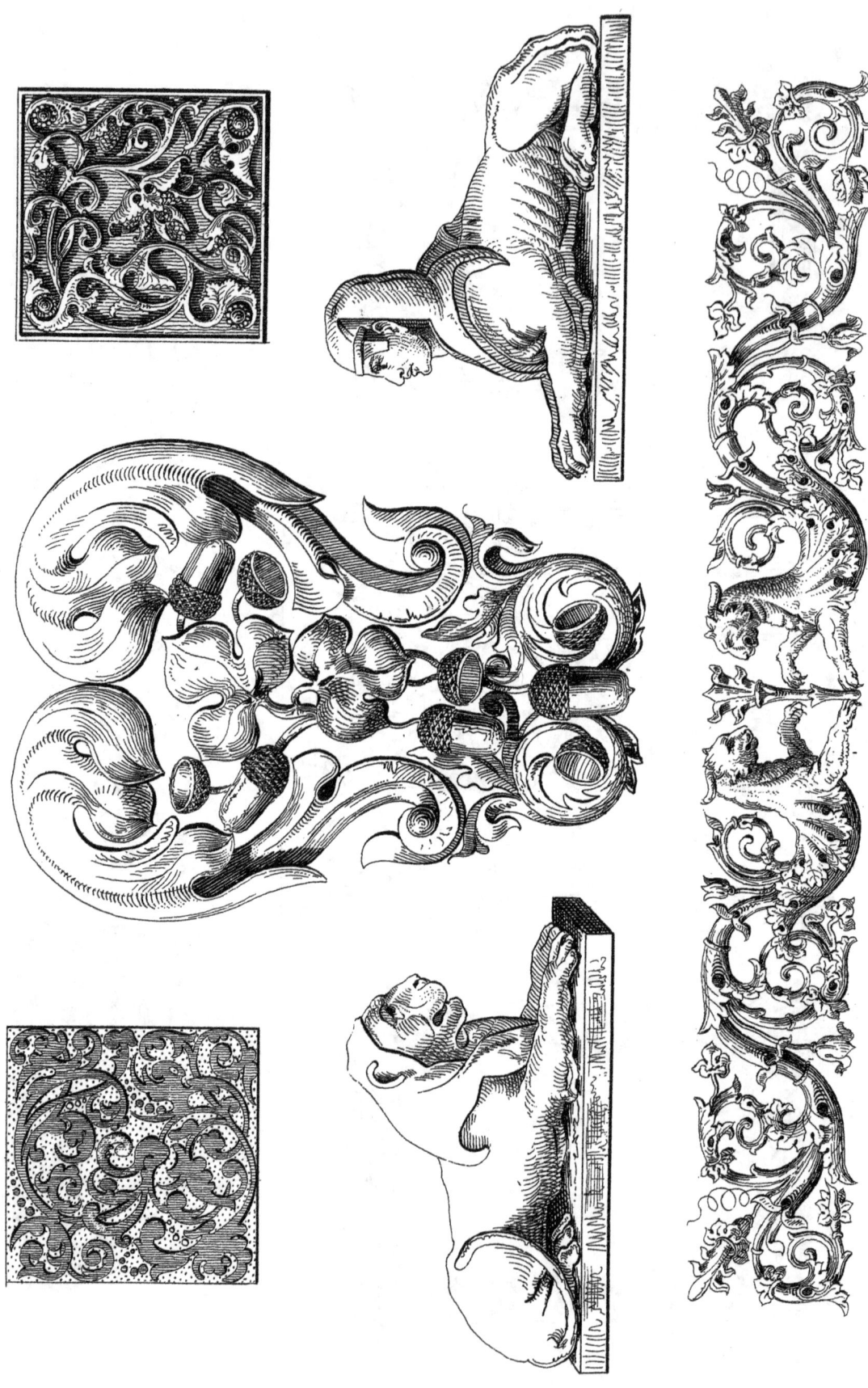

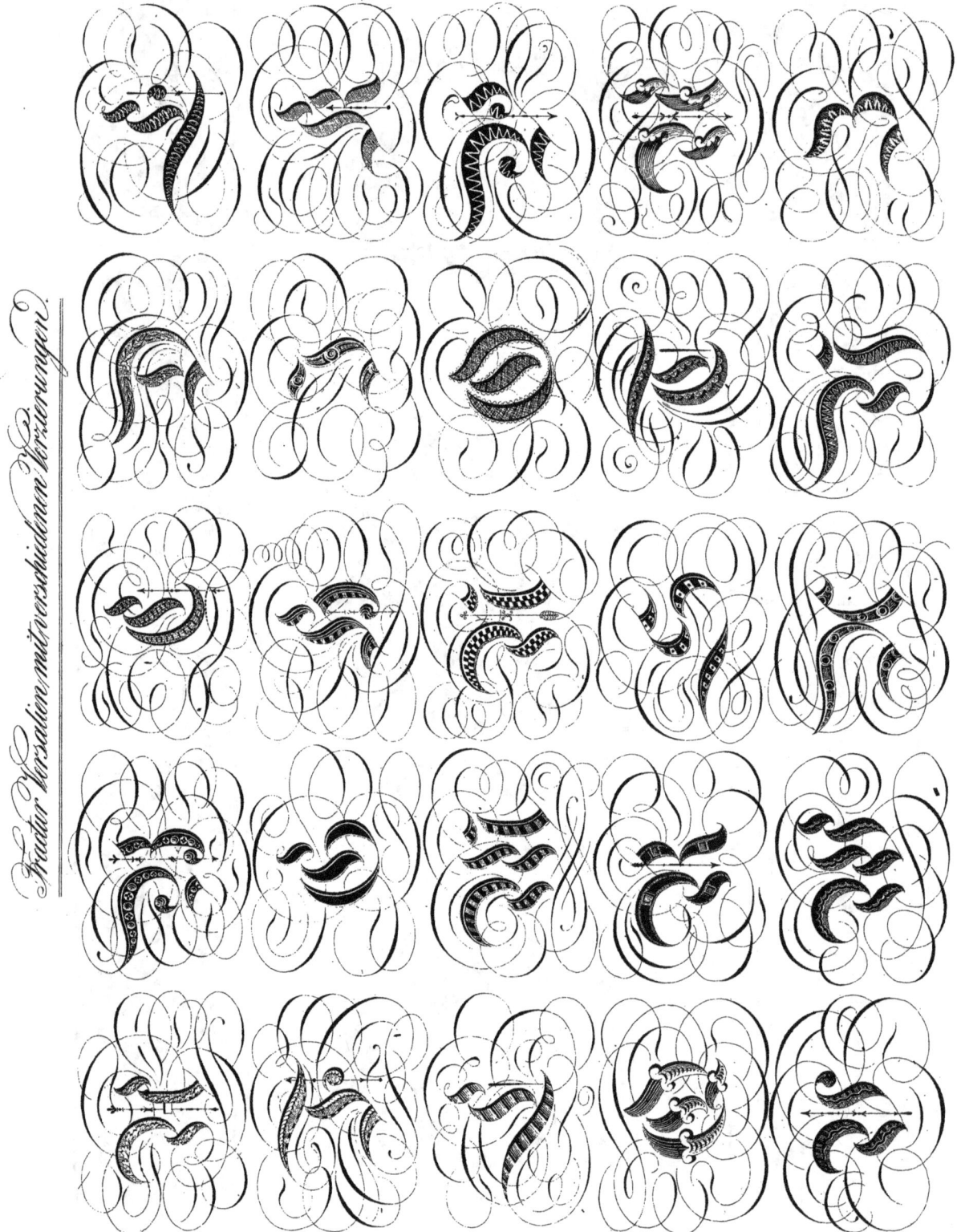

Fraktur-Versalien mit verschiedenen Verzierungen.

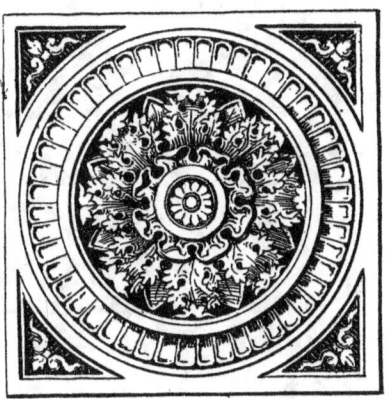

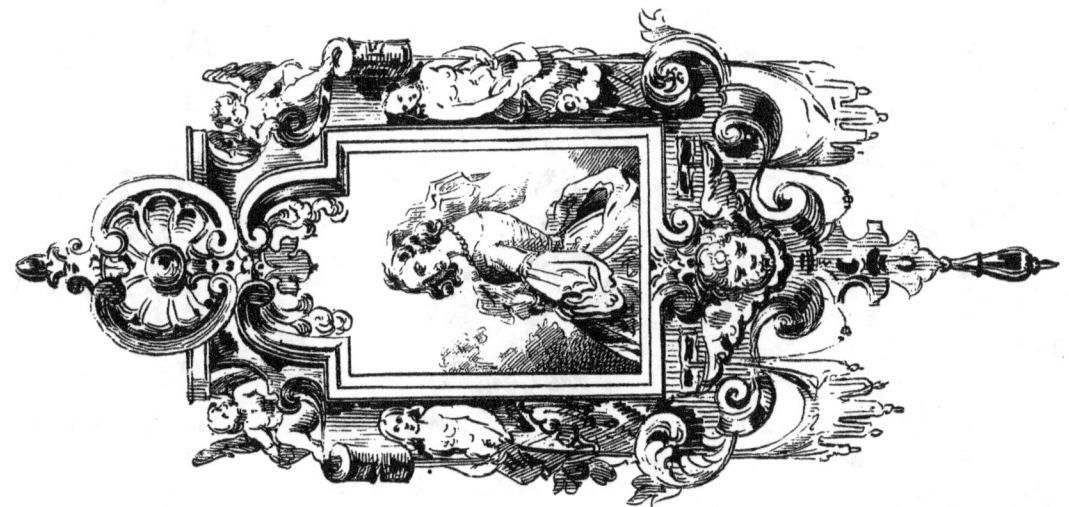

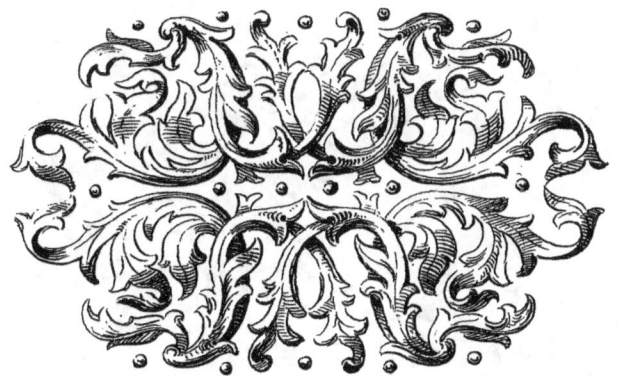

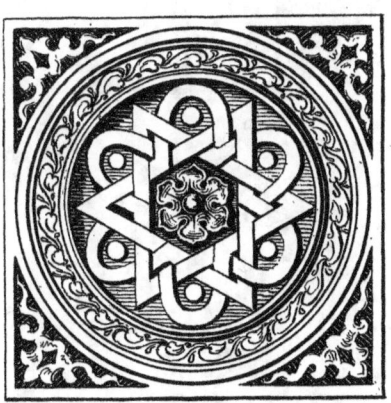

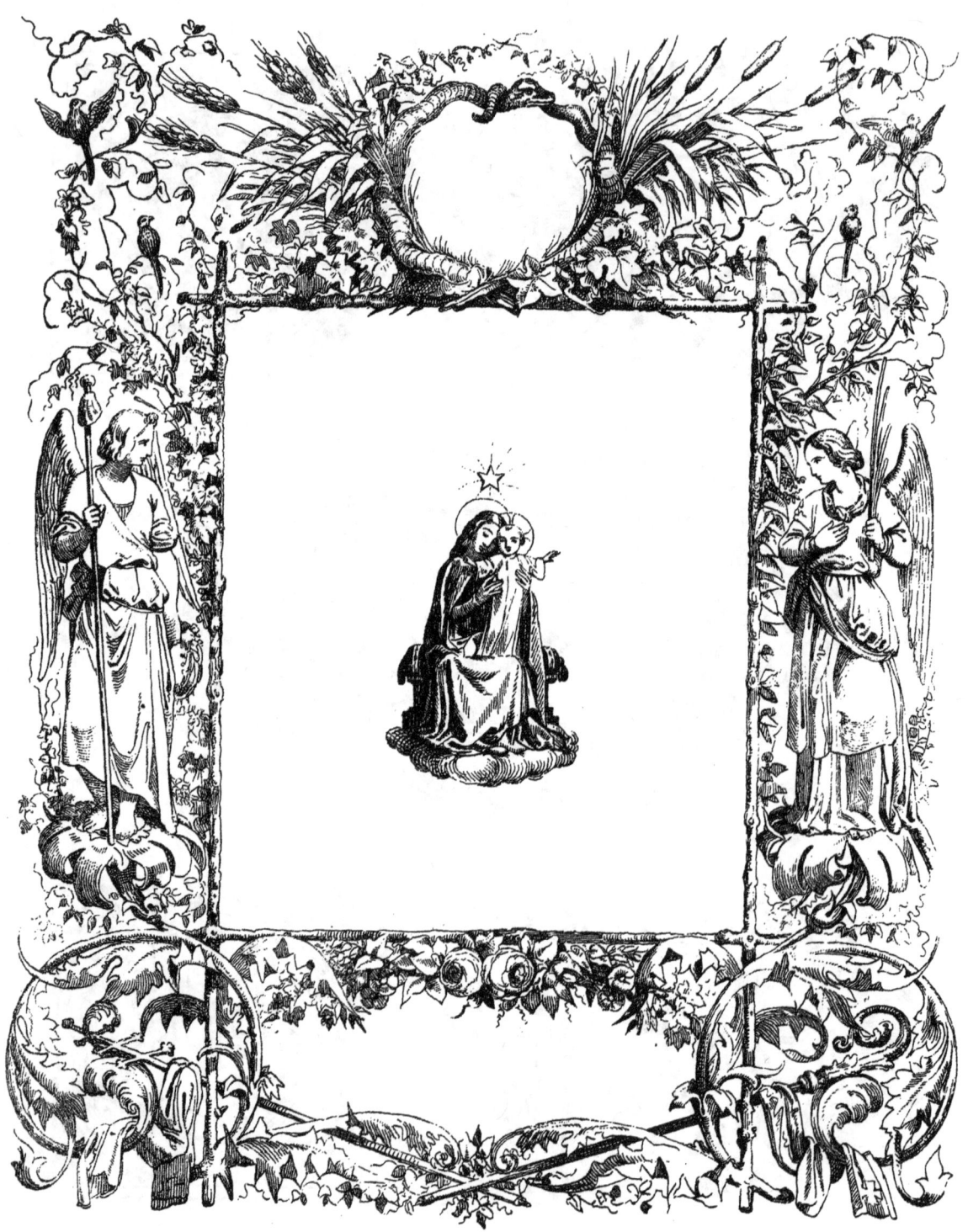

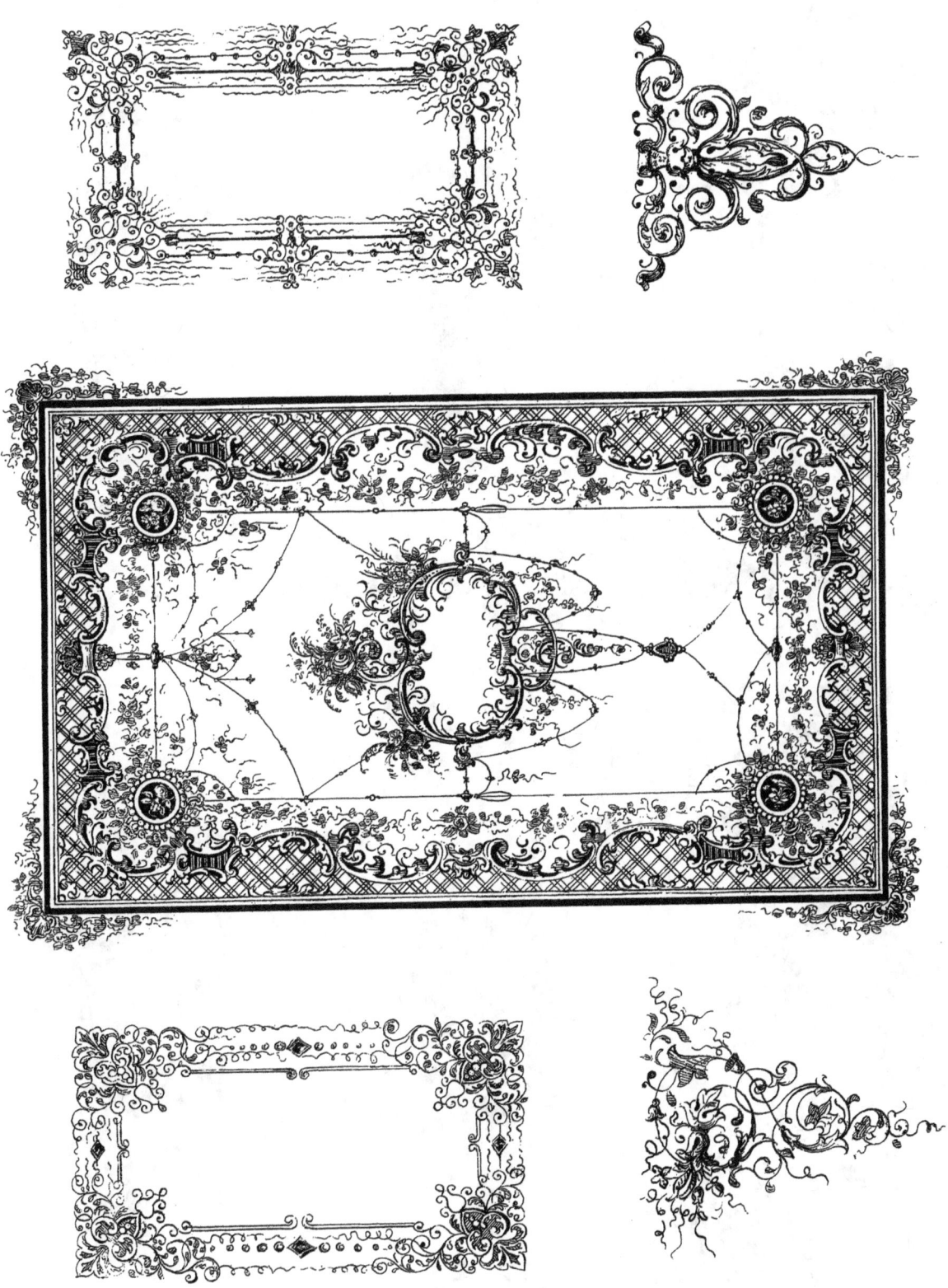

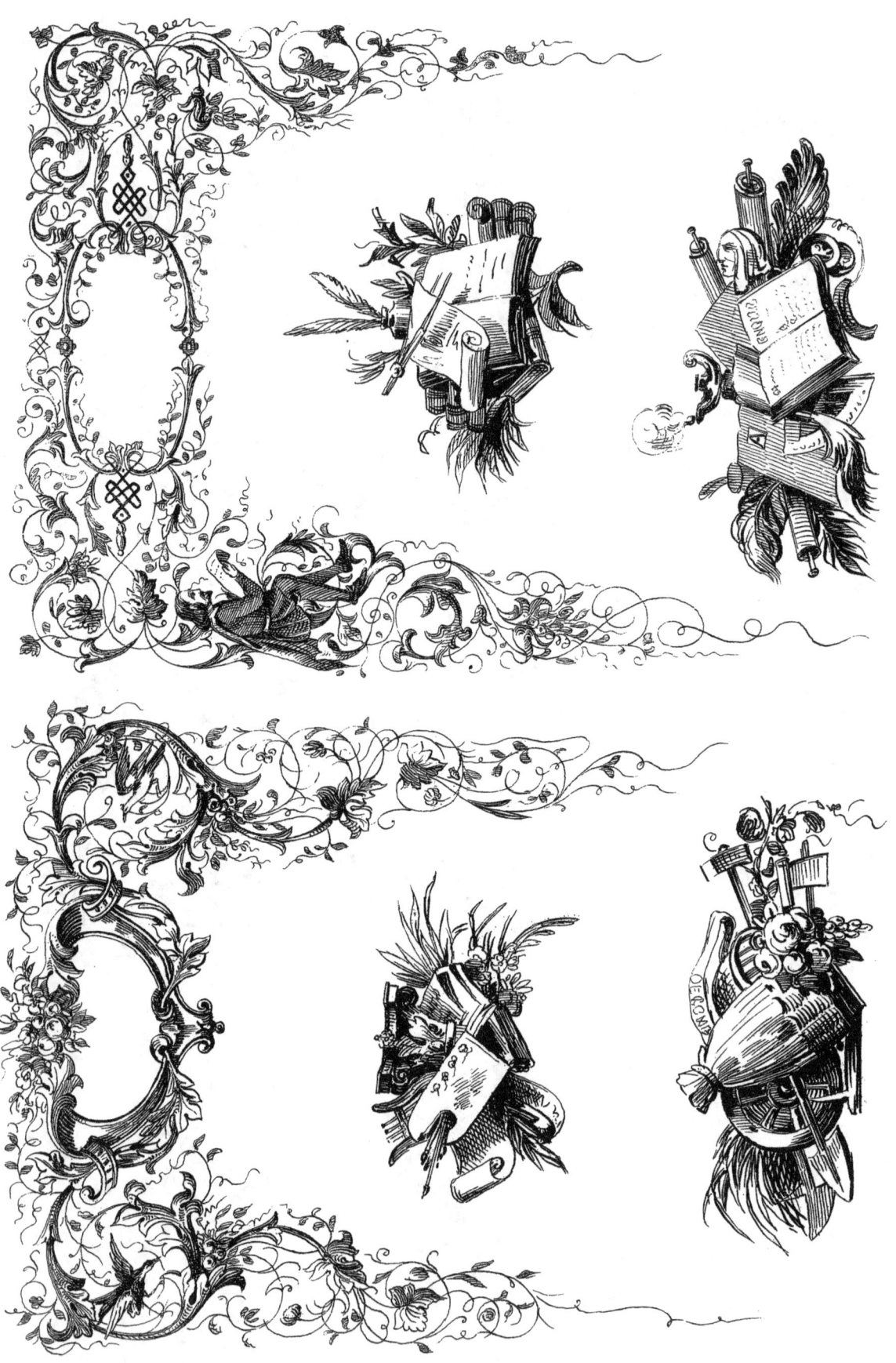

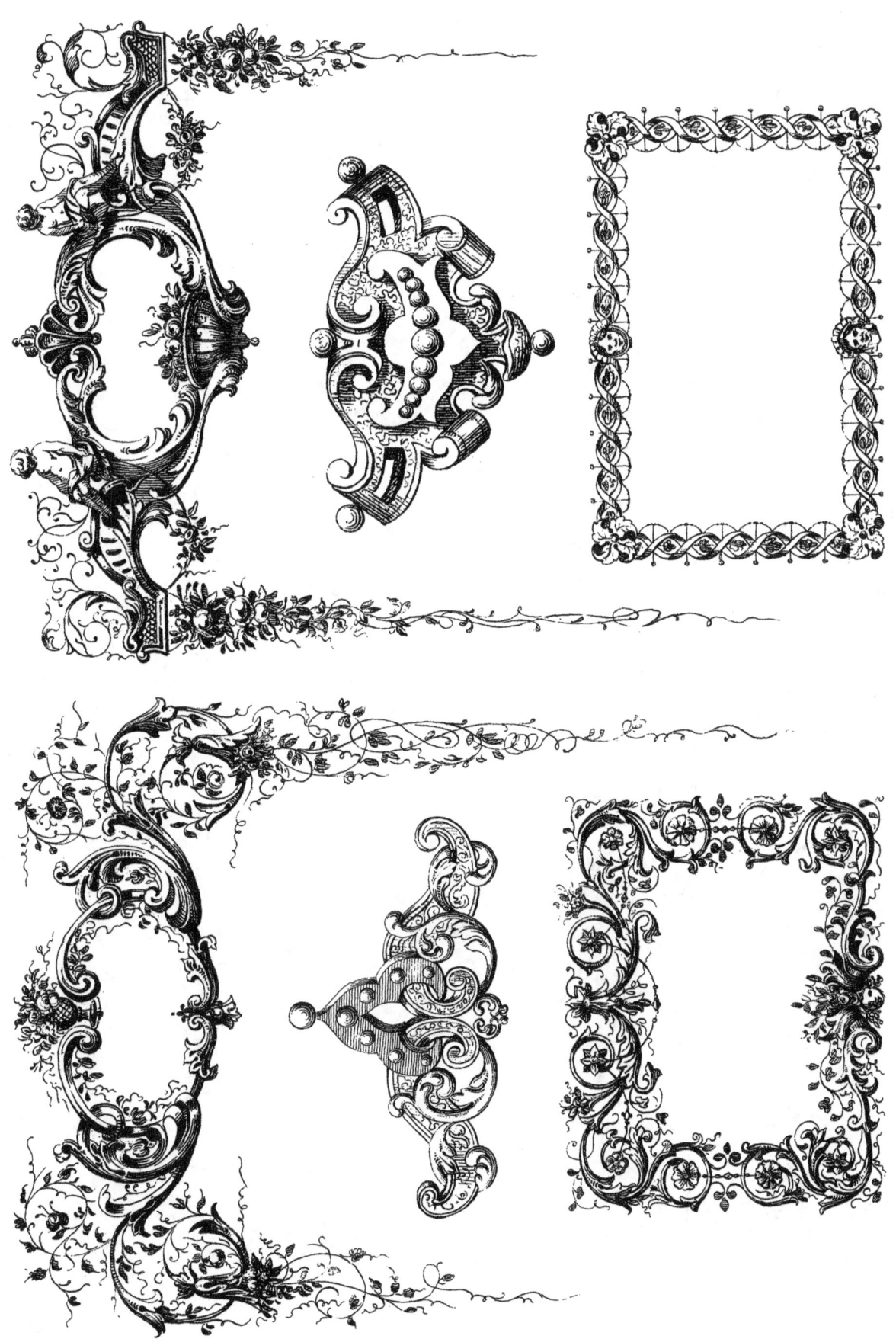

41

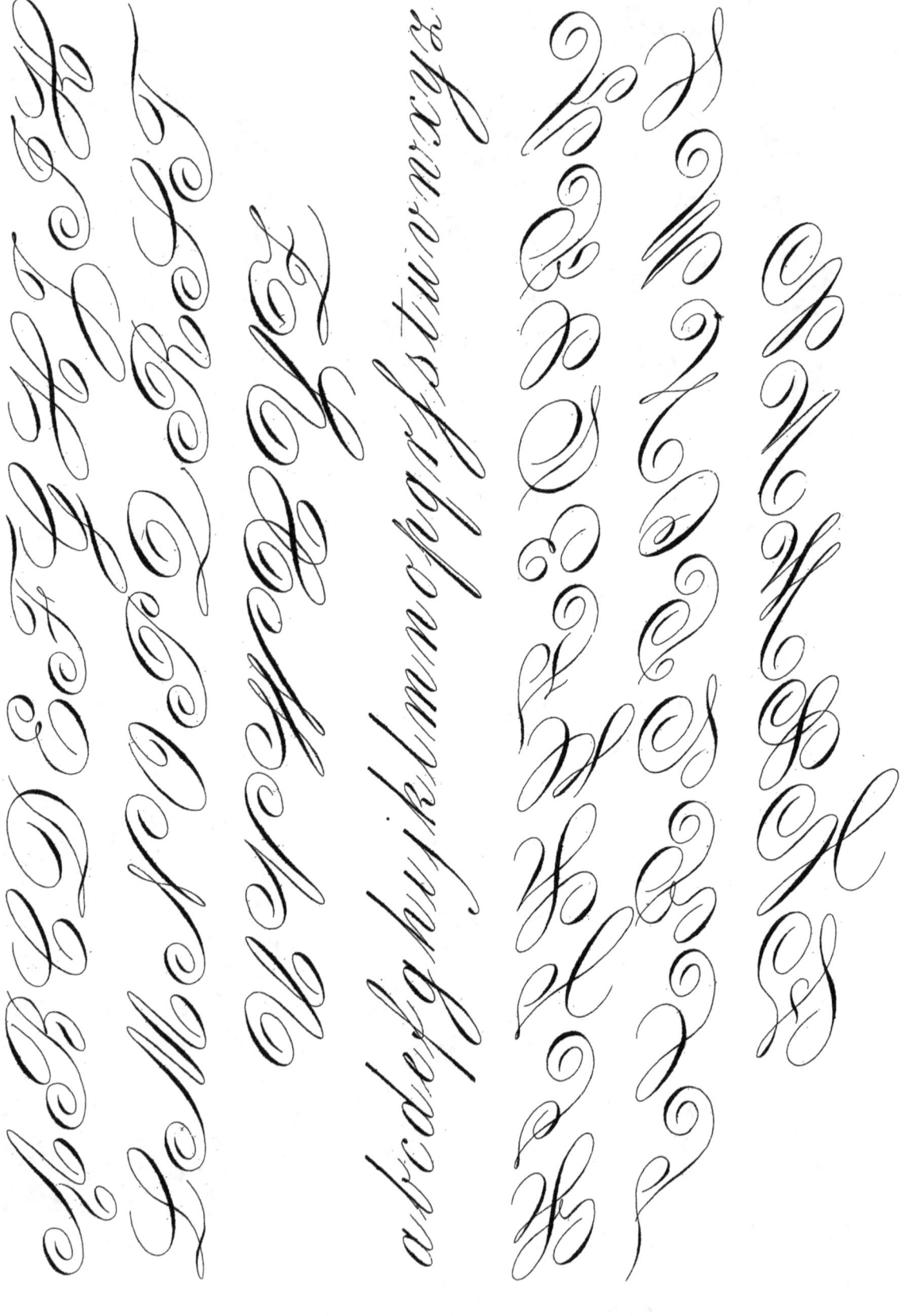

Italienische Alphabete.

42

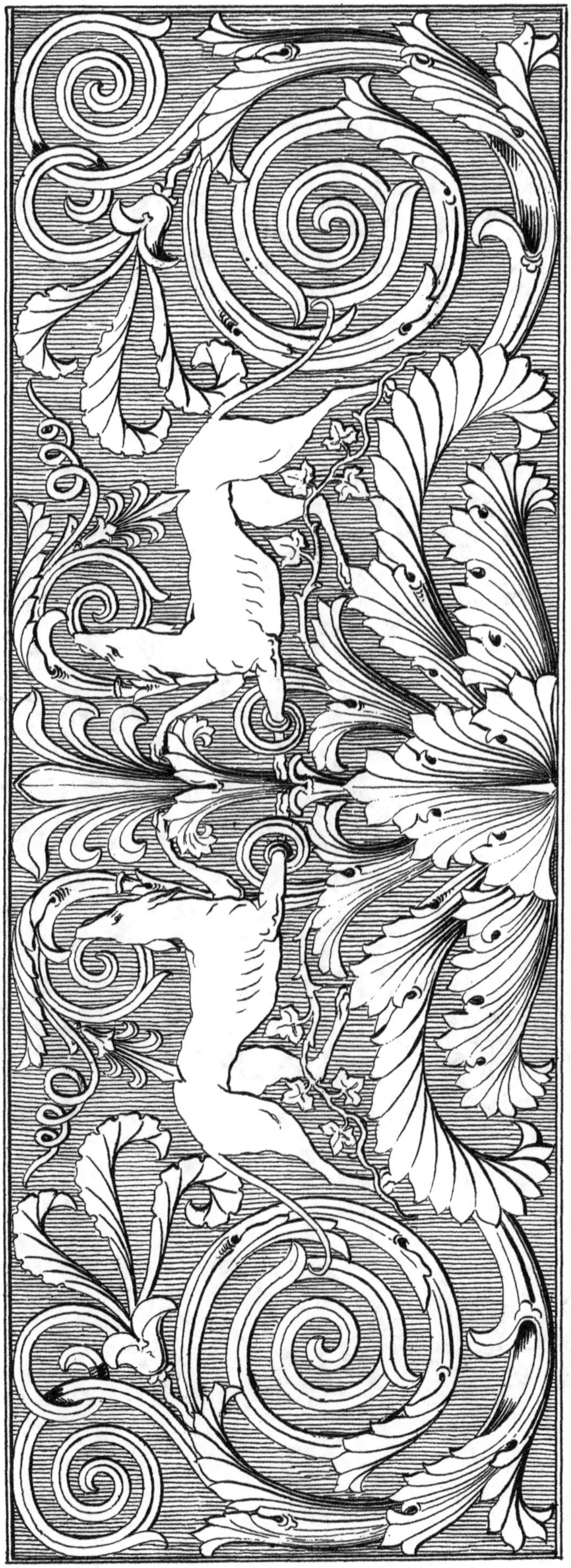

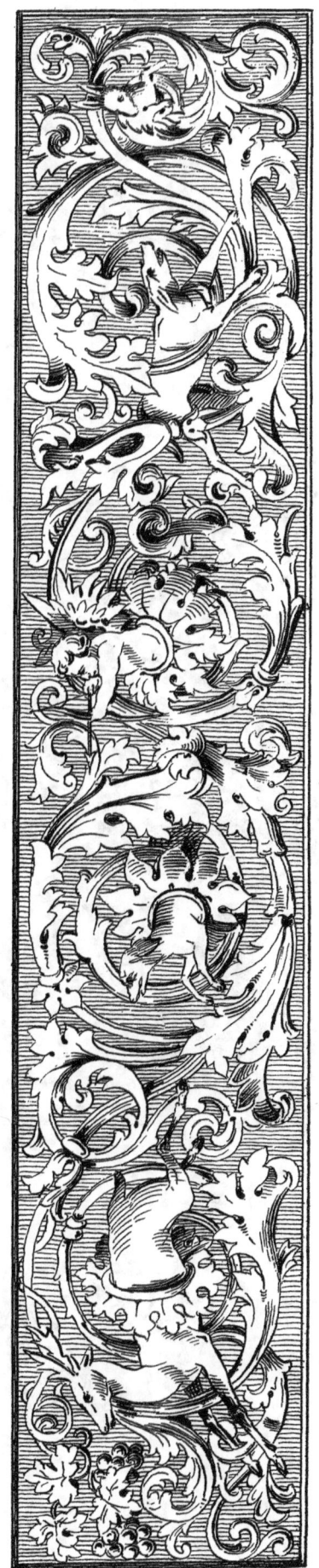

43

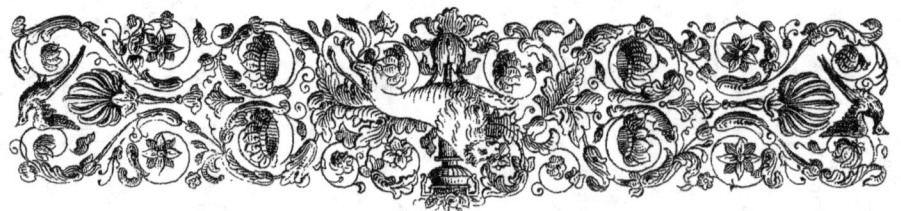

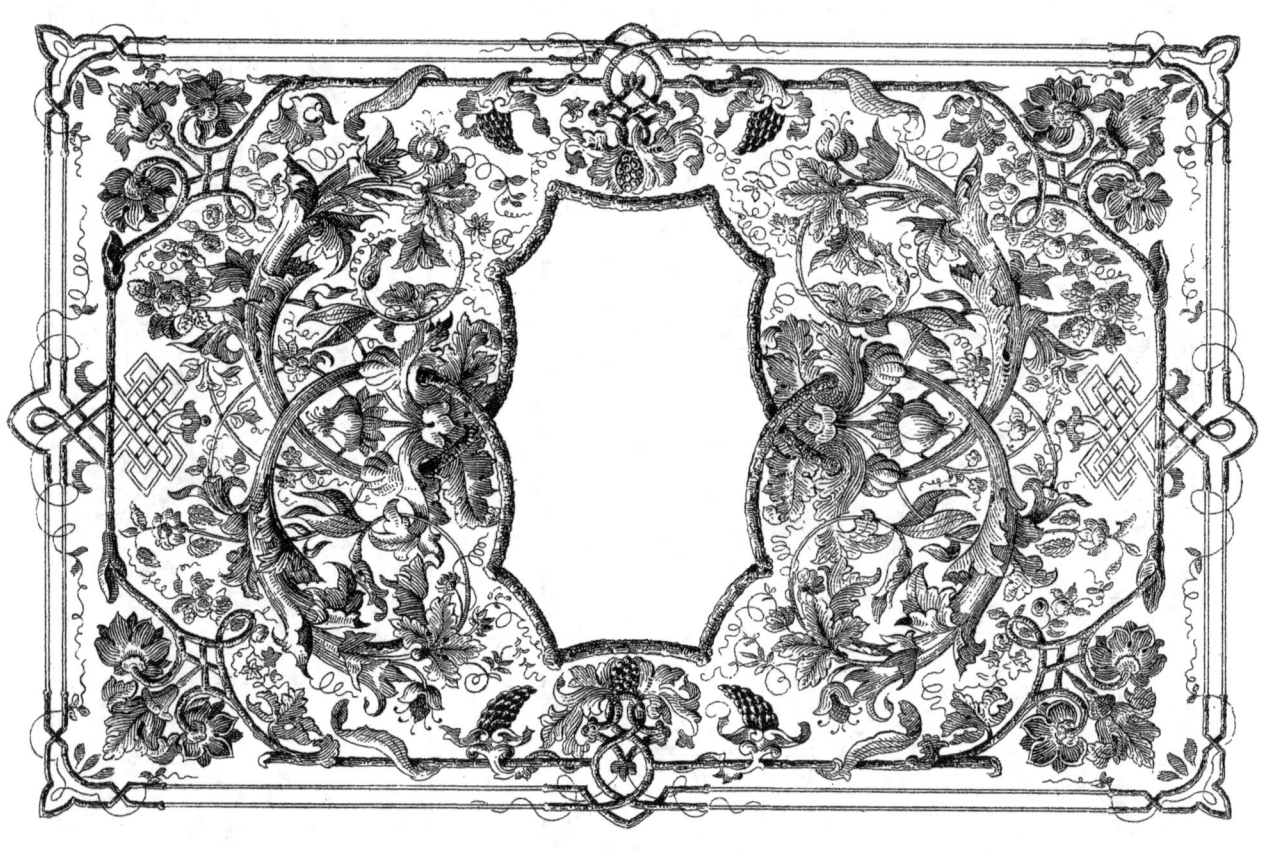

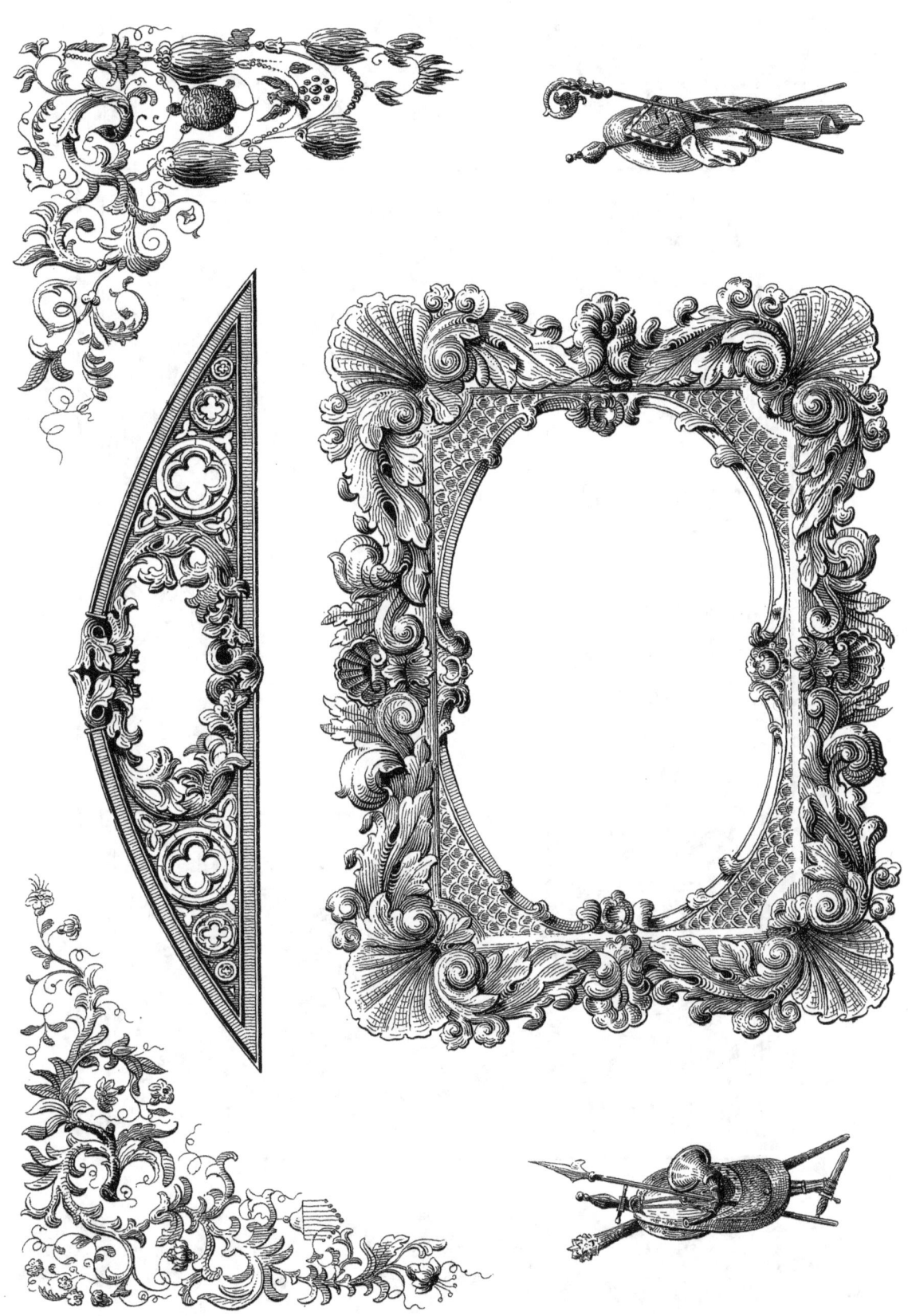

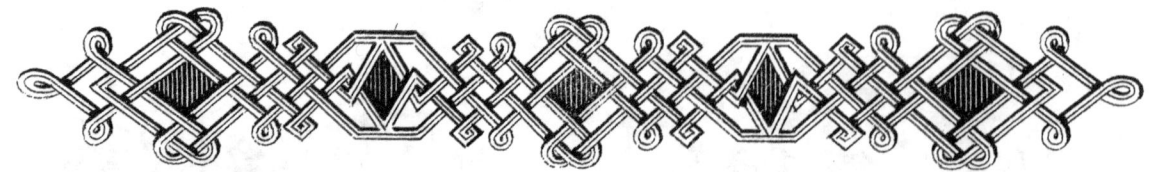

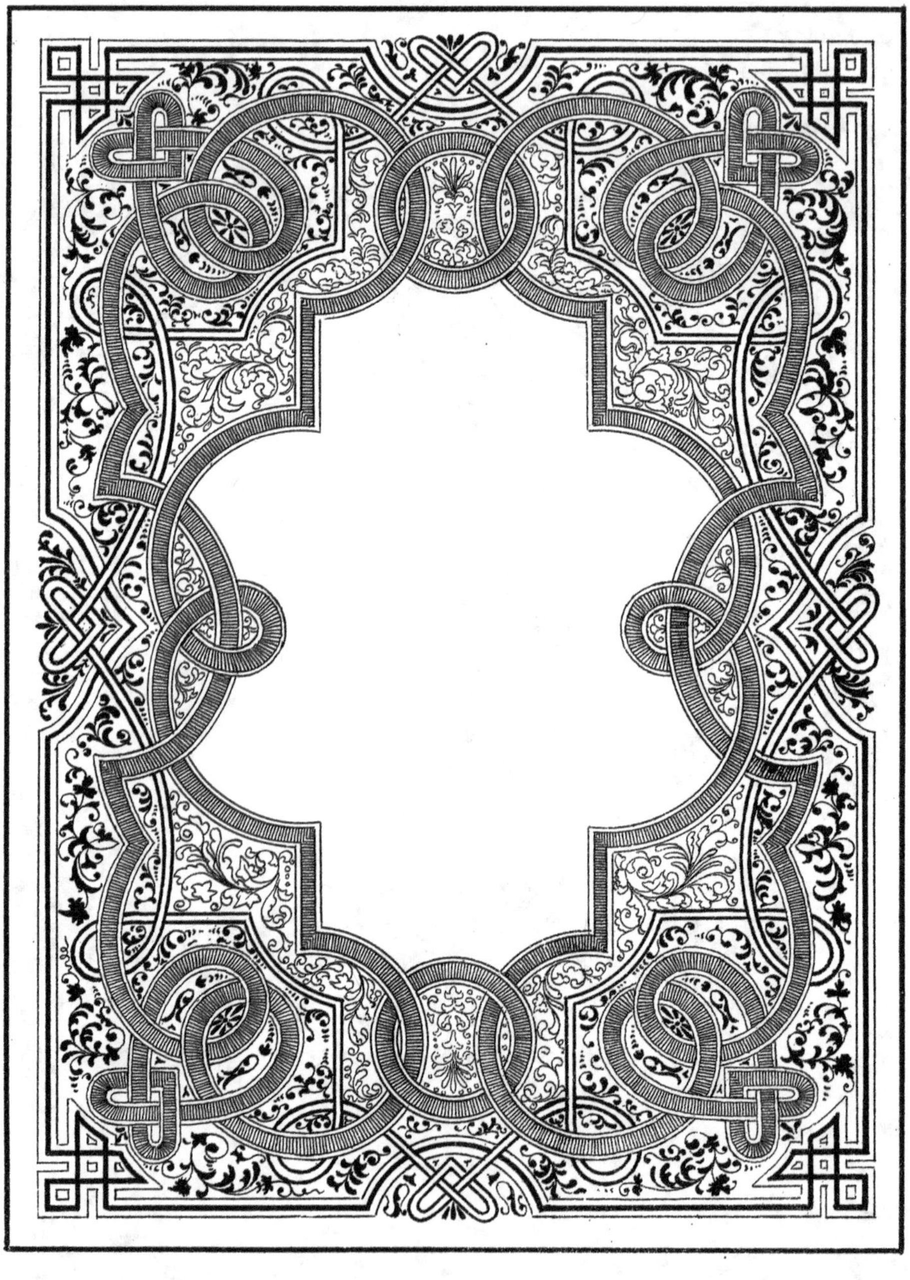

46

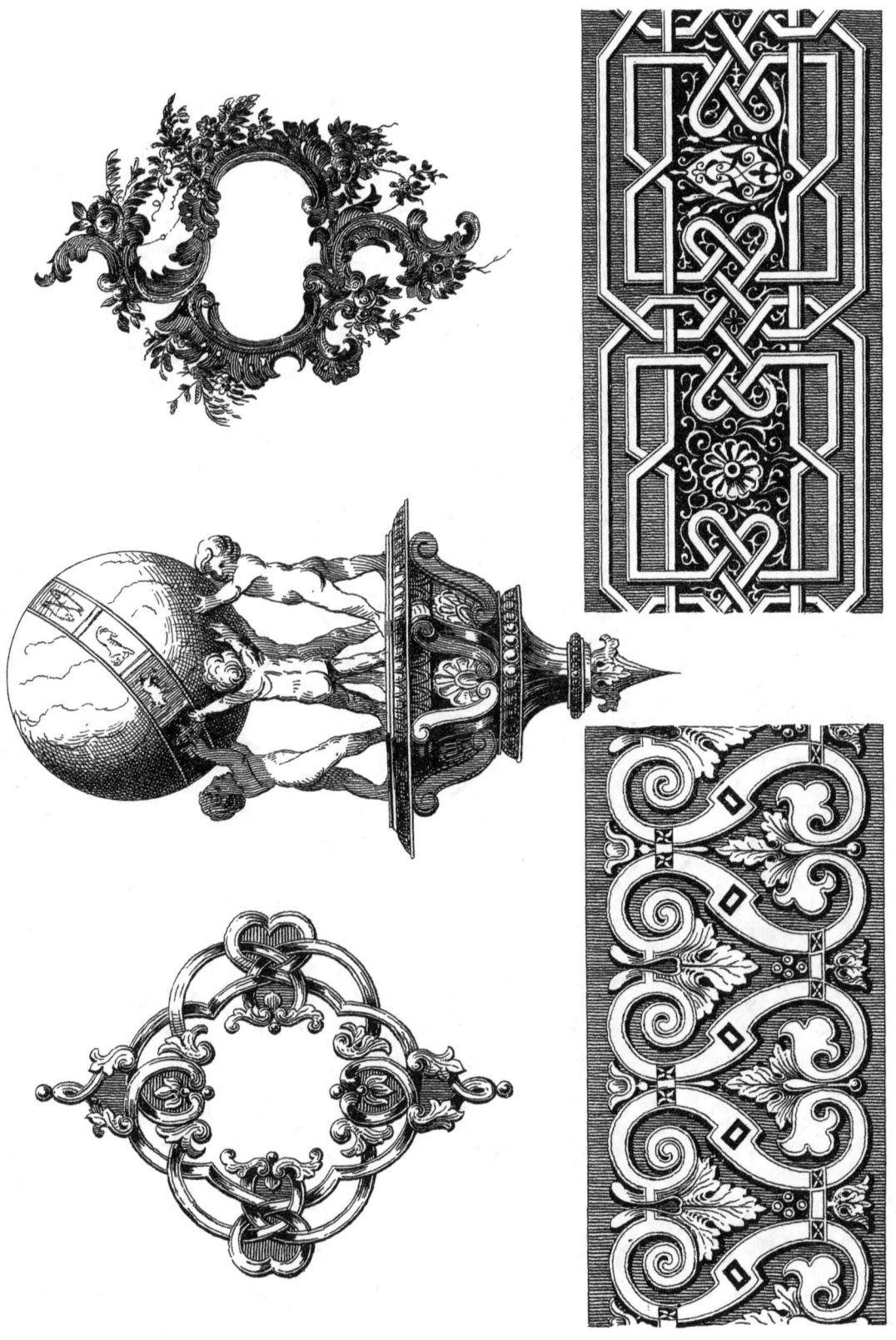

Französische Alphabete.
(Bâtarde oder Coulée.)

(Ronde.)

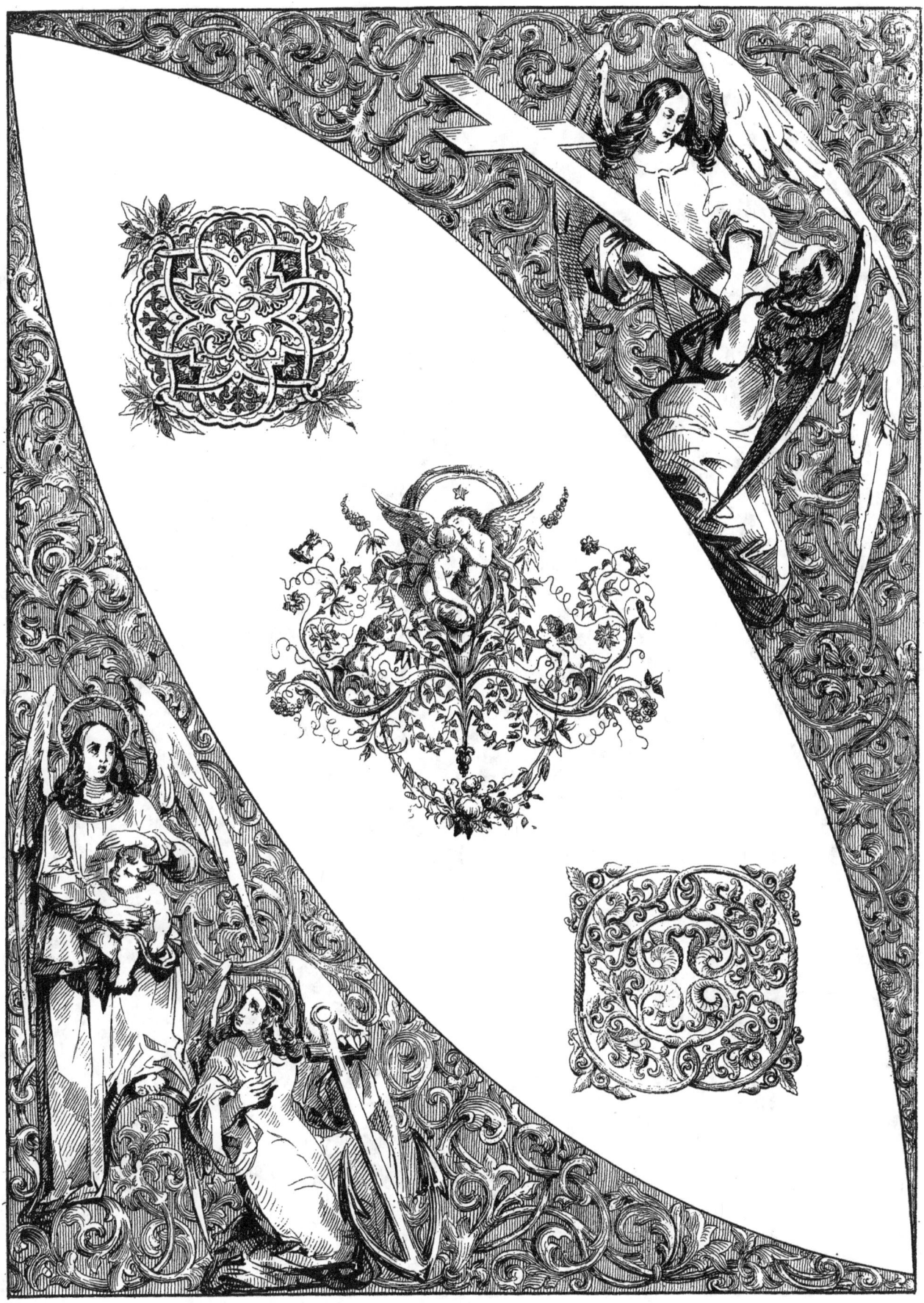

49

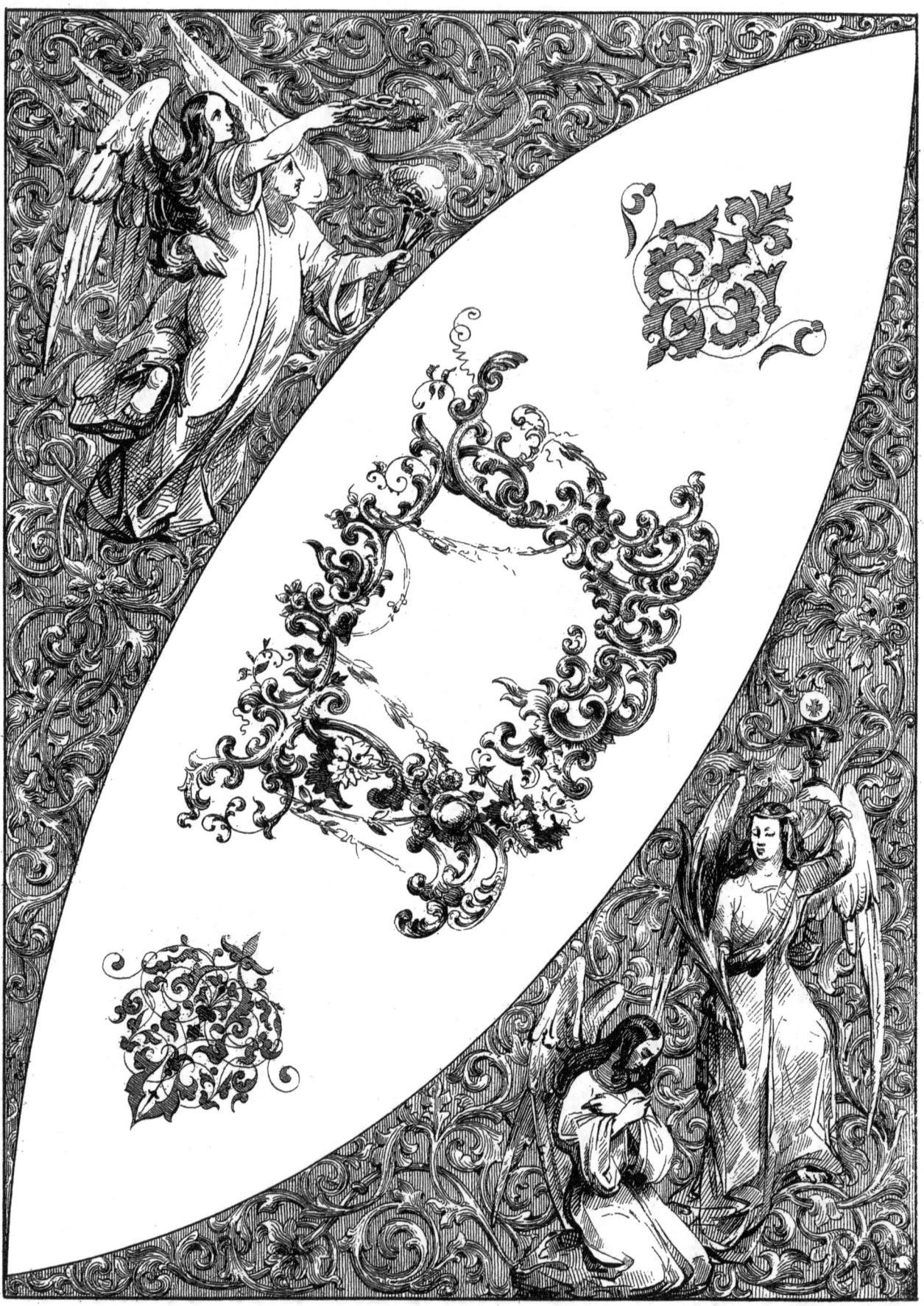

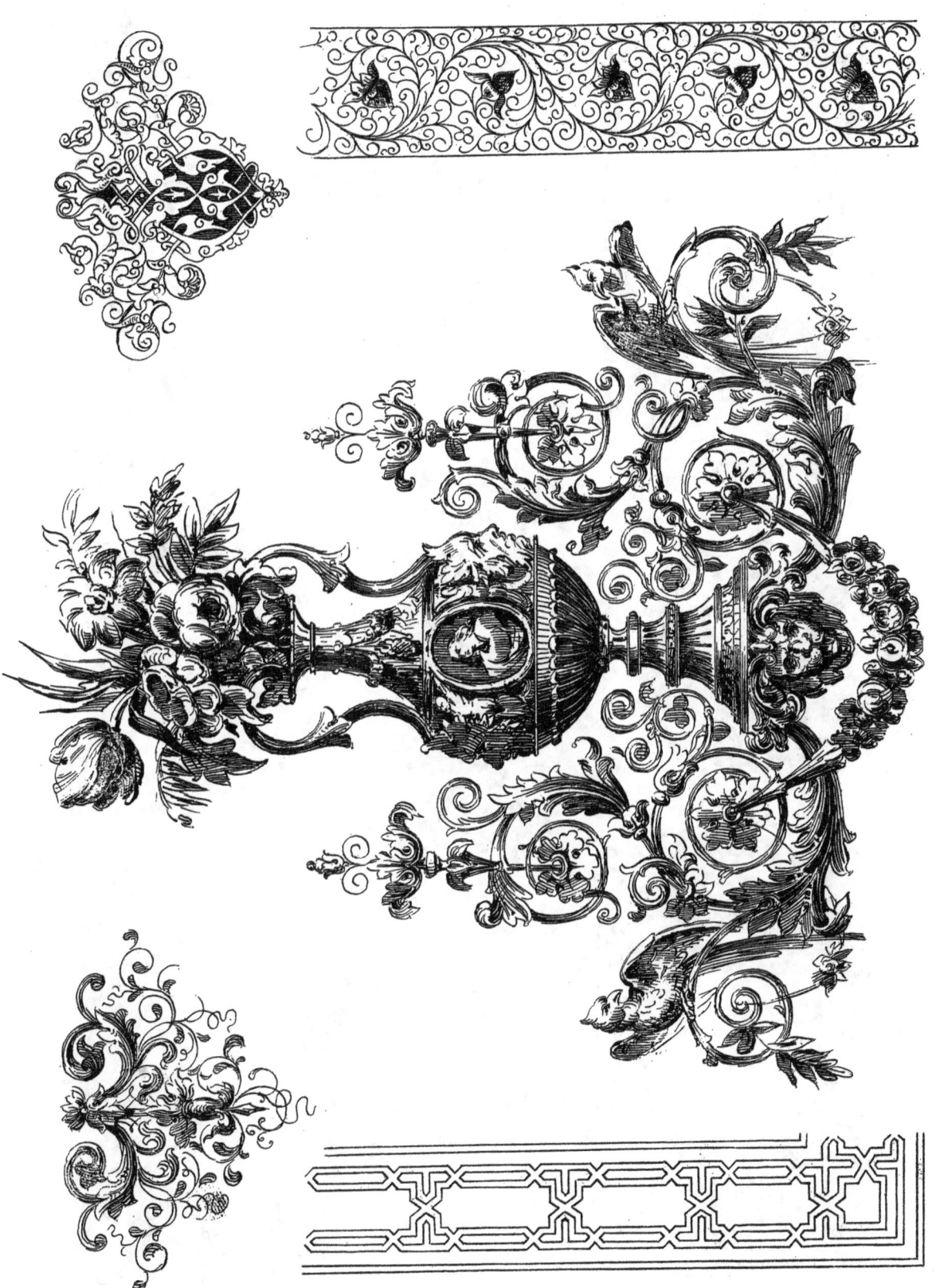

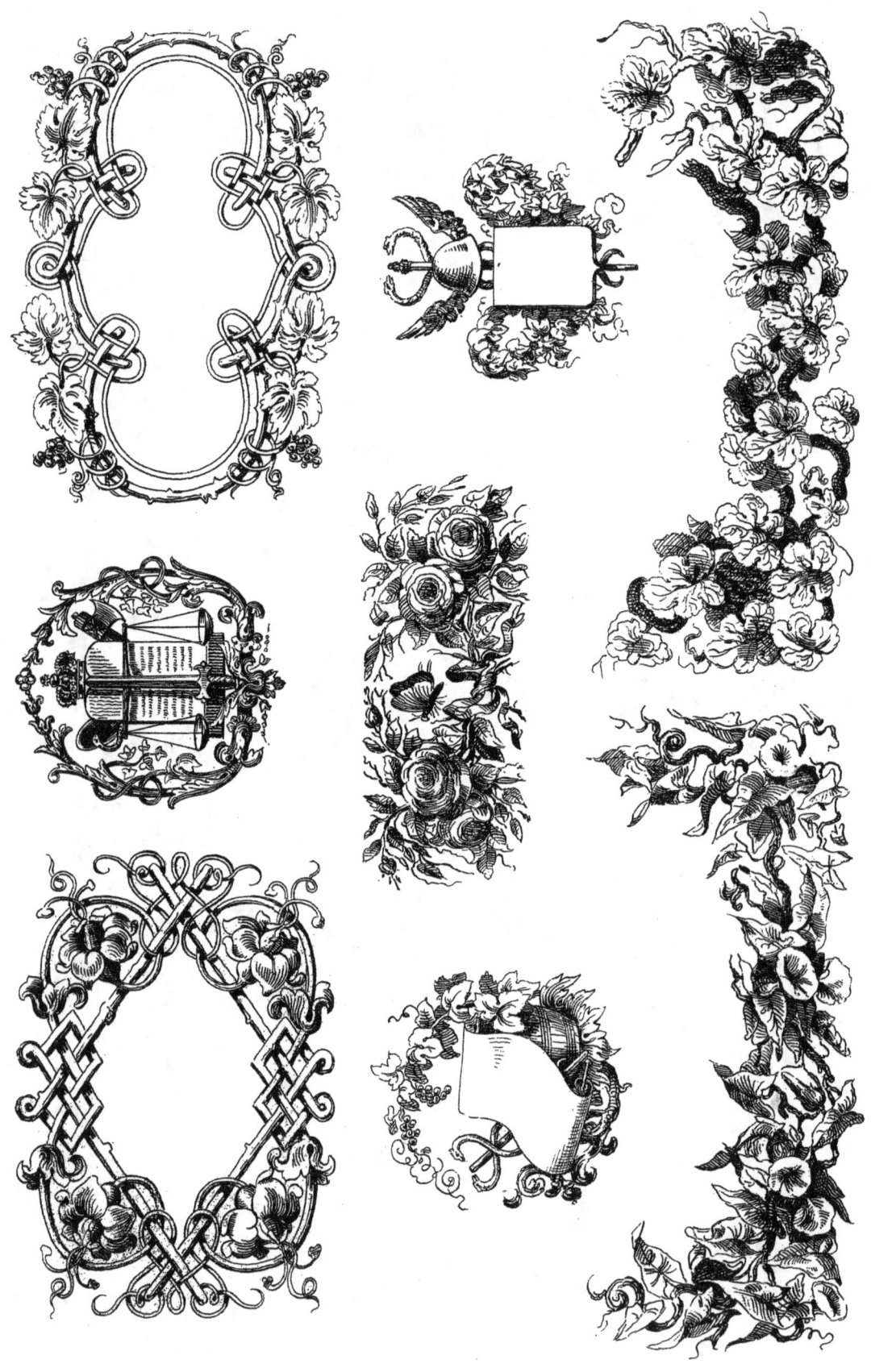

52

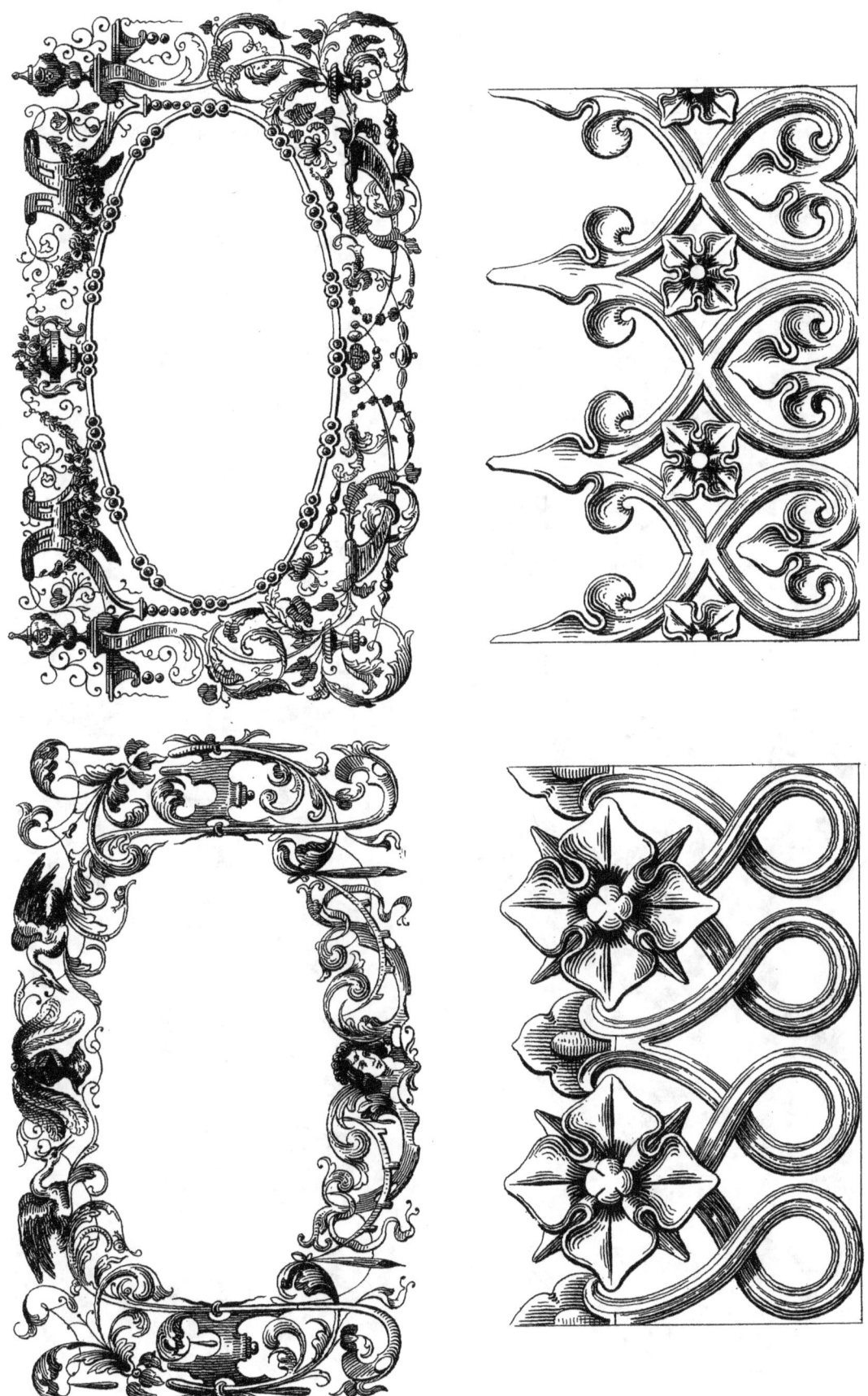

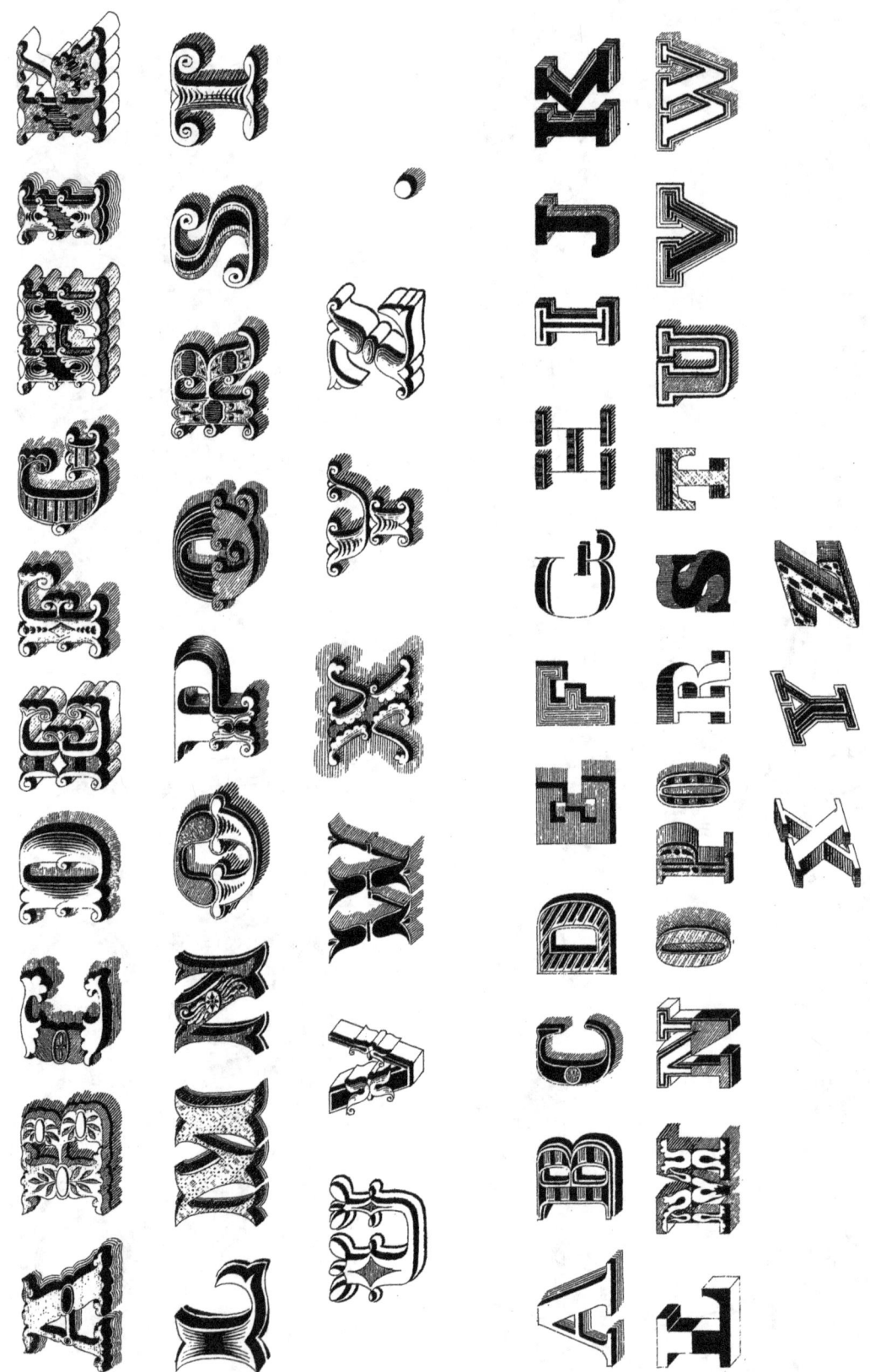

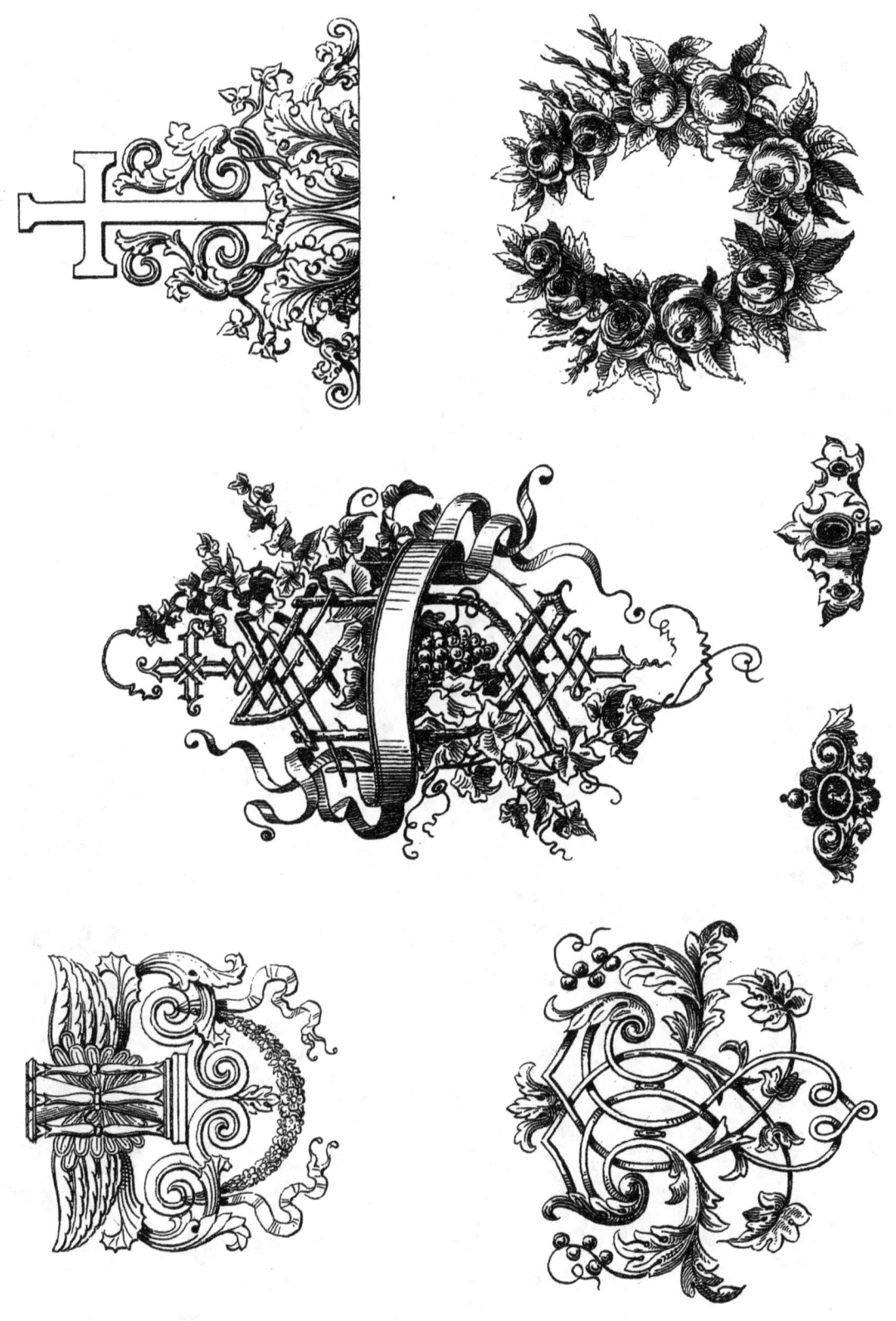

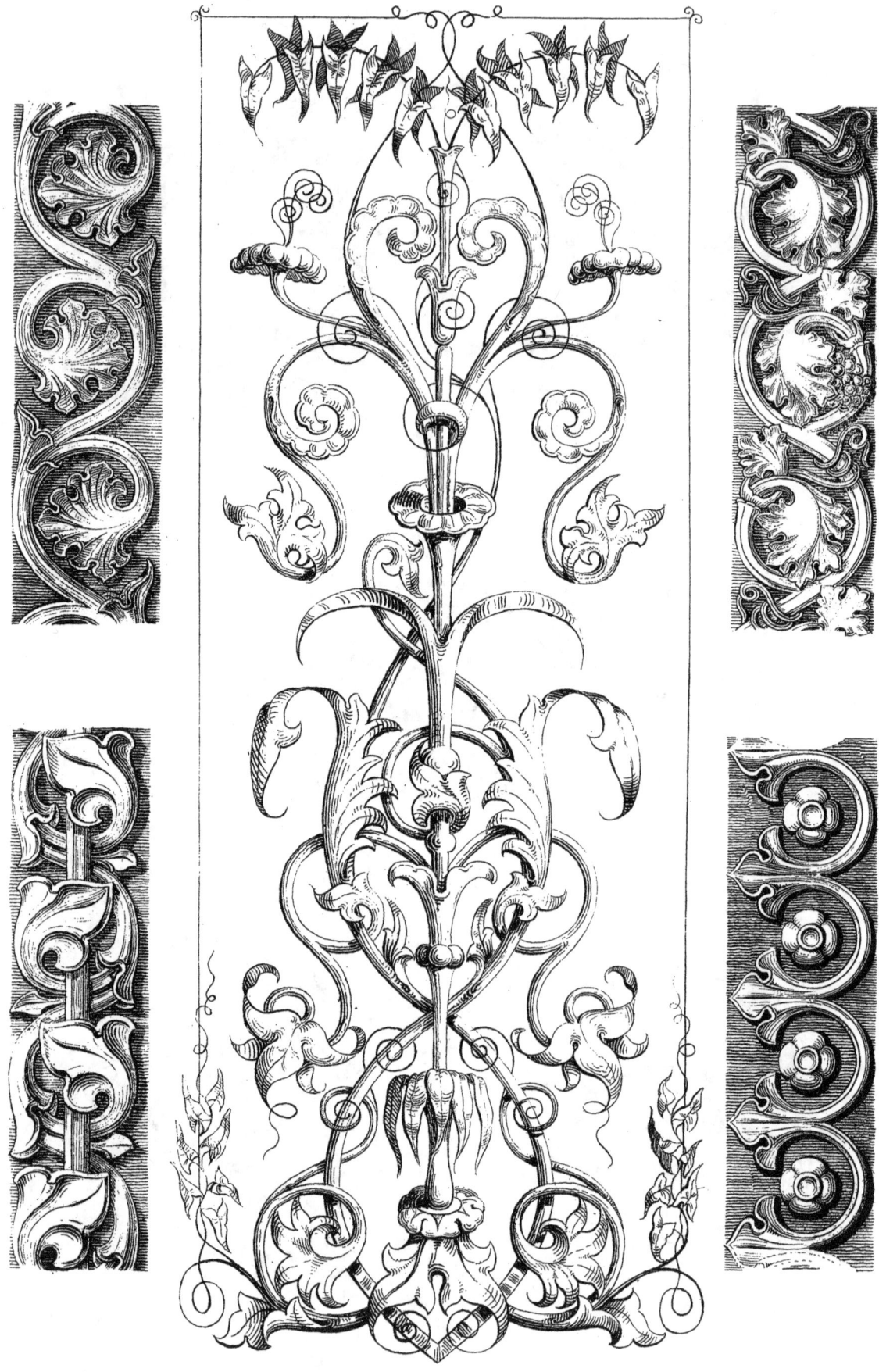

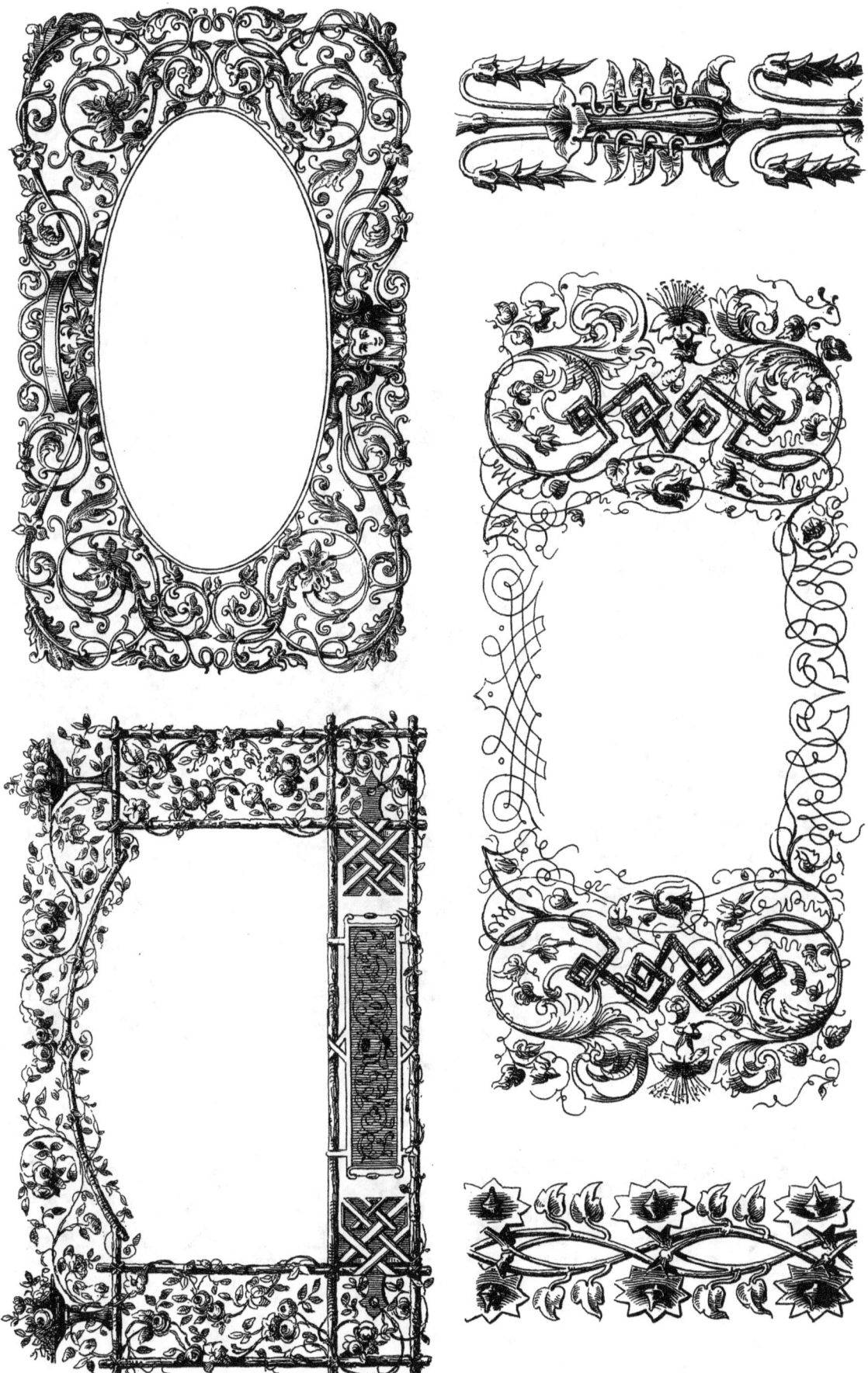

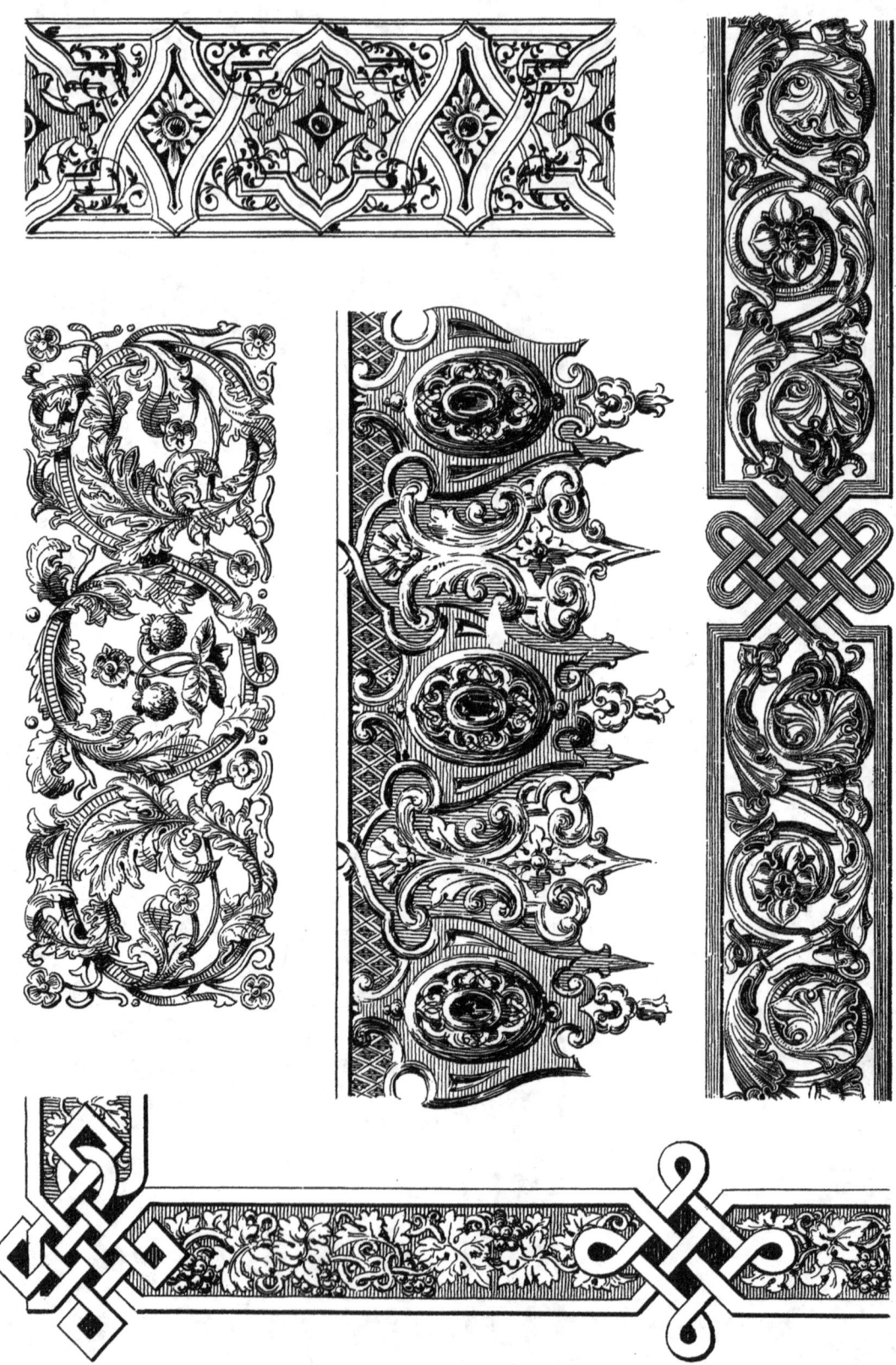

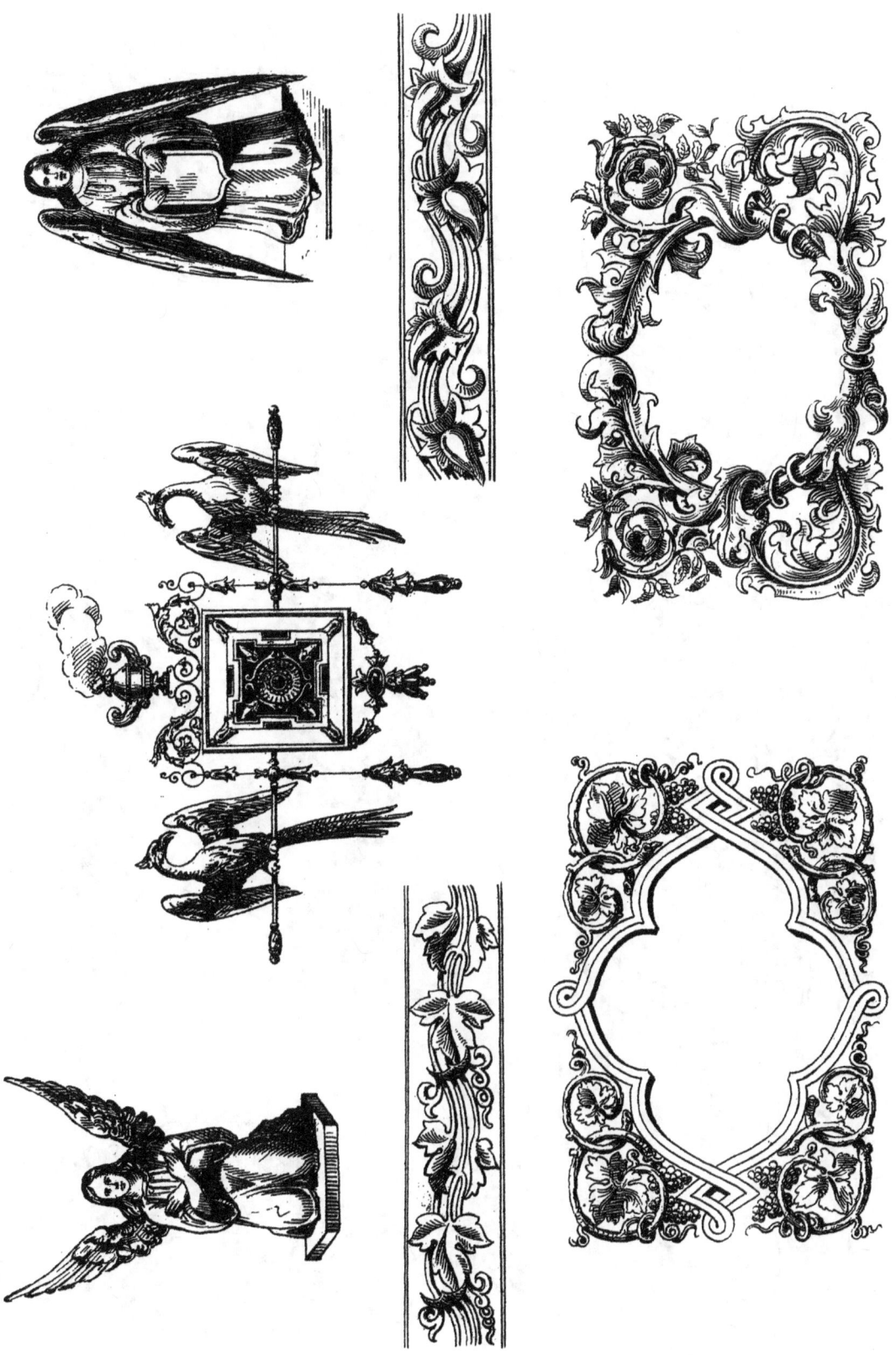

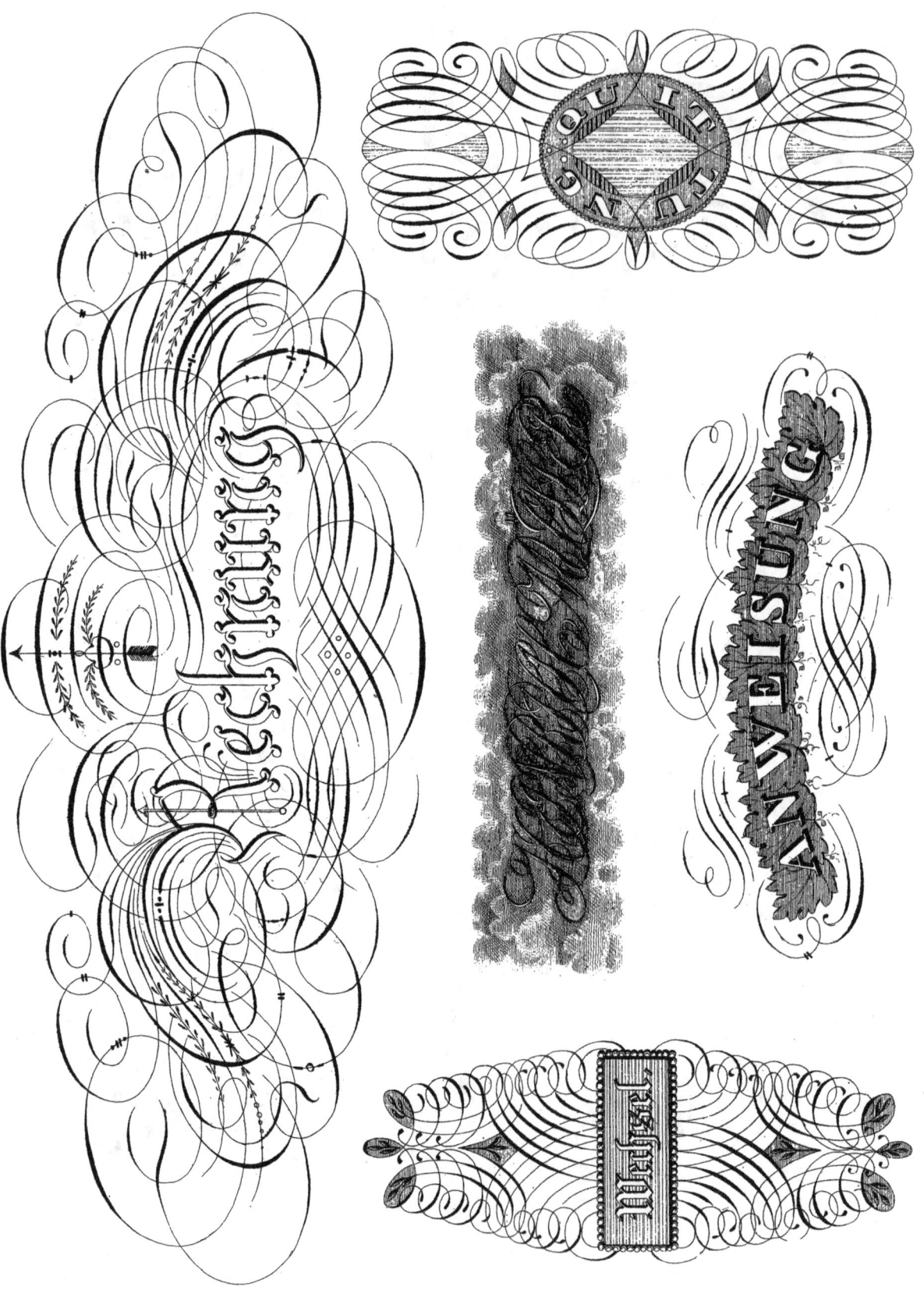

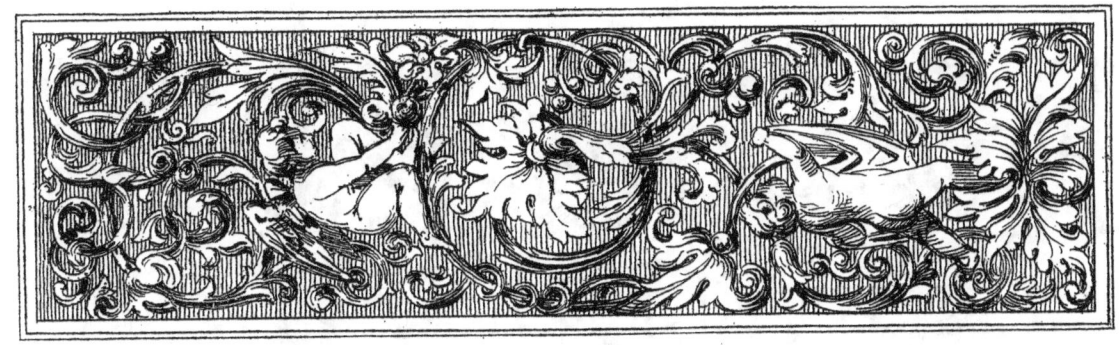

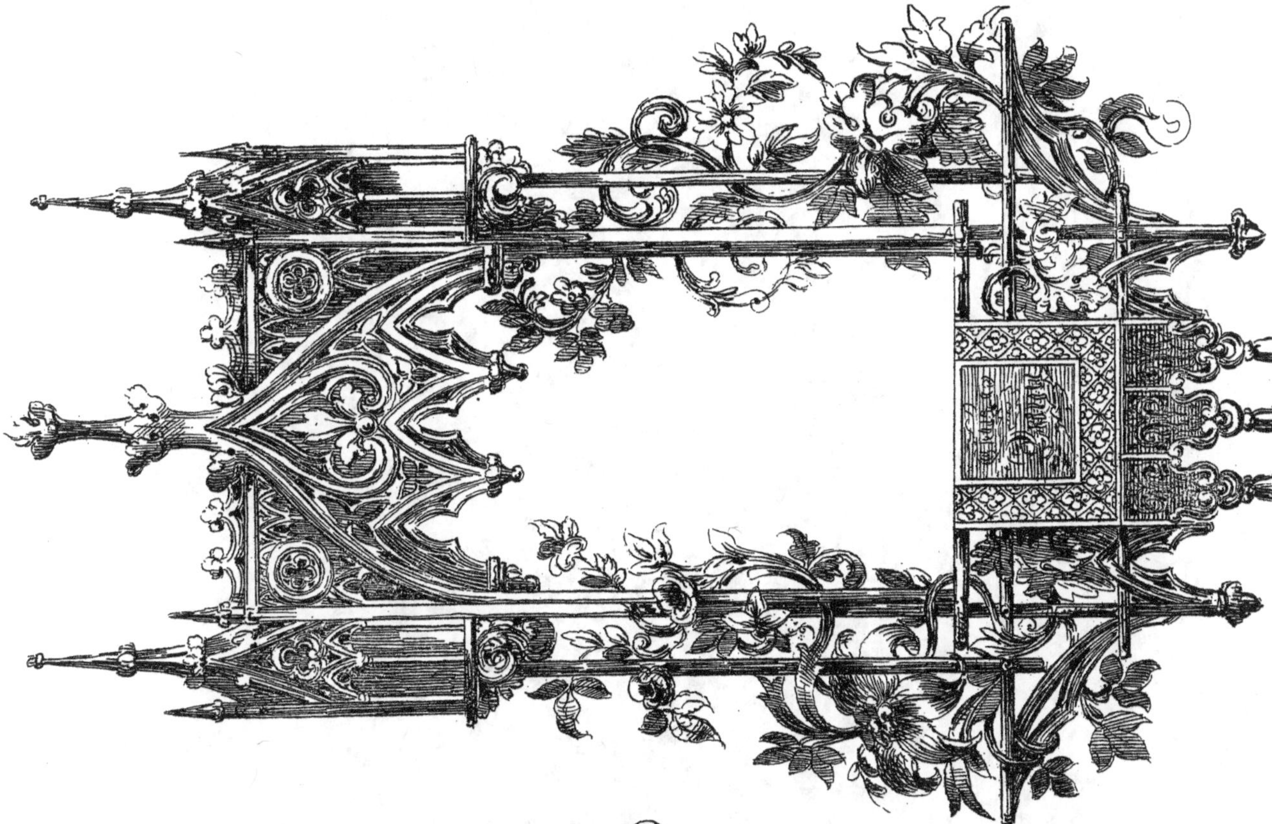

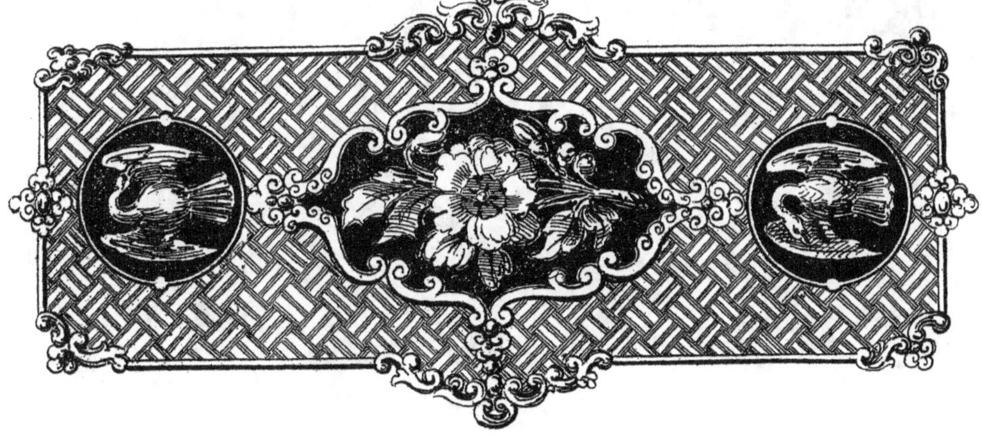

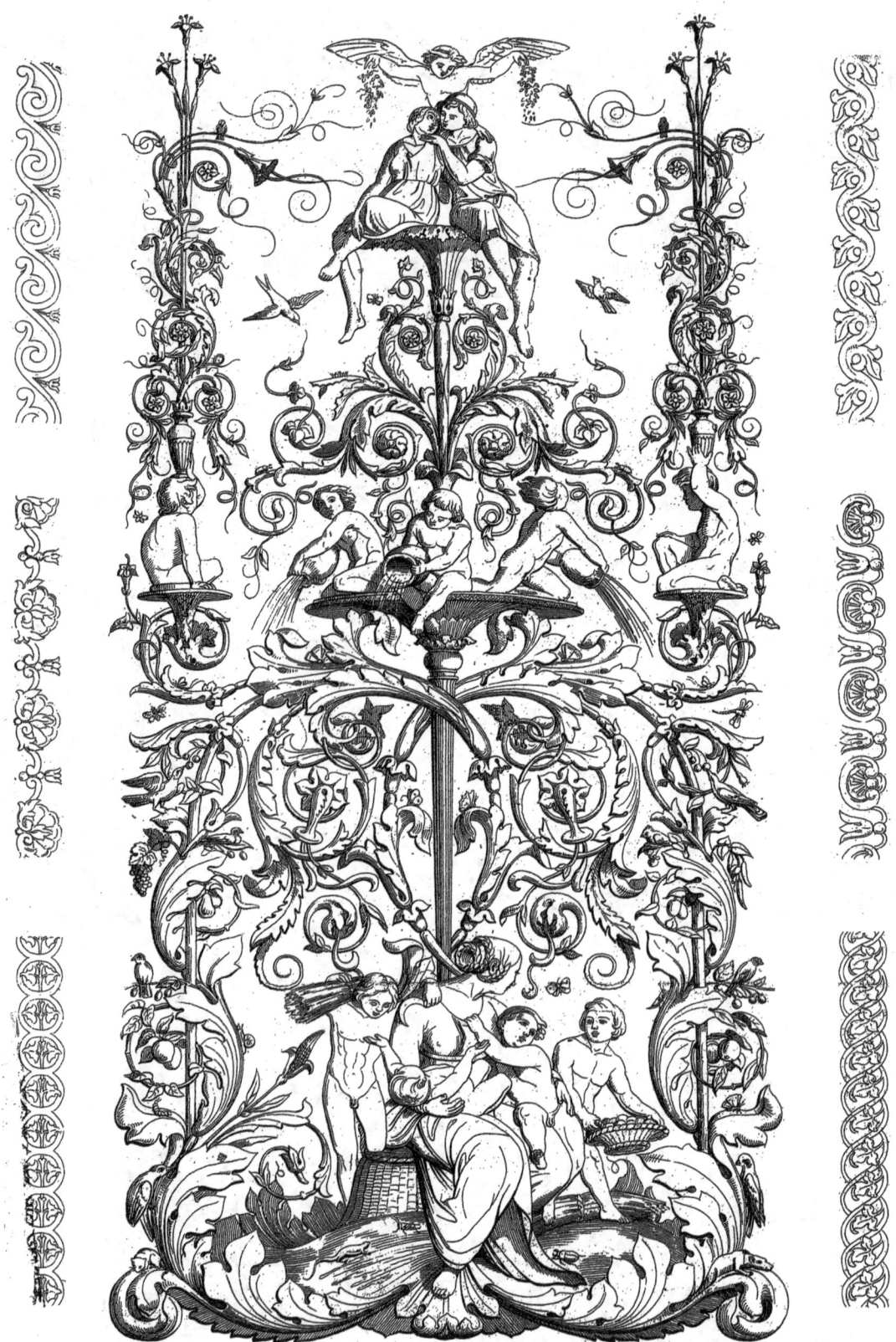

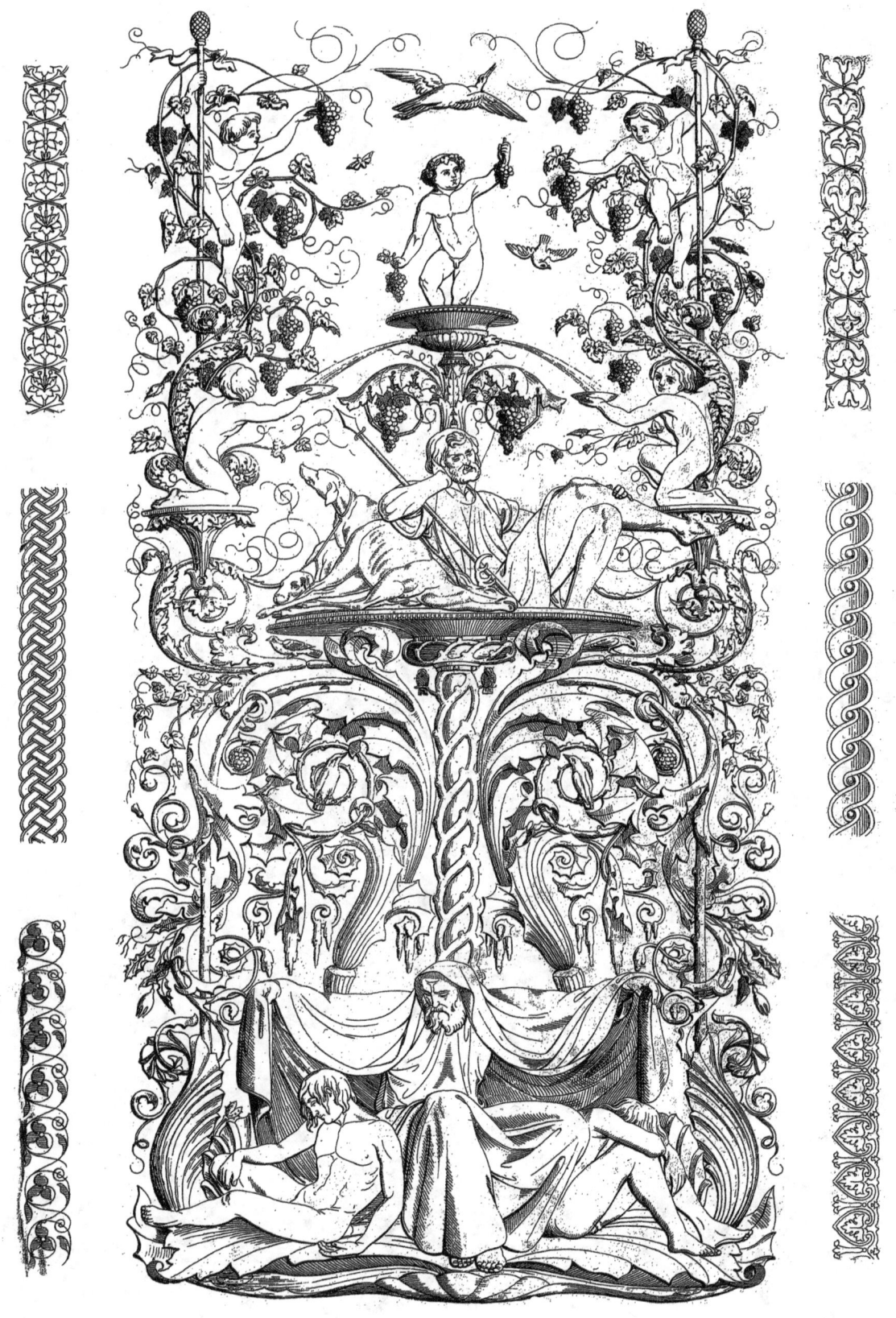

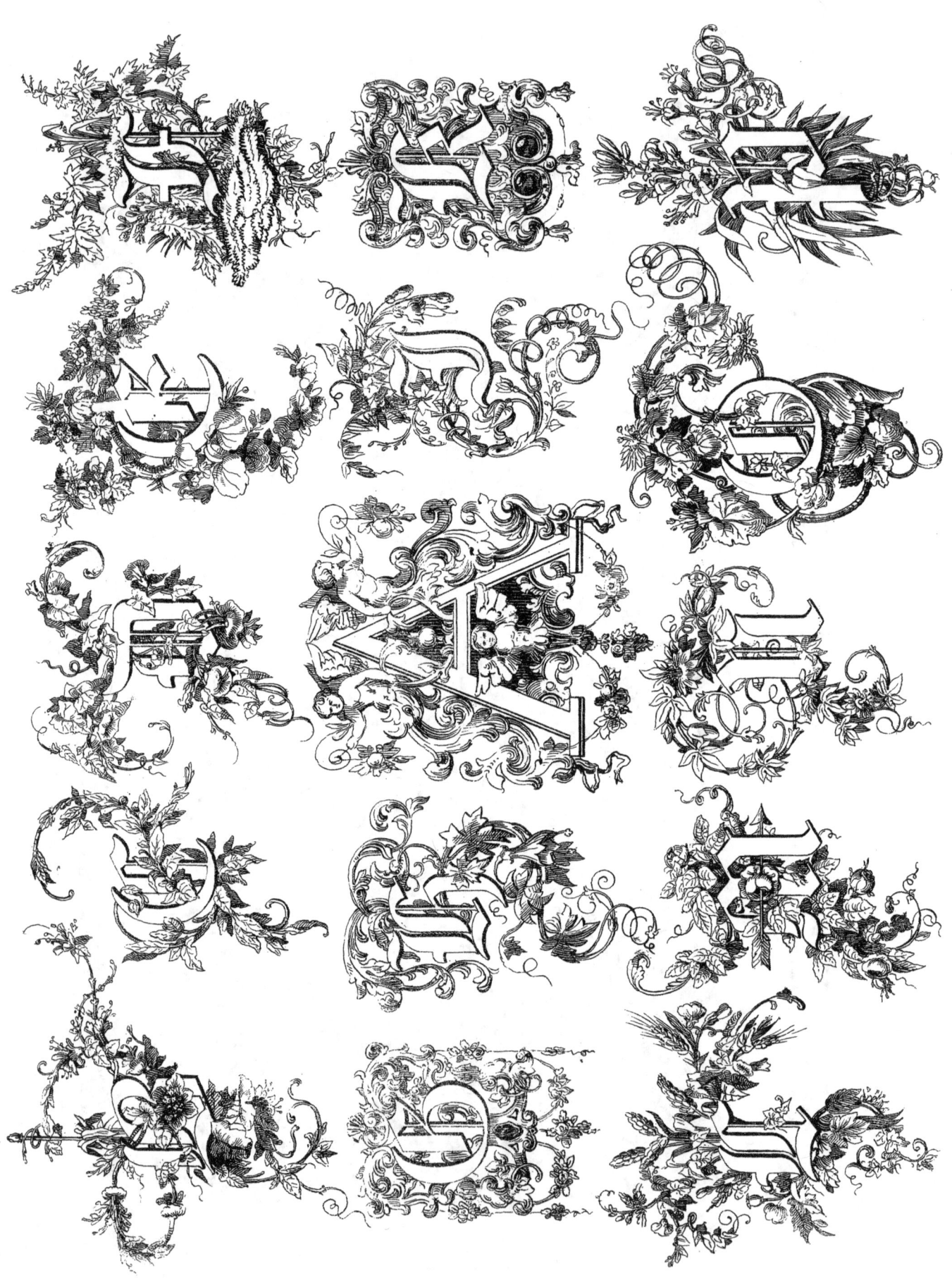

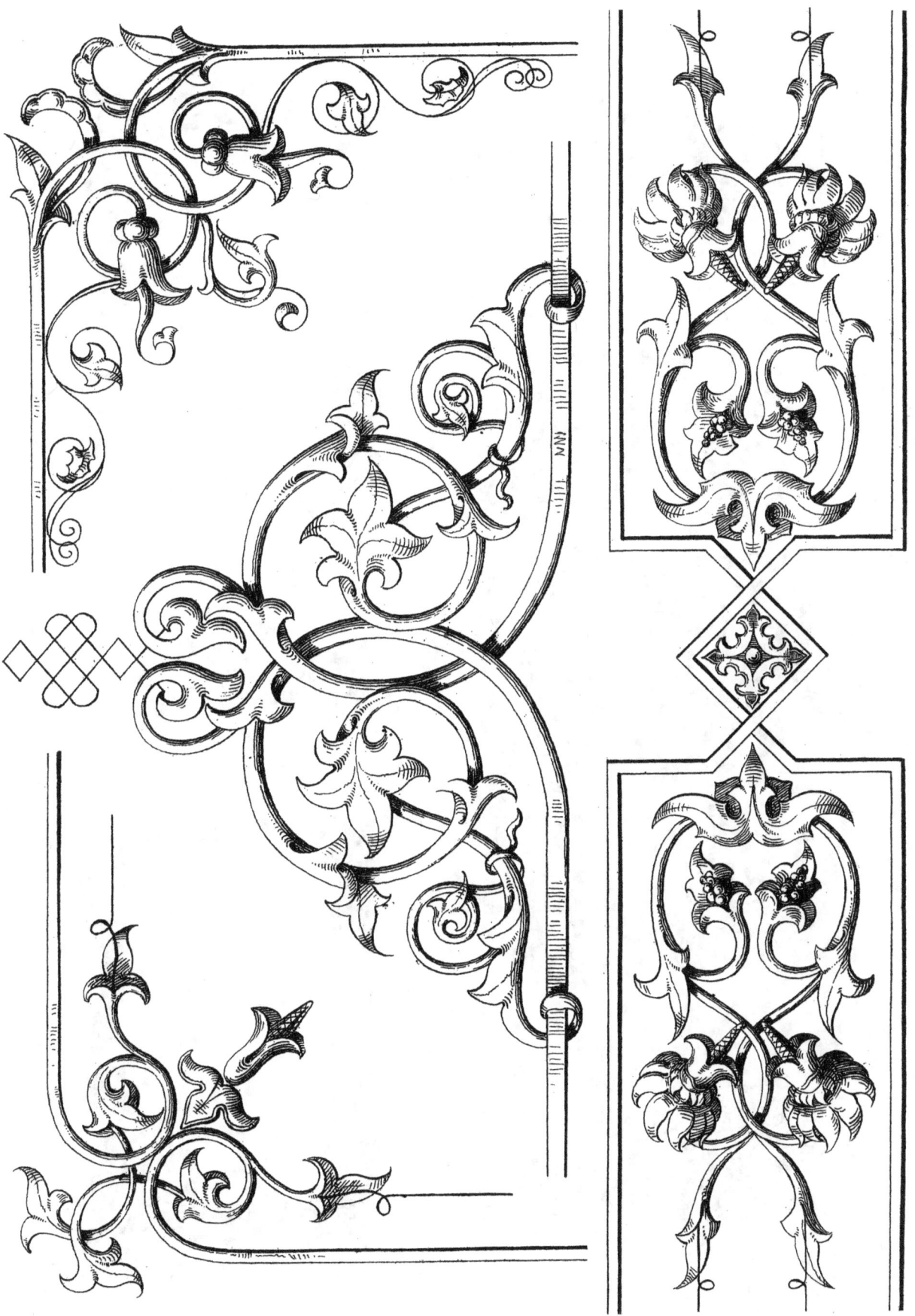

65

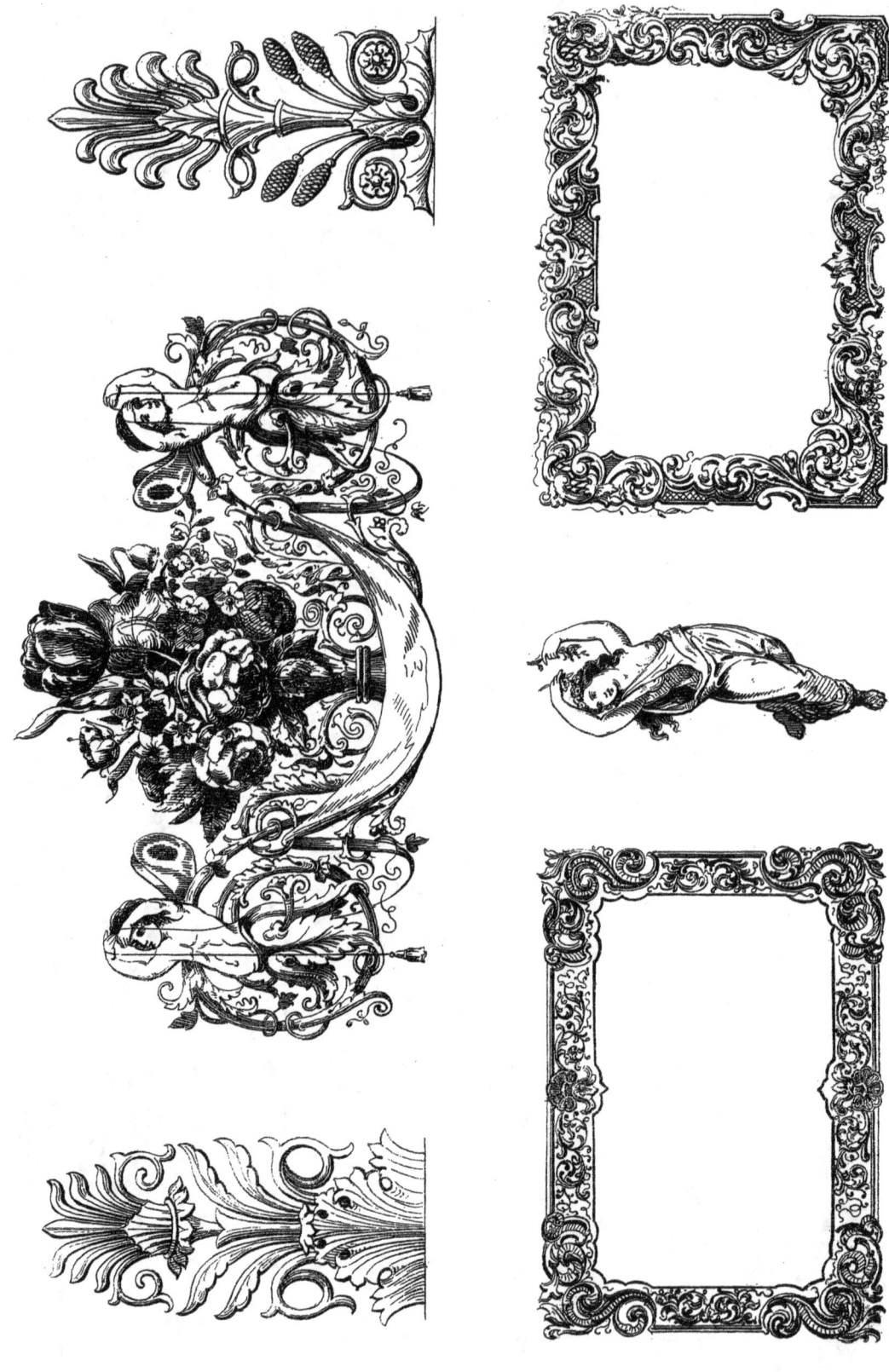

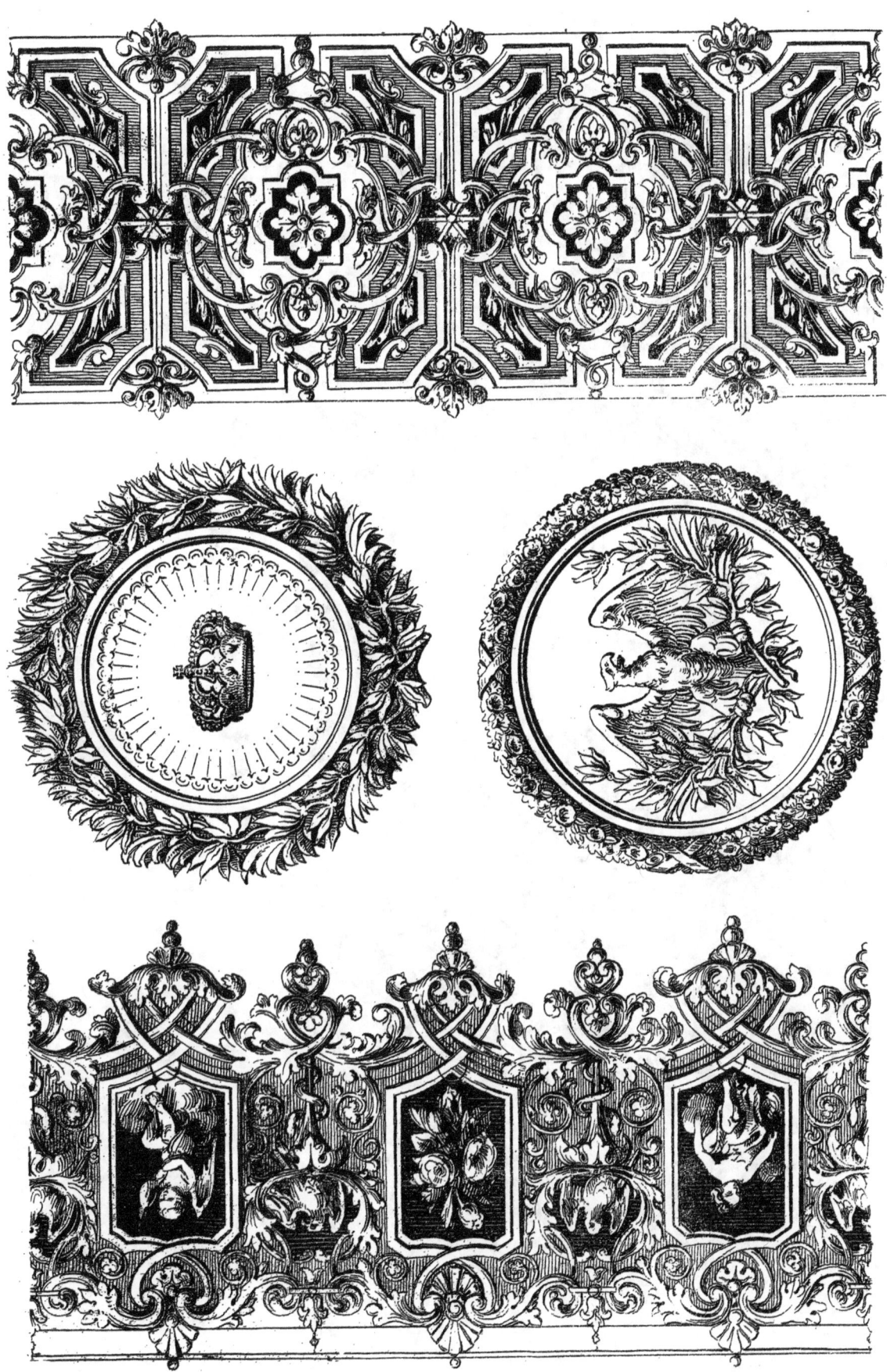

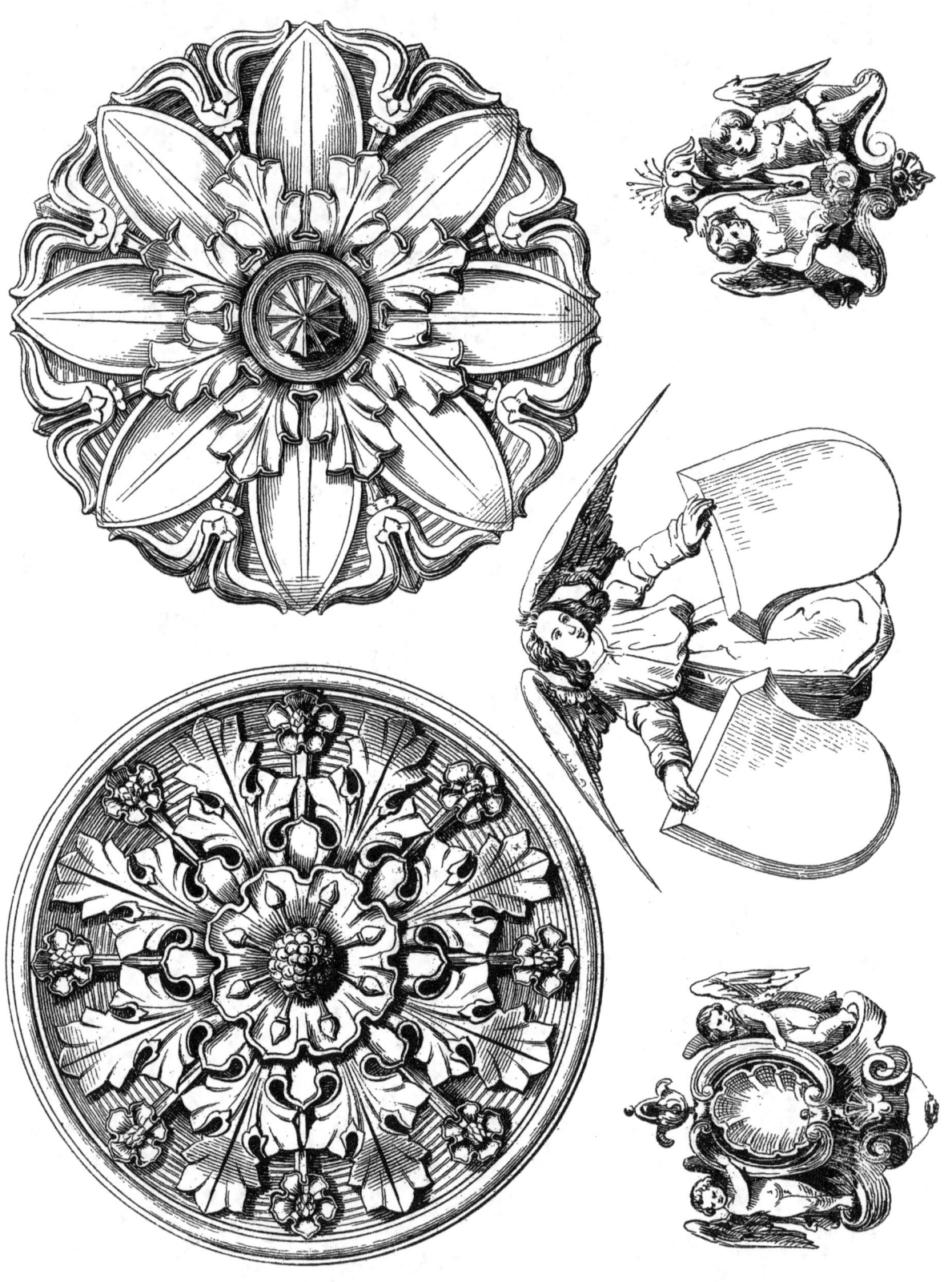

68

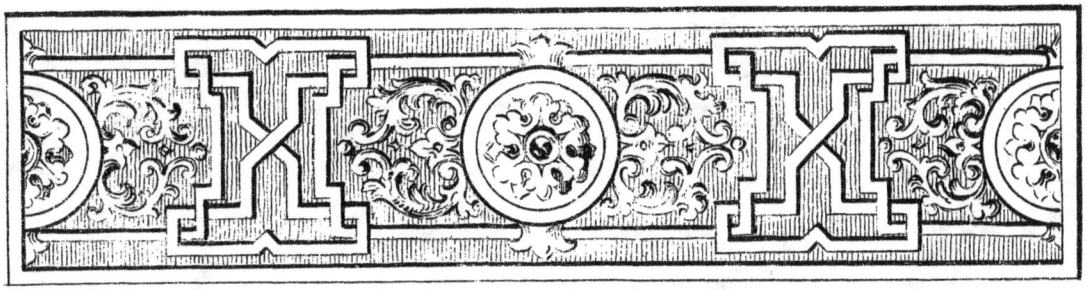

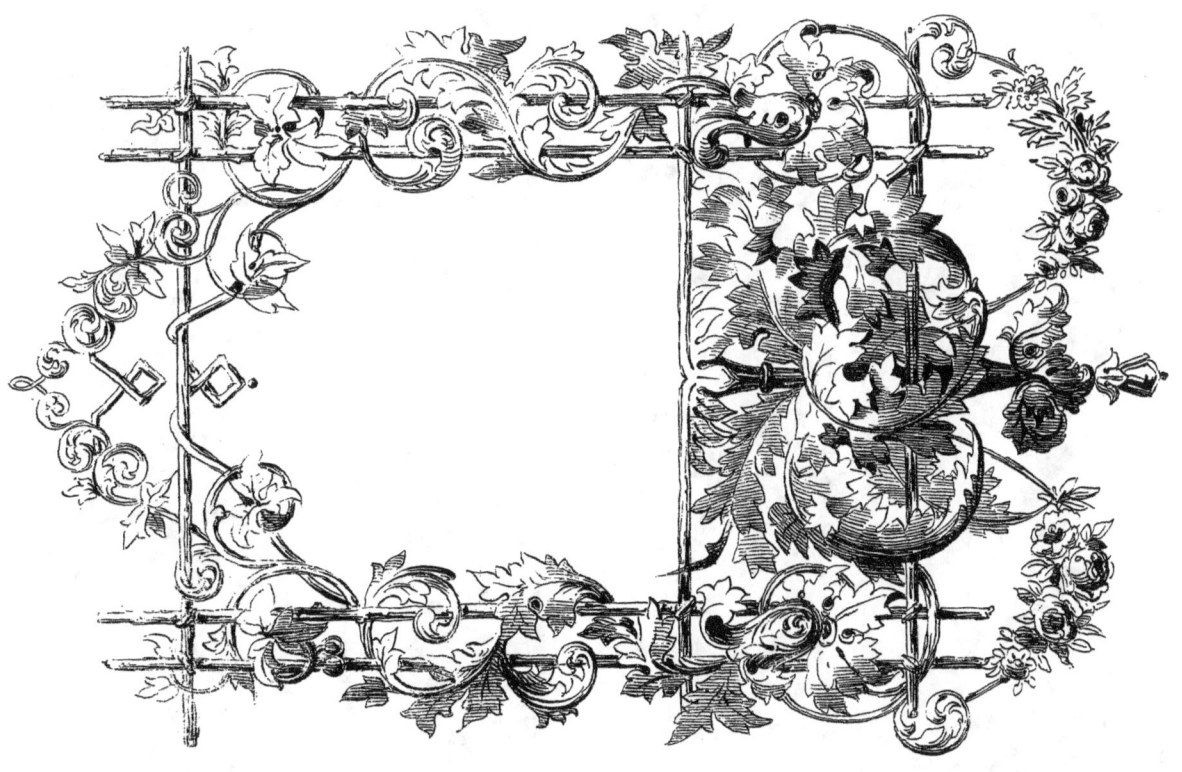

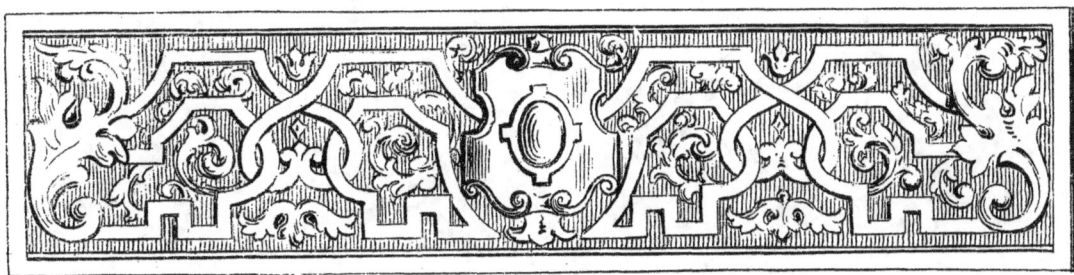

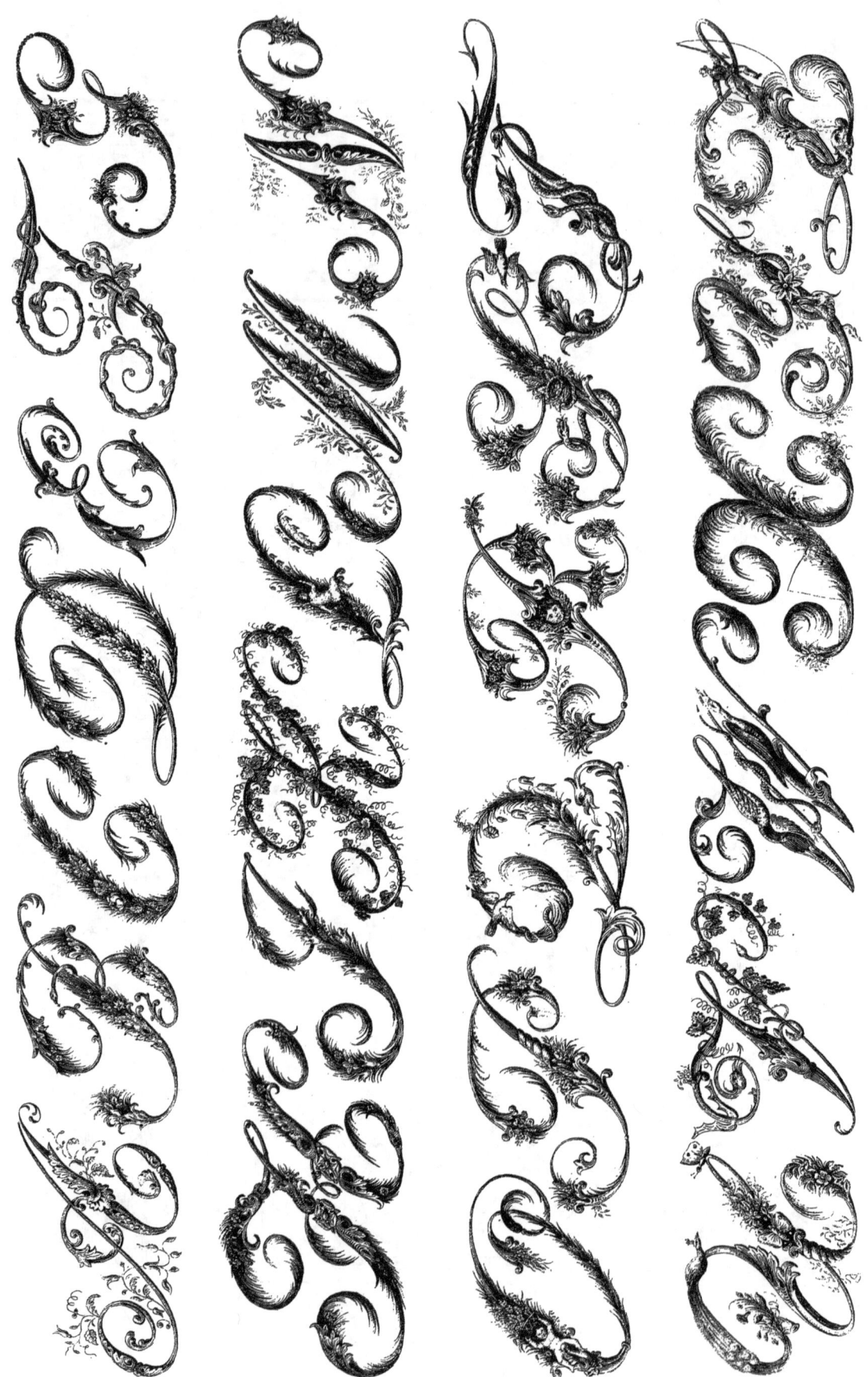

70

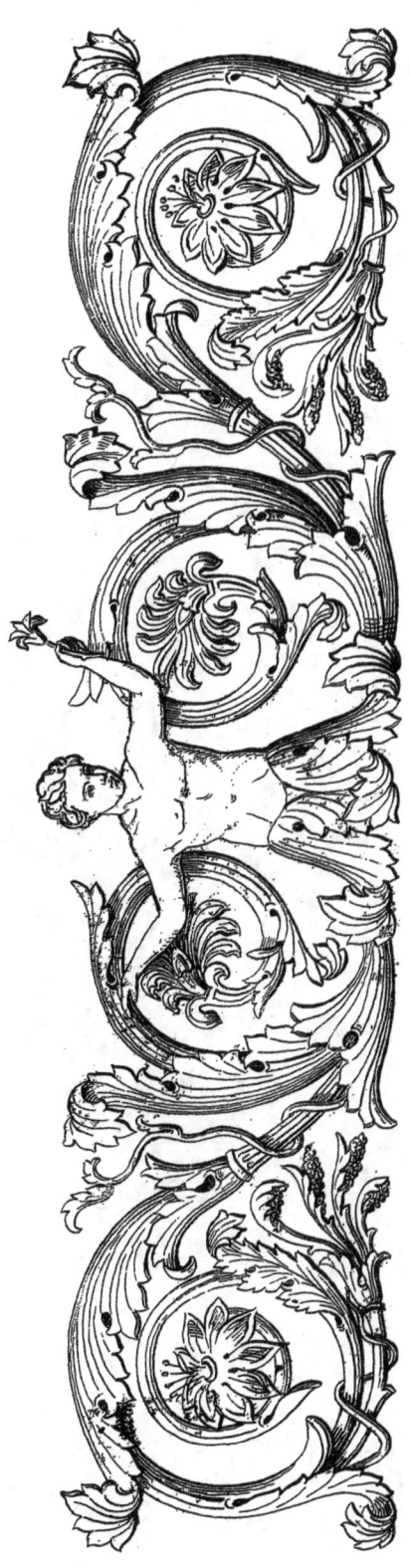

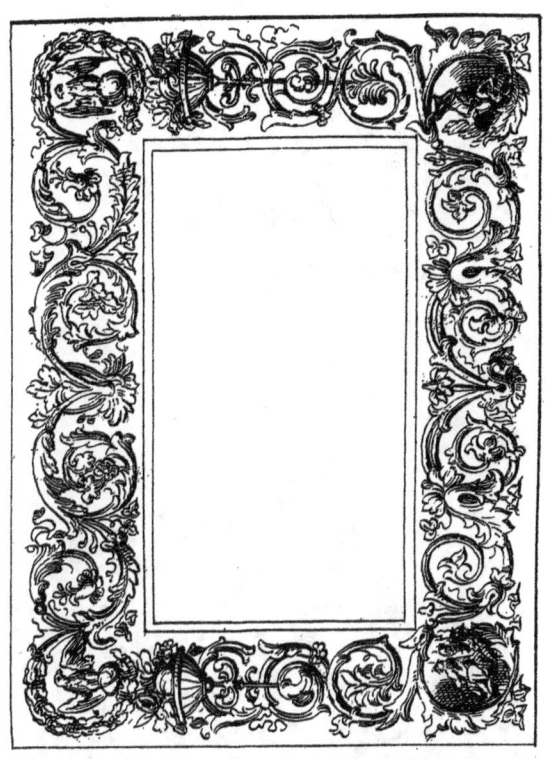

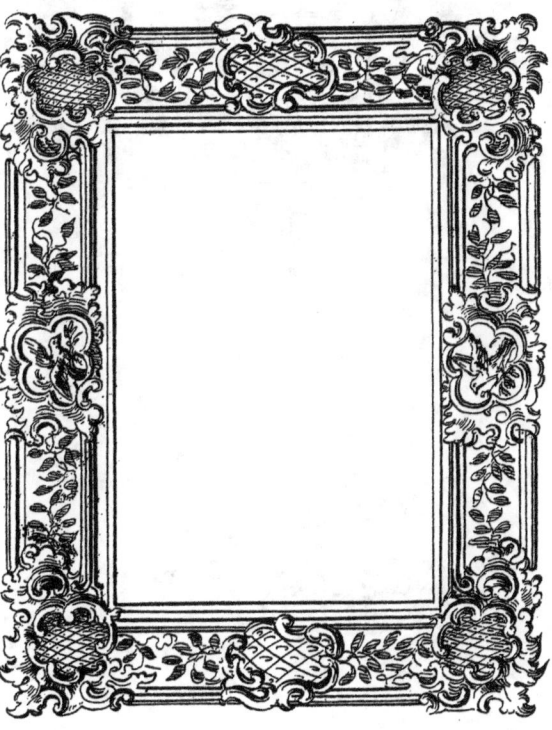

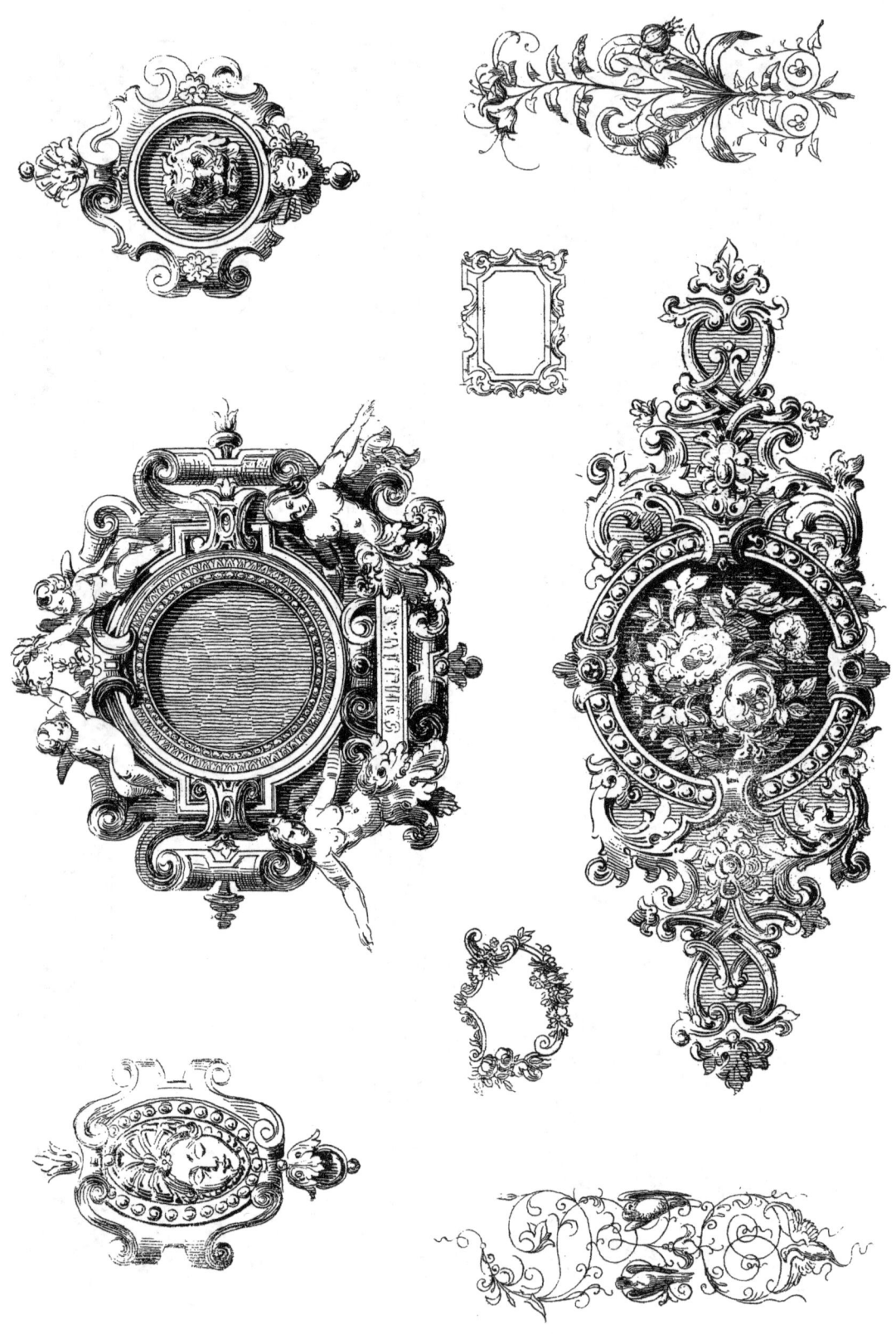

72

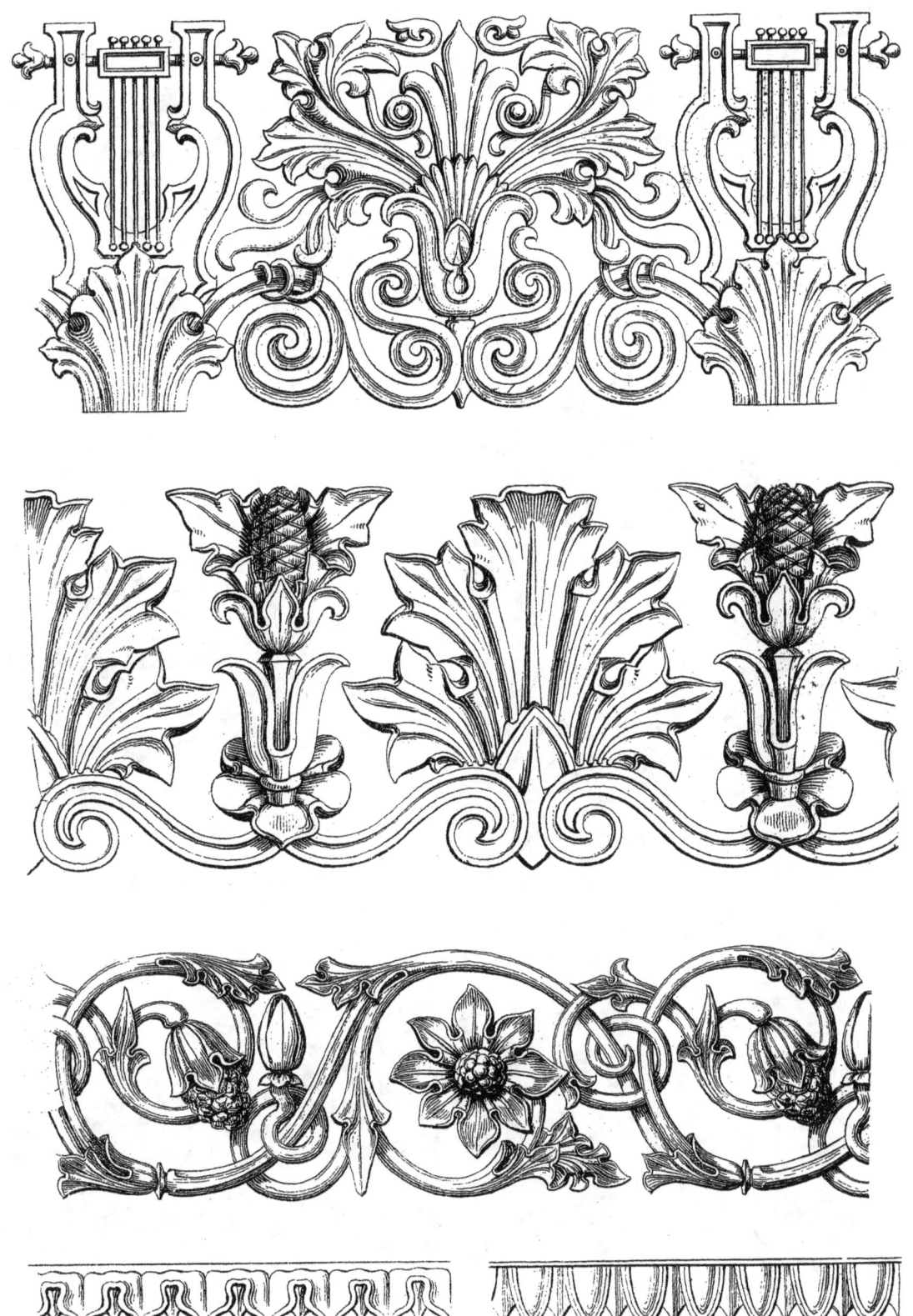

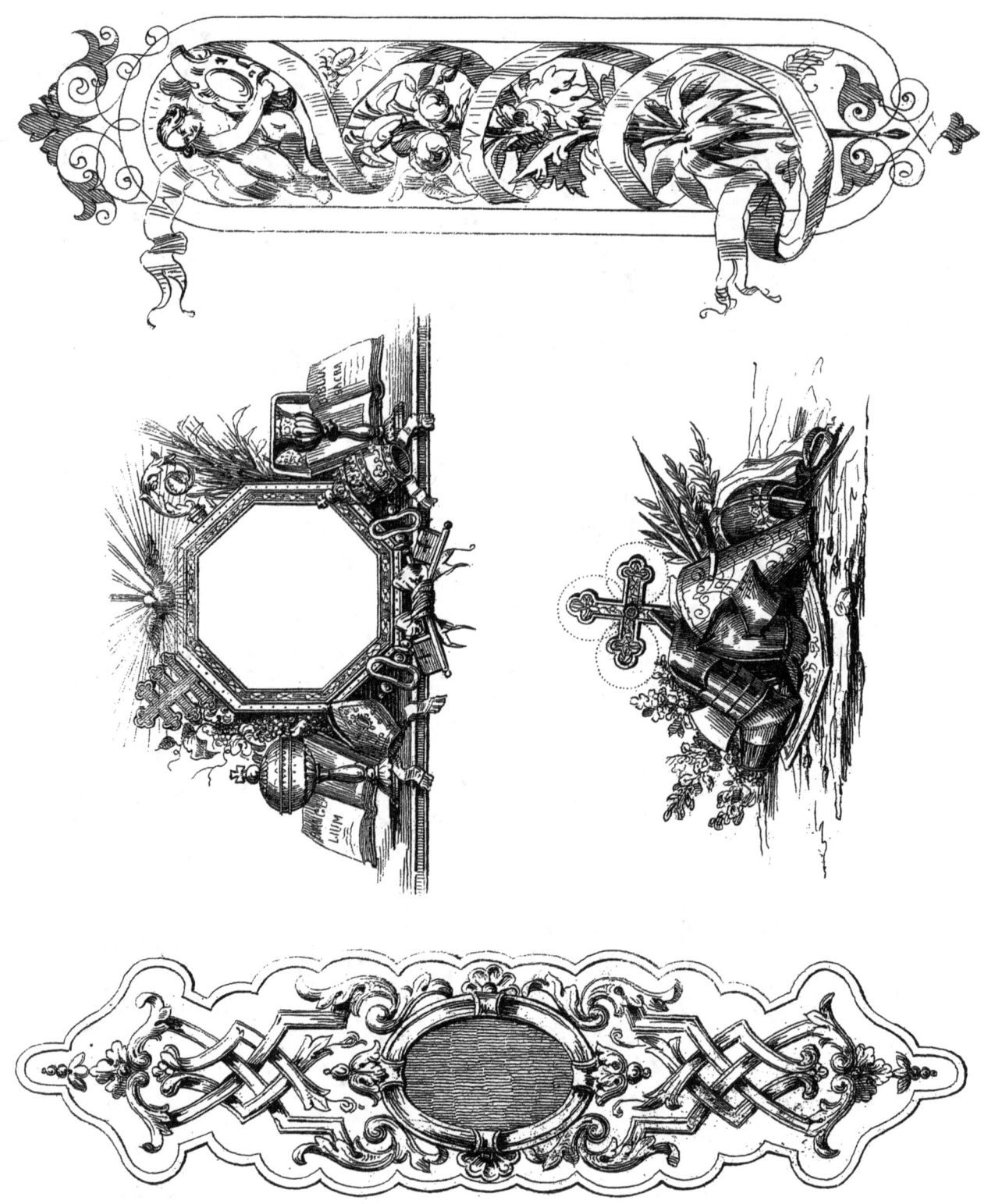

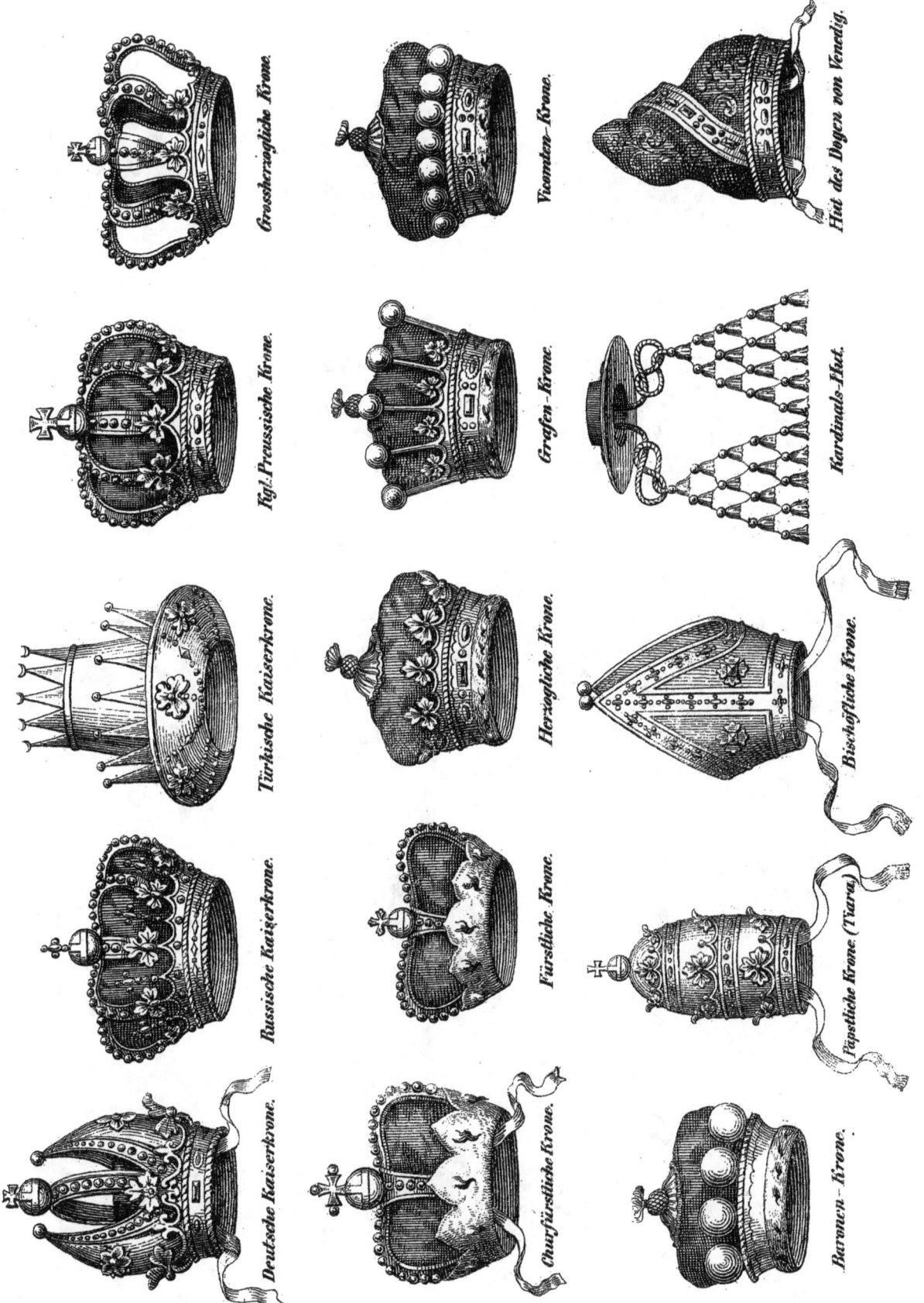

Grossherzogliche Krone.

Vicomten-Krone.

Hut des Dogen von Venedig.

Kgl. Preussische Krone.

Grafen-Krone.

Kardinals-Hut.

Türkische Kaiserkrone.

Herzogliche Krone.

Bischöfliche Krone.

Russische Kaiserkrone.

Fürstliche Krone.

Päpstliche Krone. (Tiara.)

Deutsche Kaiserkrone.

Churfürstliche Krone.

Baronen-Krone.

75

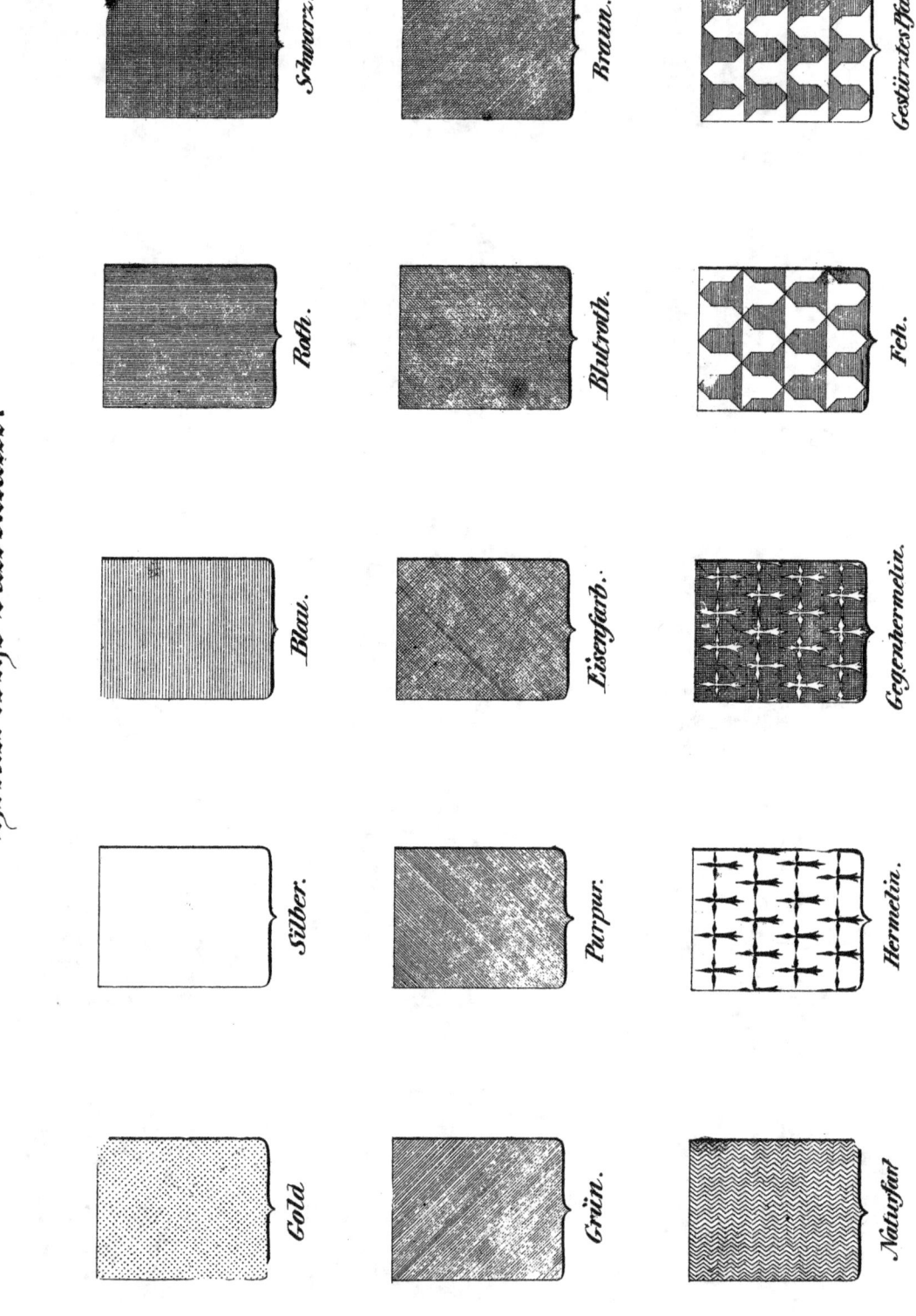

Heraldische Farbentafel.

Schwarz.

Braun.

Gestürztes Pfähleh.

Roth.

Blutroth.

Feh.

Blau.

Eisenfarb.

Gegenhermelin.

Silber.

Purpur.

Hermelin.

Gold.

Grün.

Naturfarb.

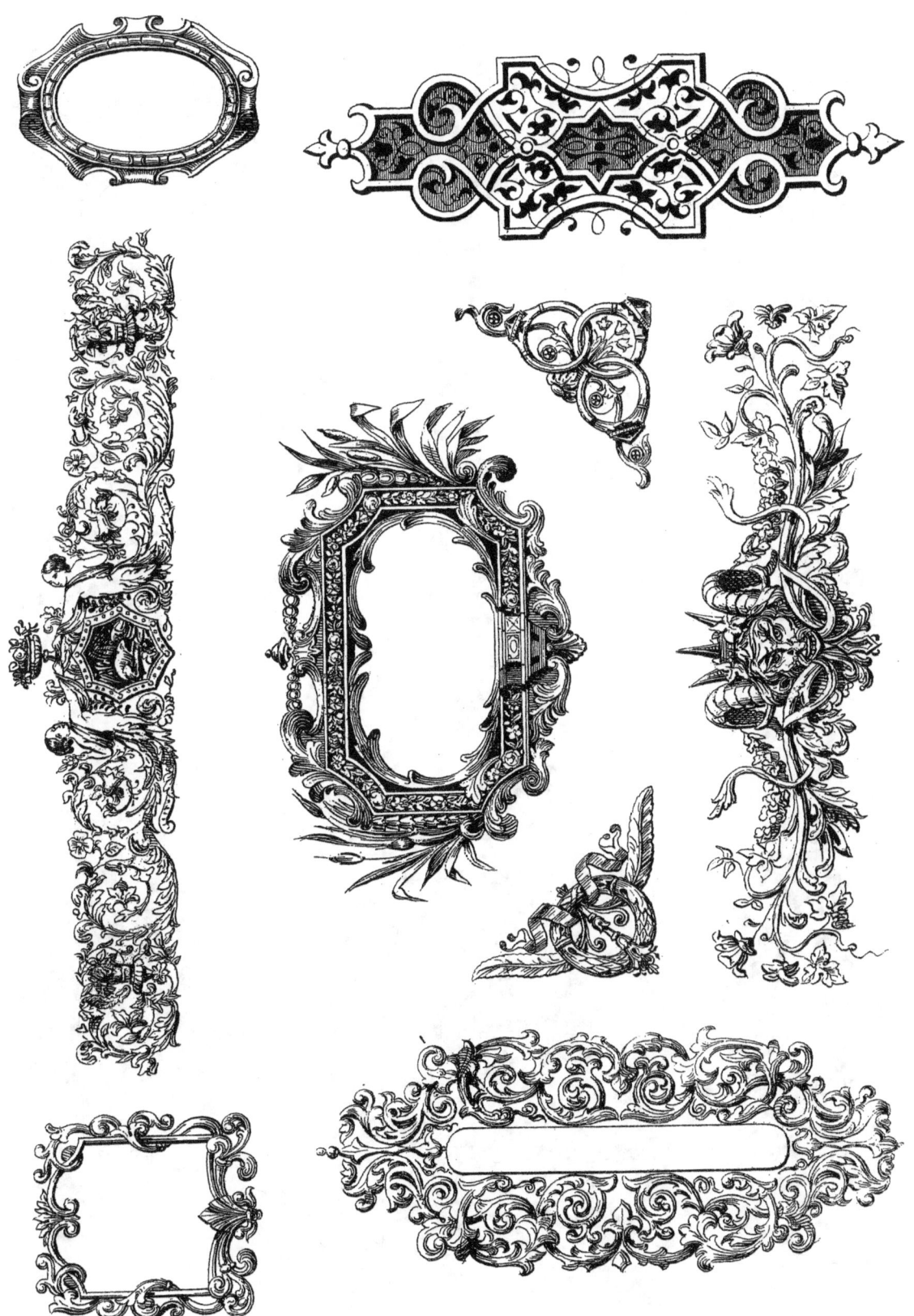

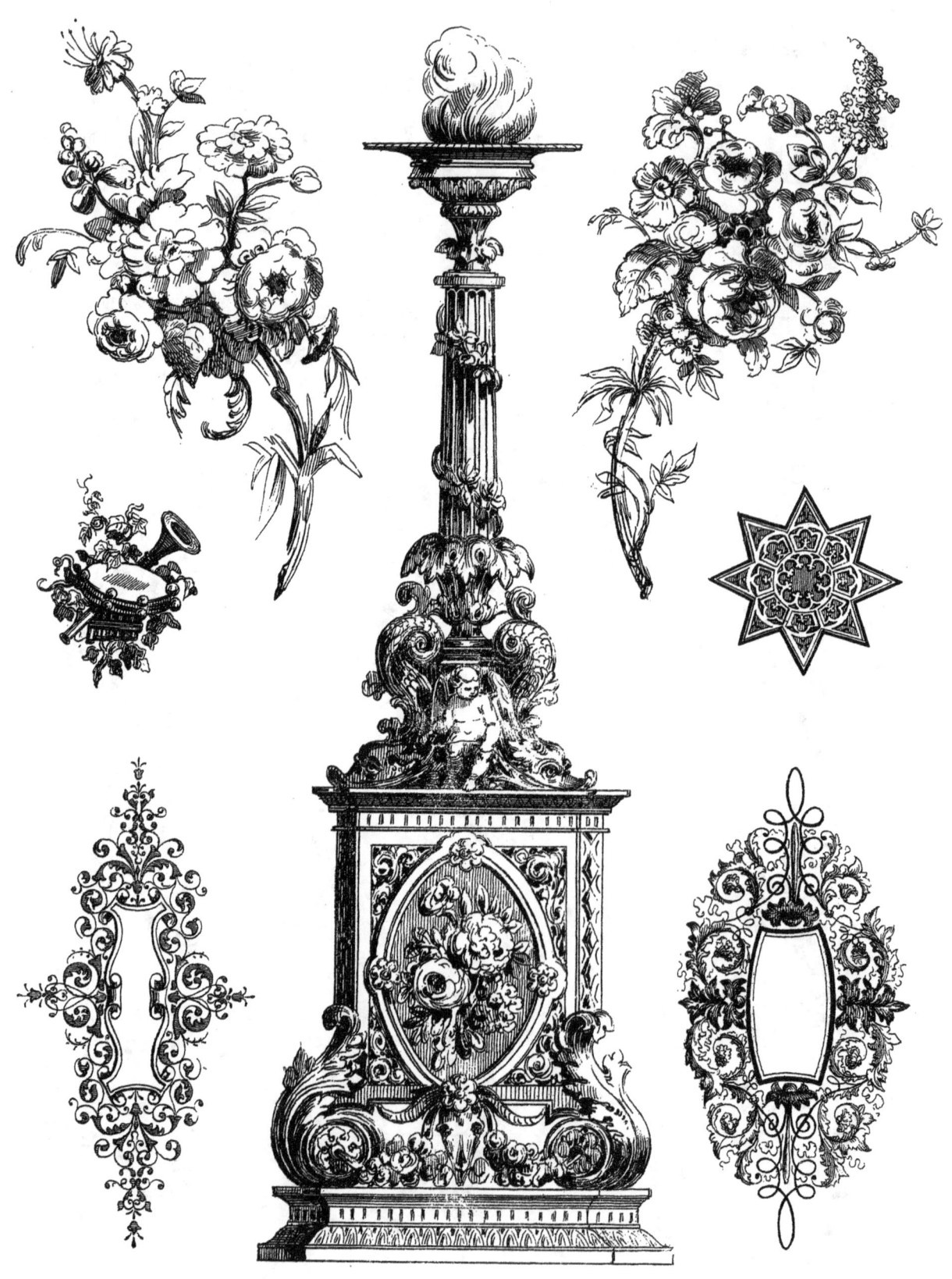

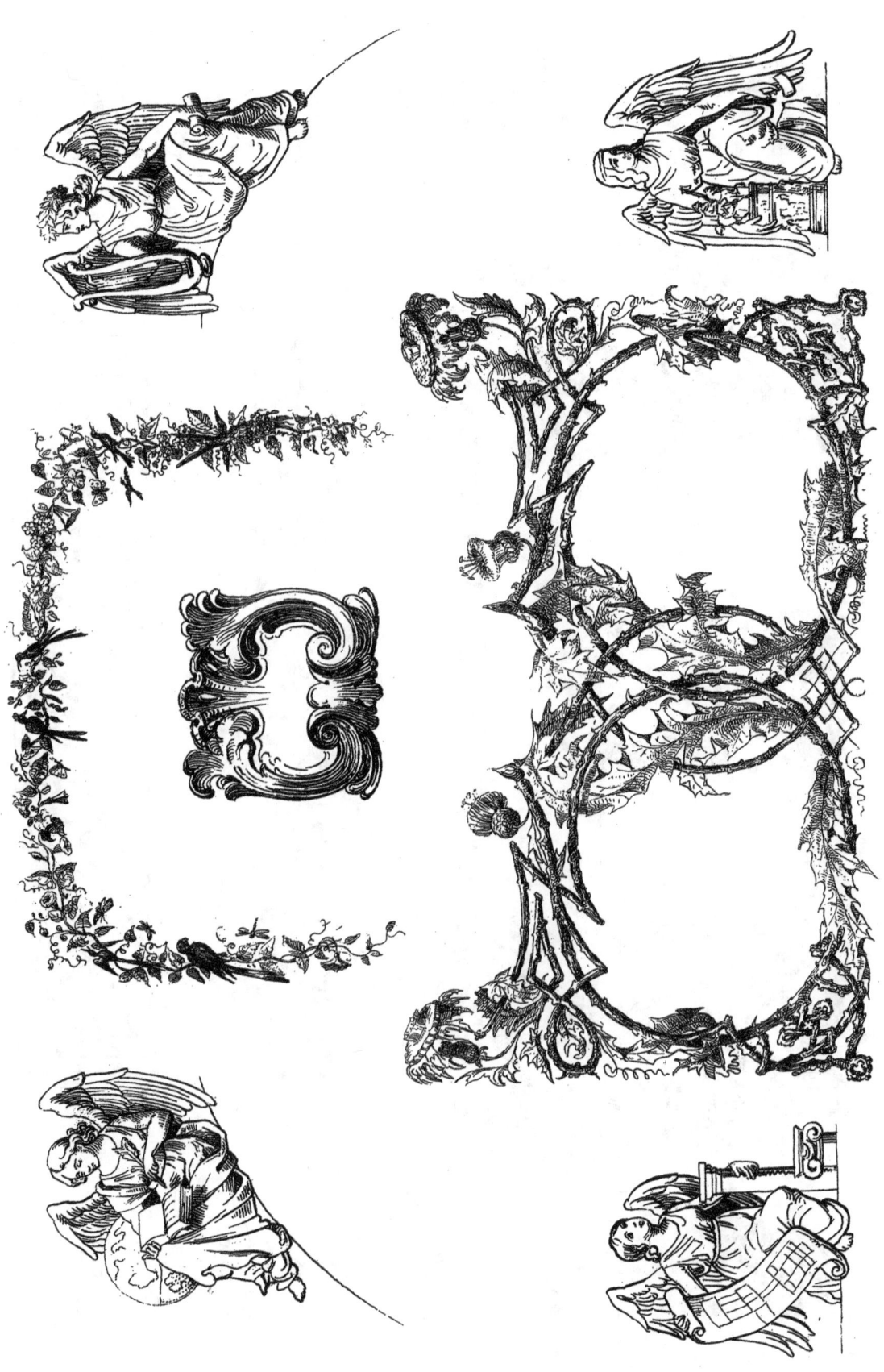

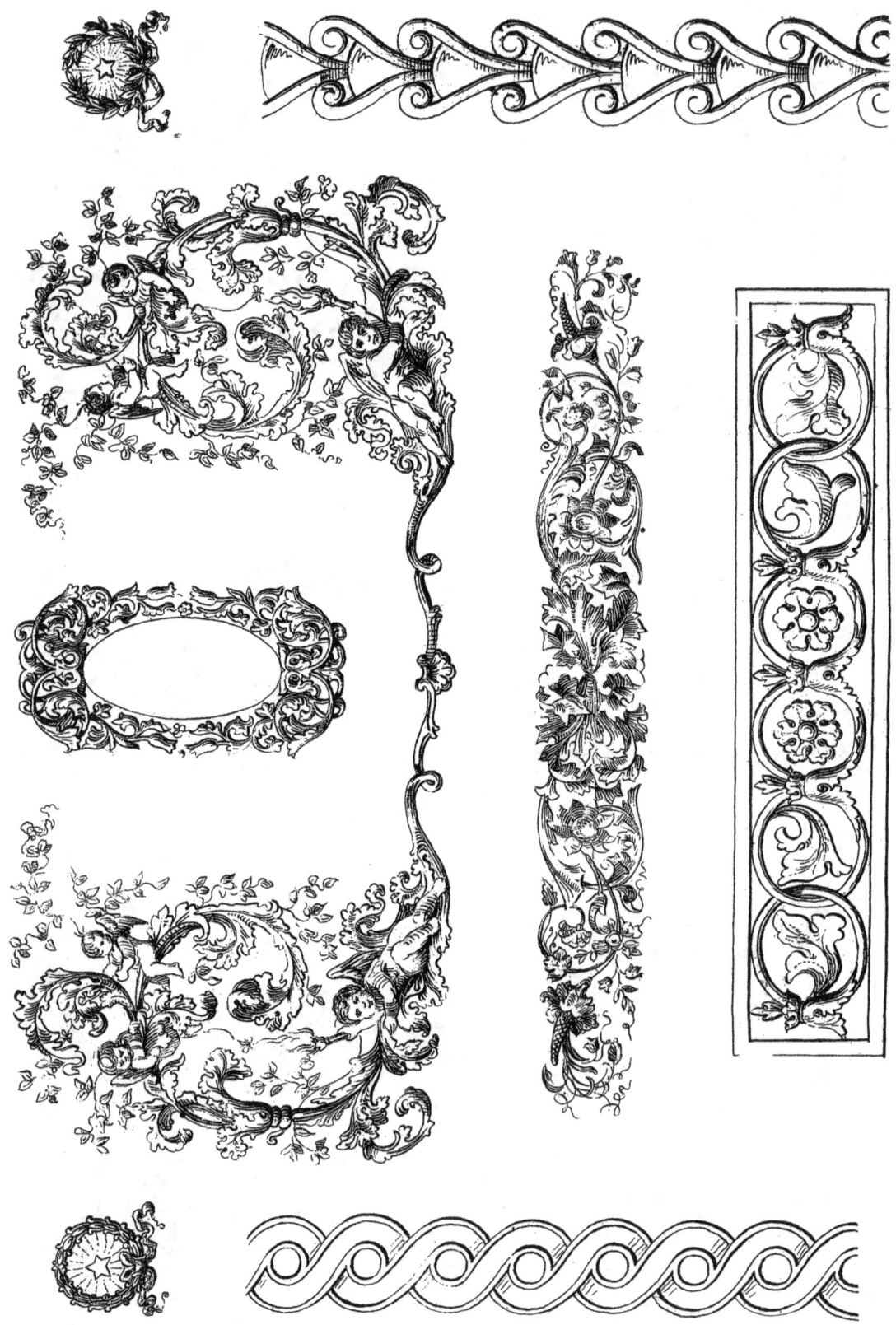

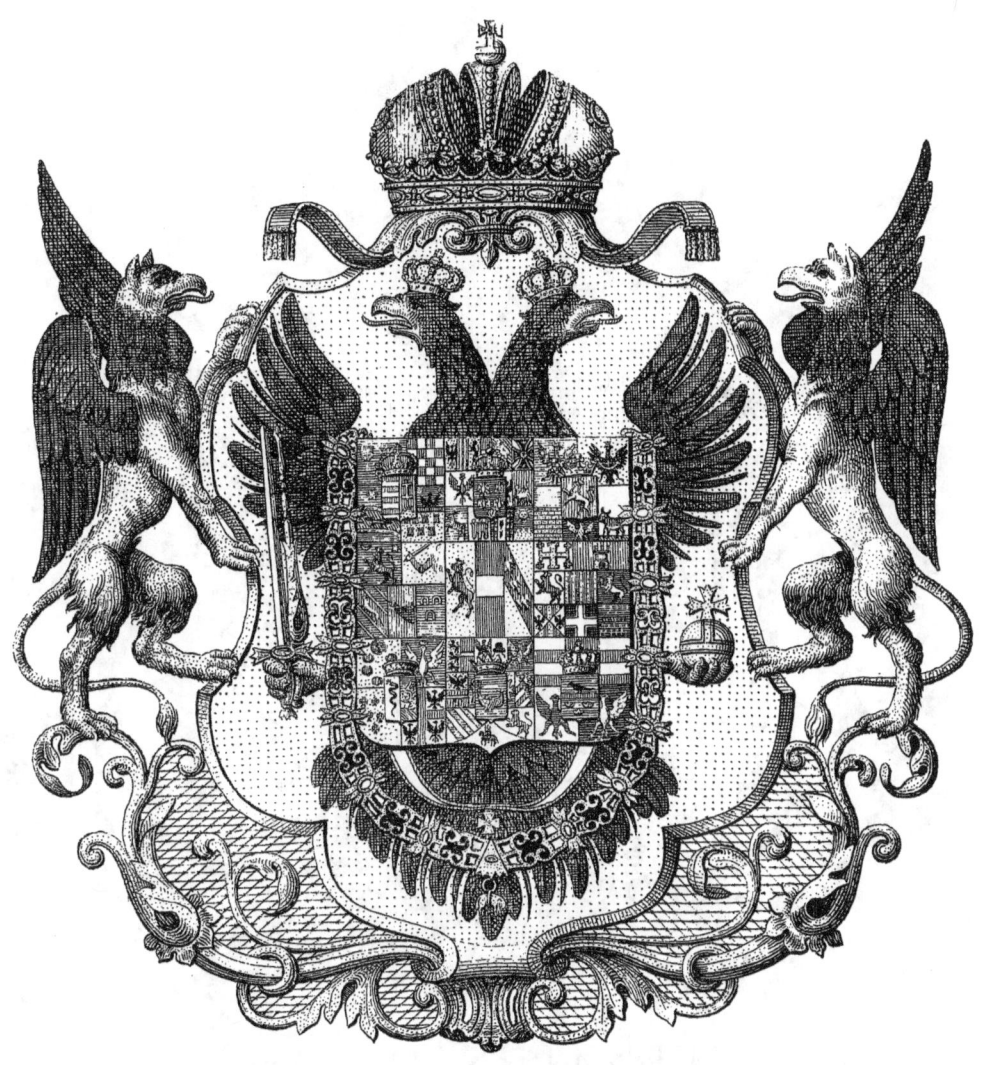

WAPPEN DES KAISERS VON OESTERREICH.

1 Oesterreich.		33 Brixen.		
2 Habsburg.		34 Hohenems.		
3 Lothringen.		35 Feldkirch.		
4 Alt. } Ungarn.		36 Bregenz.		
5 Neu.		37 Sonnenberg.		
6 Dalmatien.		38 Illyrien.		
7 Croatien.		39 Kärnthen.		
8 Slavonien.		40 Krain.		
9 Siebenbürgen.		41 Windische Mark.		
10 Böhmen.		42 Friaul.		
11 Mähren.		43 Triest.		
12 Schlesien.		44 Jstrien.		
13 Ober Lausitz.		45 Gradiska.		
14 Teschen.		46 Görz.		
15 Nieder Lausitz.		47 Ragusa.		
16 Lombardei.		48 Zara.		
17 Venedig.		49 Cattaro.		
18 Toscana.		50 Cumanien.		
19 Modena.		51 Bosnien.		
20 Parma. Piacenza.		52 Bulgarien.		
21 Guastalla.		53 Servien.		
22 Galicien.		54 Rascien.		
23 Lodomerien.		55 Jerusalem.		
24 Auschwitz.		56 Castilien.		
25 Zator.		57 Leon.		
26 Oesterreich unter der Ens.		58 Arragonien.		
27 Oesterreich ob der Ens.		59 Jndien.		
28 Salzburg.		60 Sicilien.		
29 Steiermark.		61 Calabrien.		
30 Deutscher Orden.		62 Anjou.		
31 Tirol.		a Erzherzogs Hut.		
32 Trient.		b Kronen.		

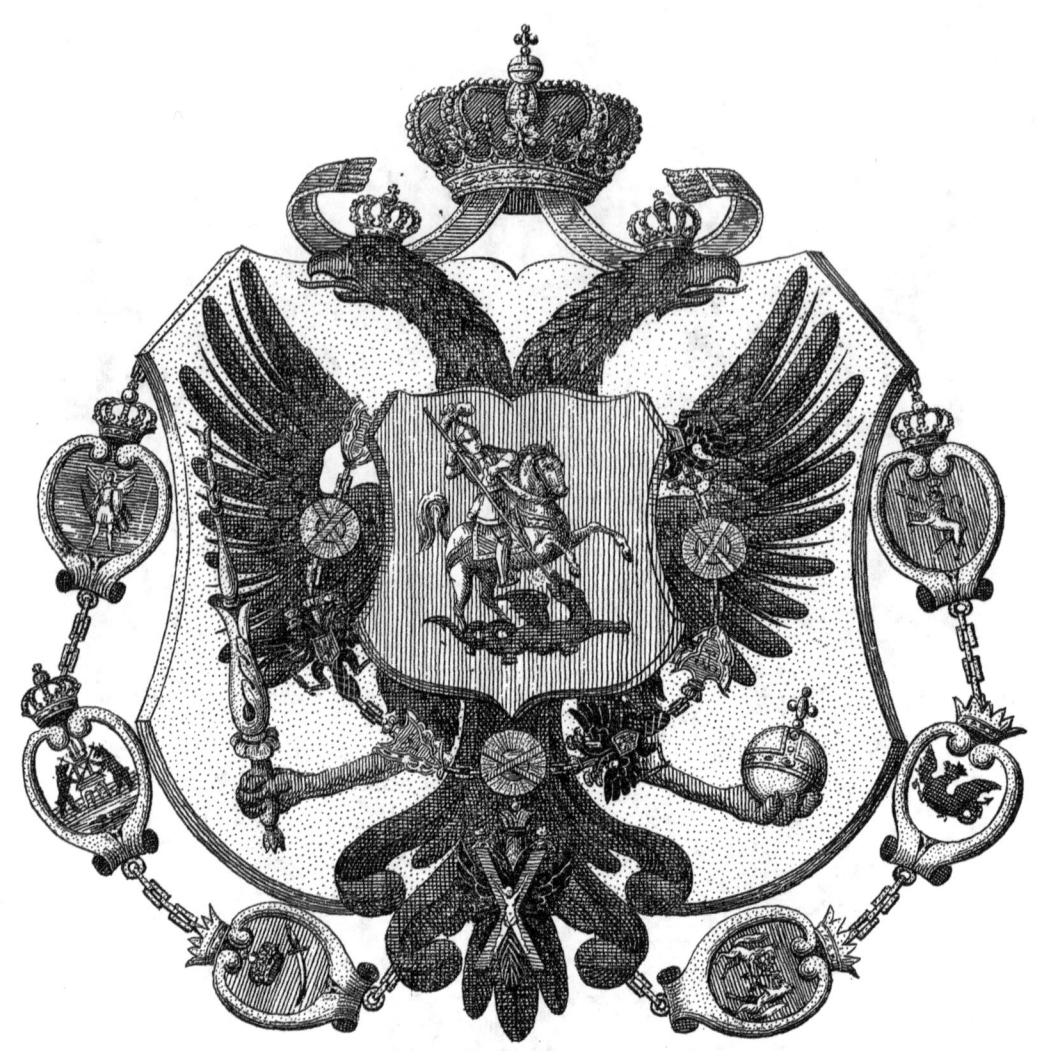

WAPPEN DES KAISERS VON RUSSLAND.

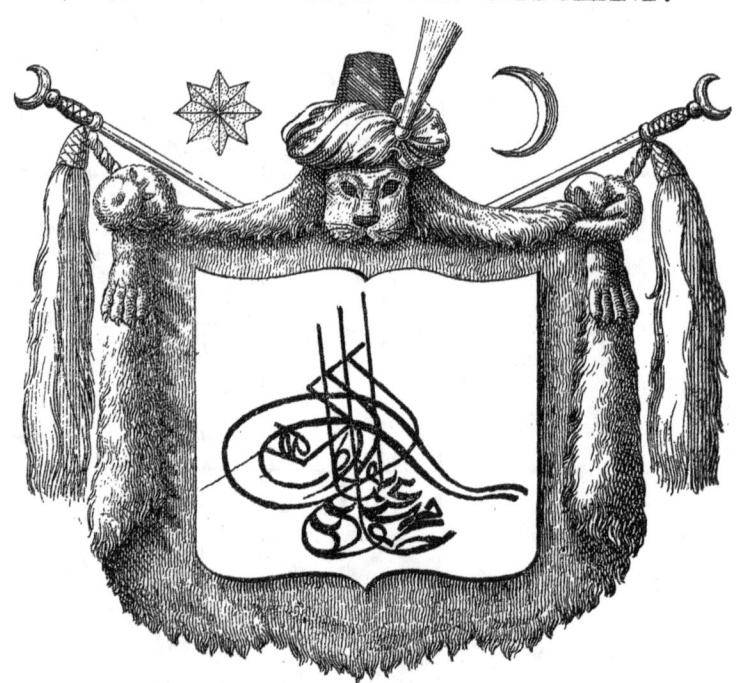

WAPPEN DES GROSSSULTANS.

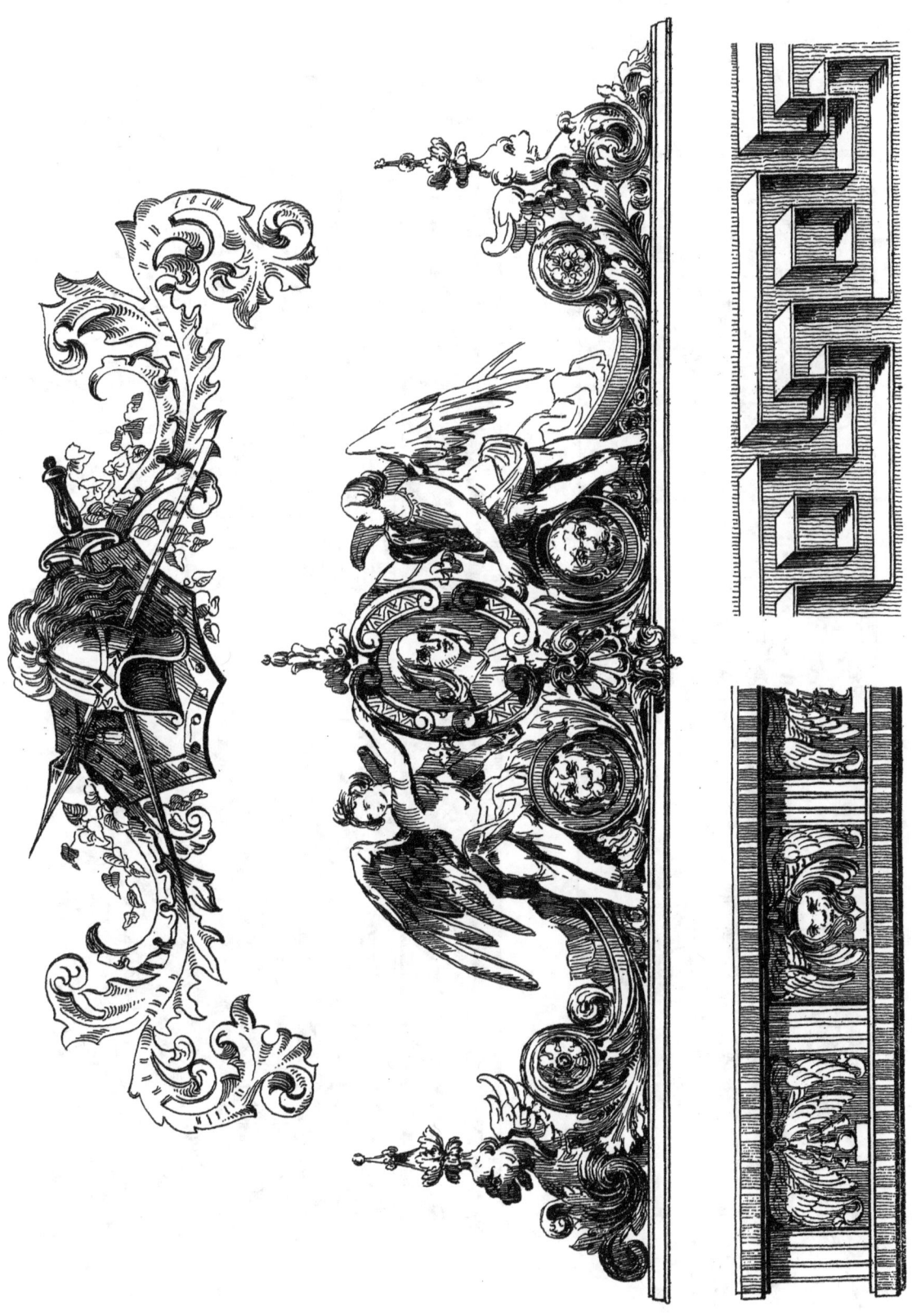

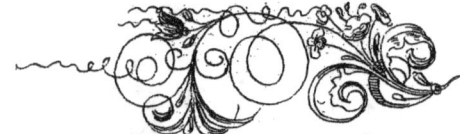

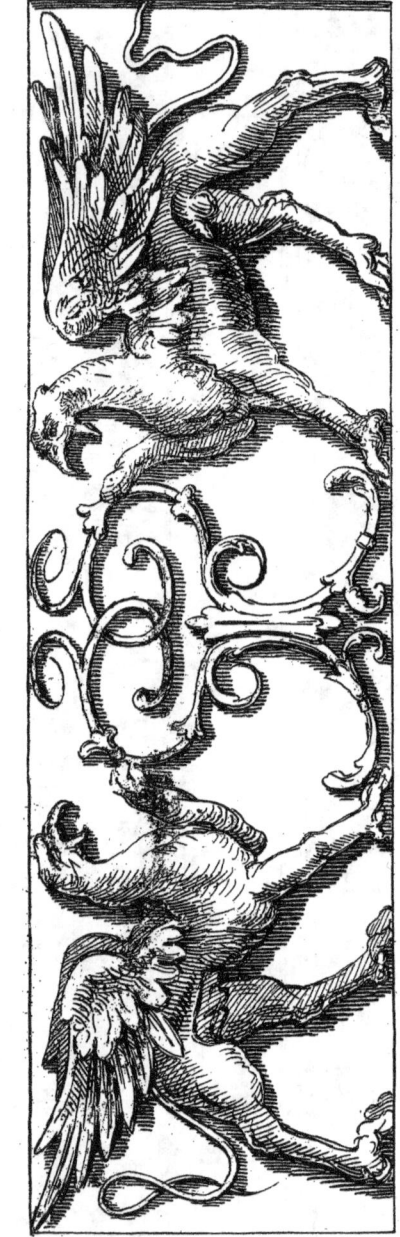

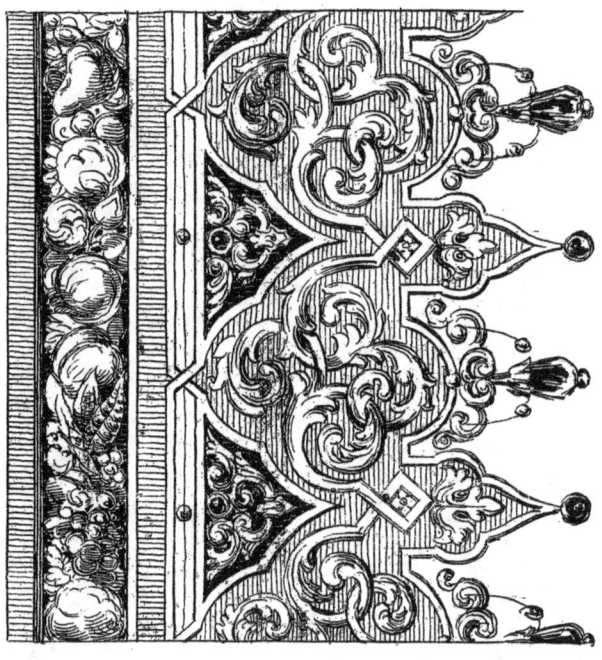

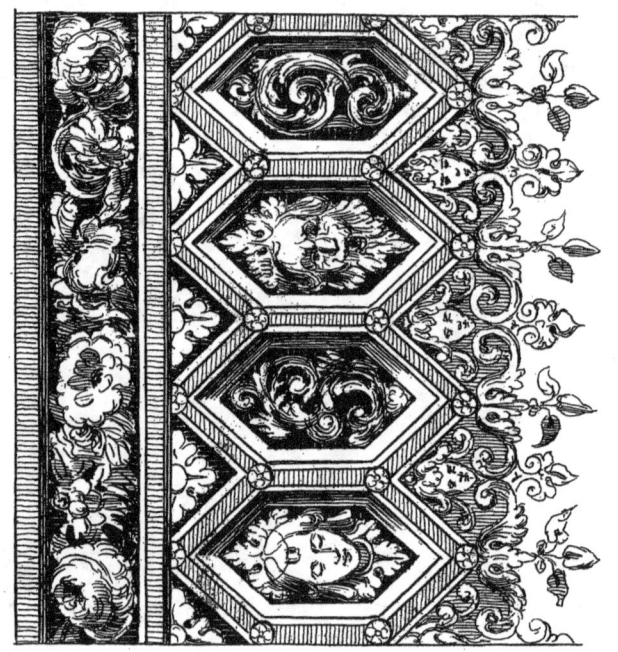

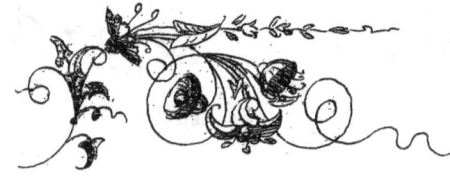

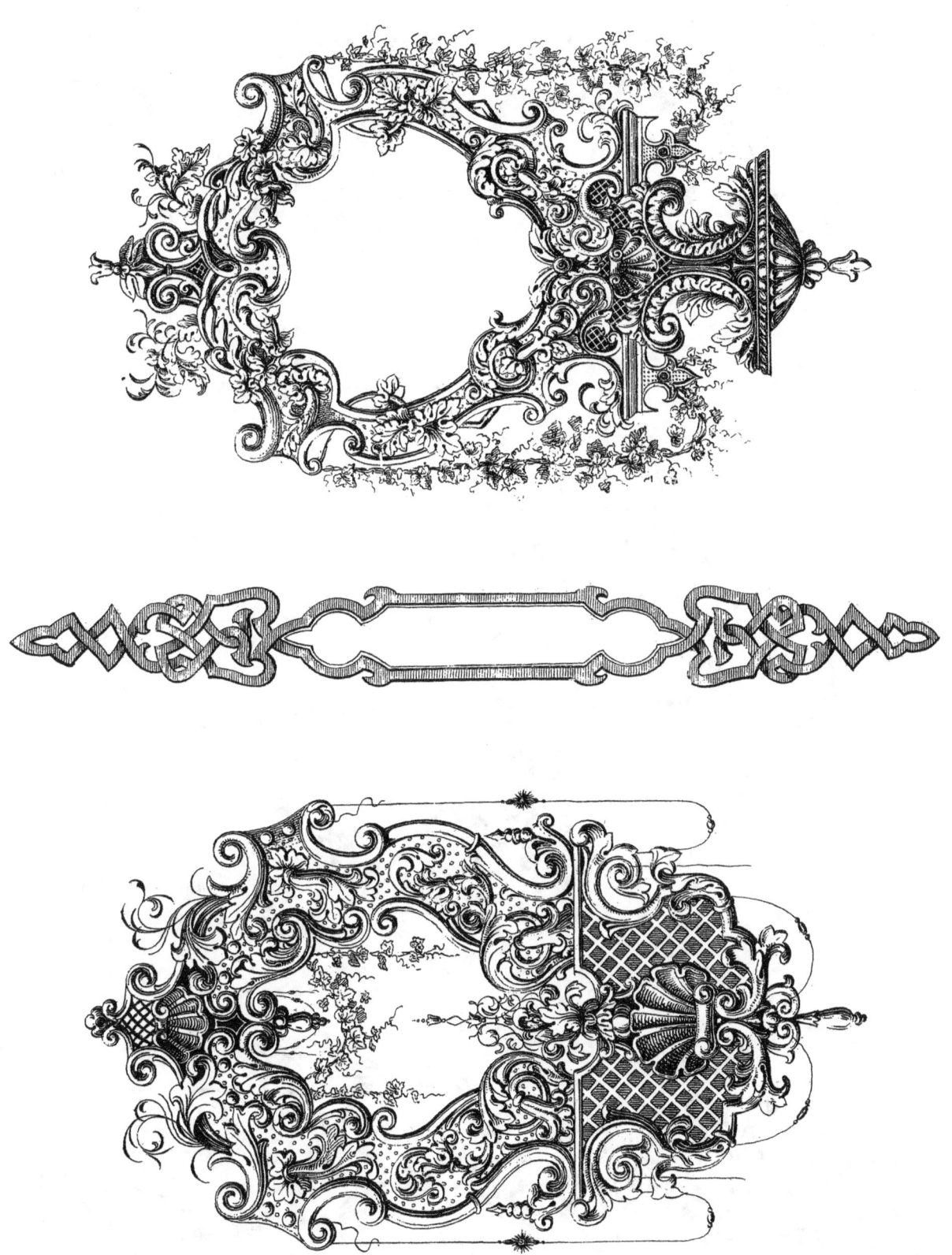

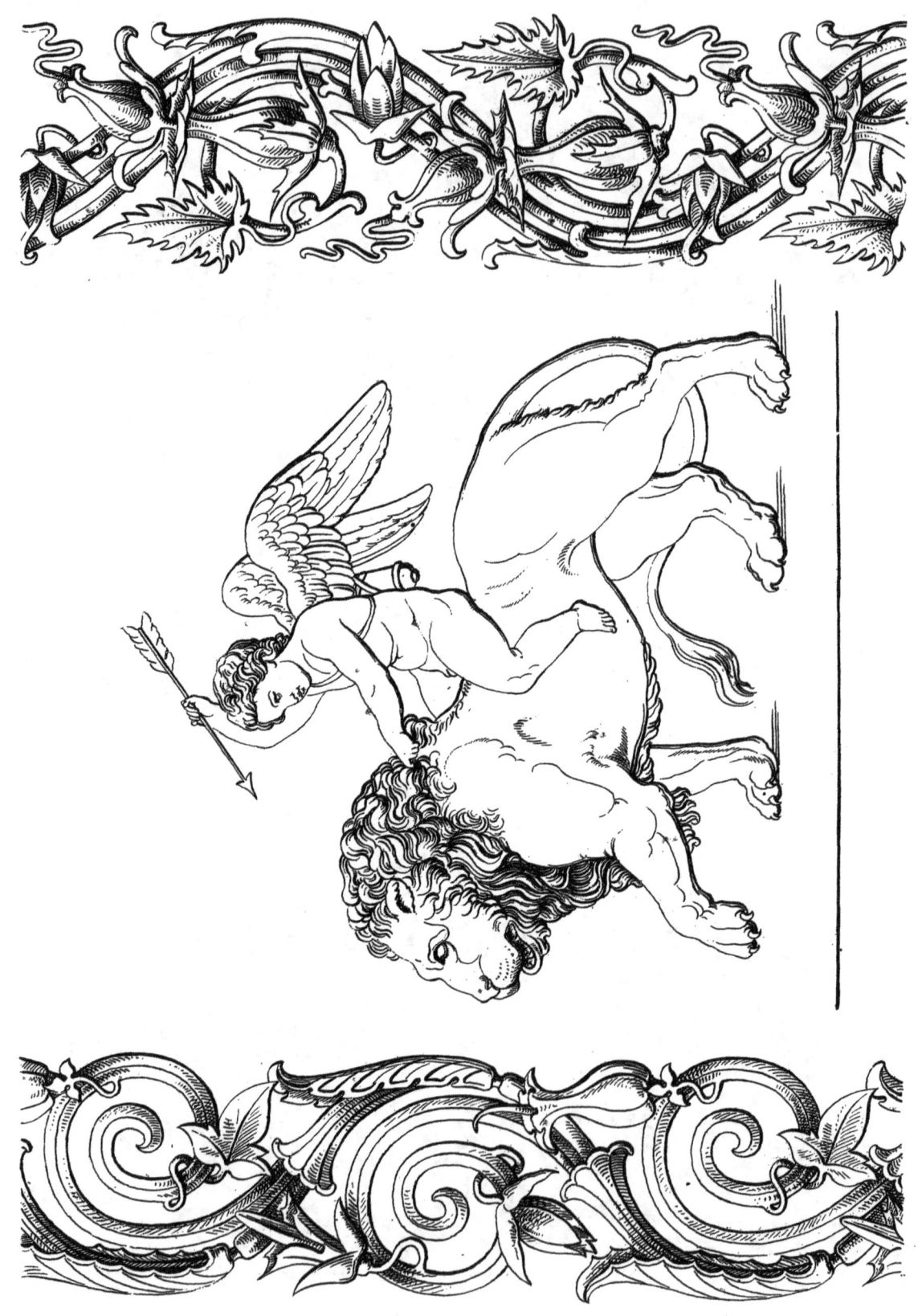

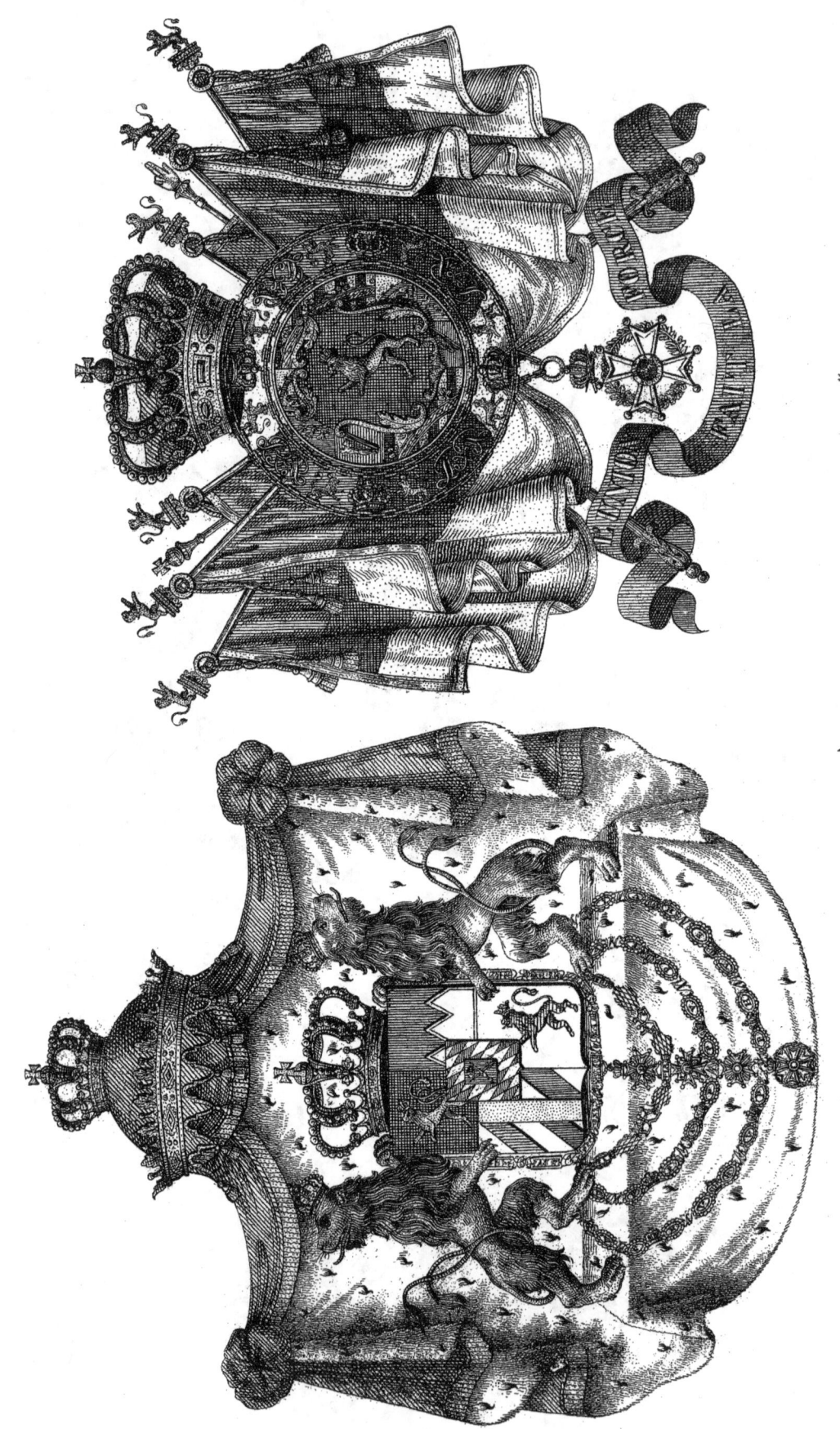

WAPPEN DES KÖNIGS DER BELGIER.

WAPPEN DES KÖNIGS VON BAIERN.

88

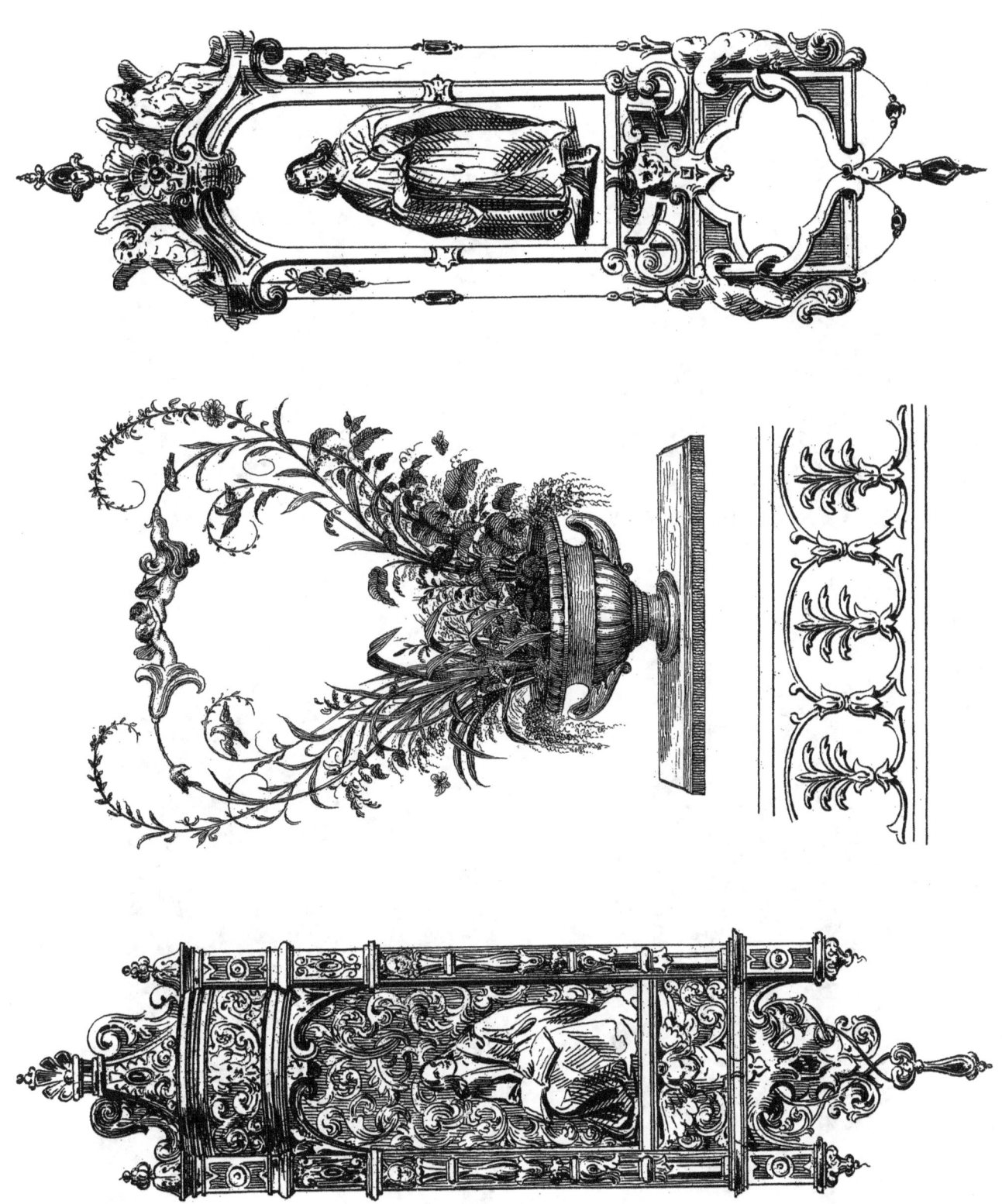

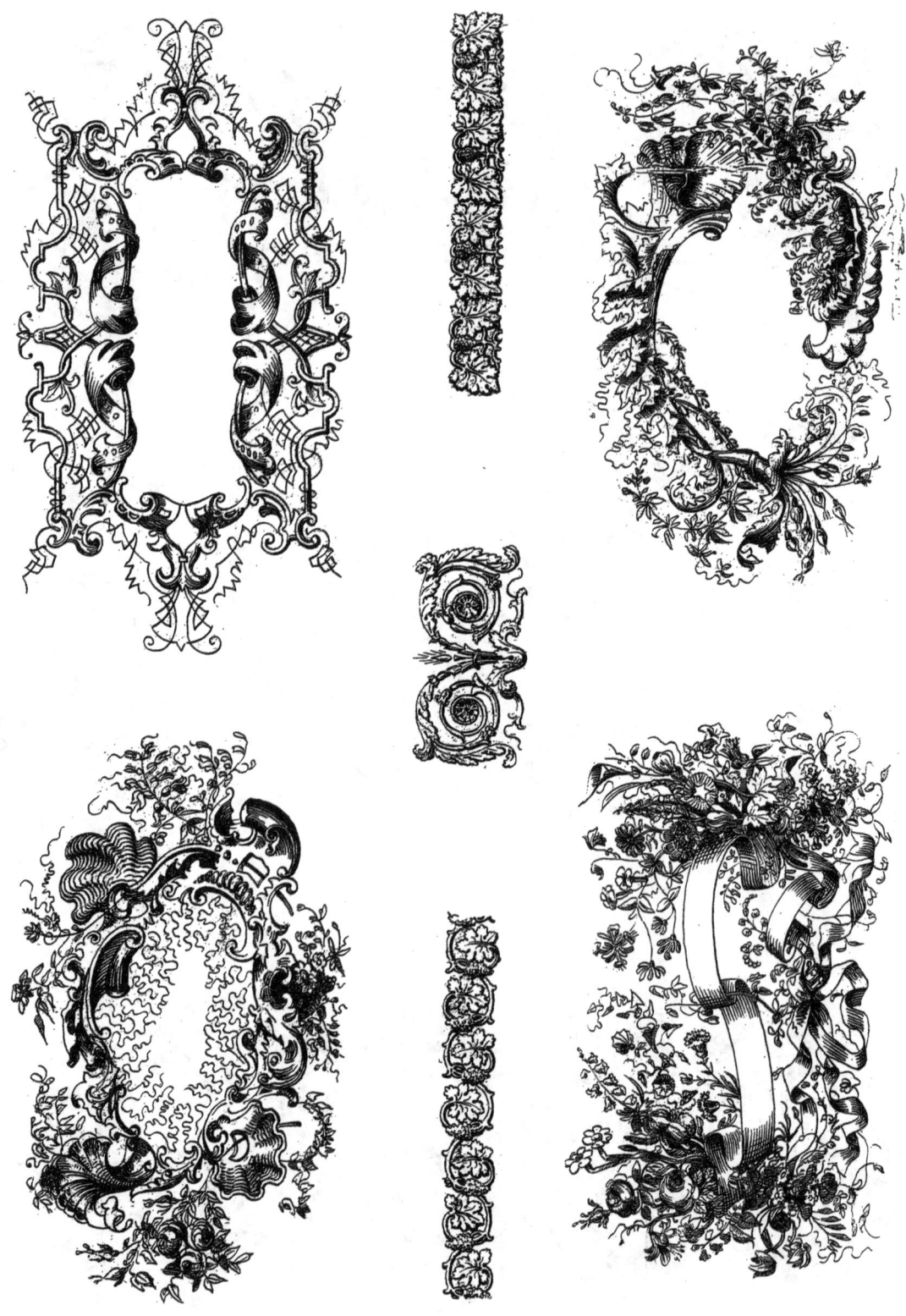

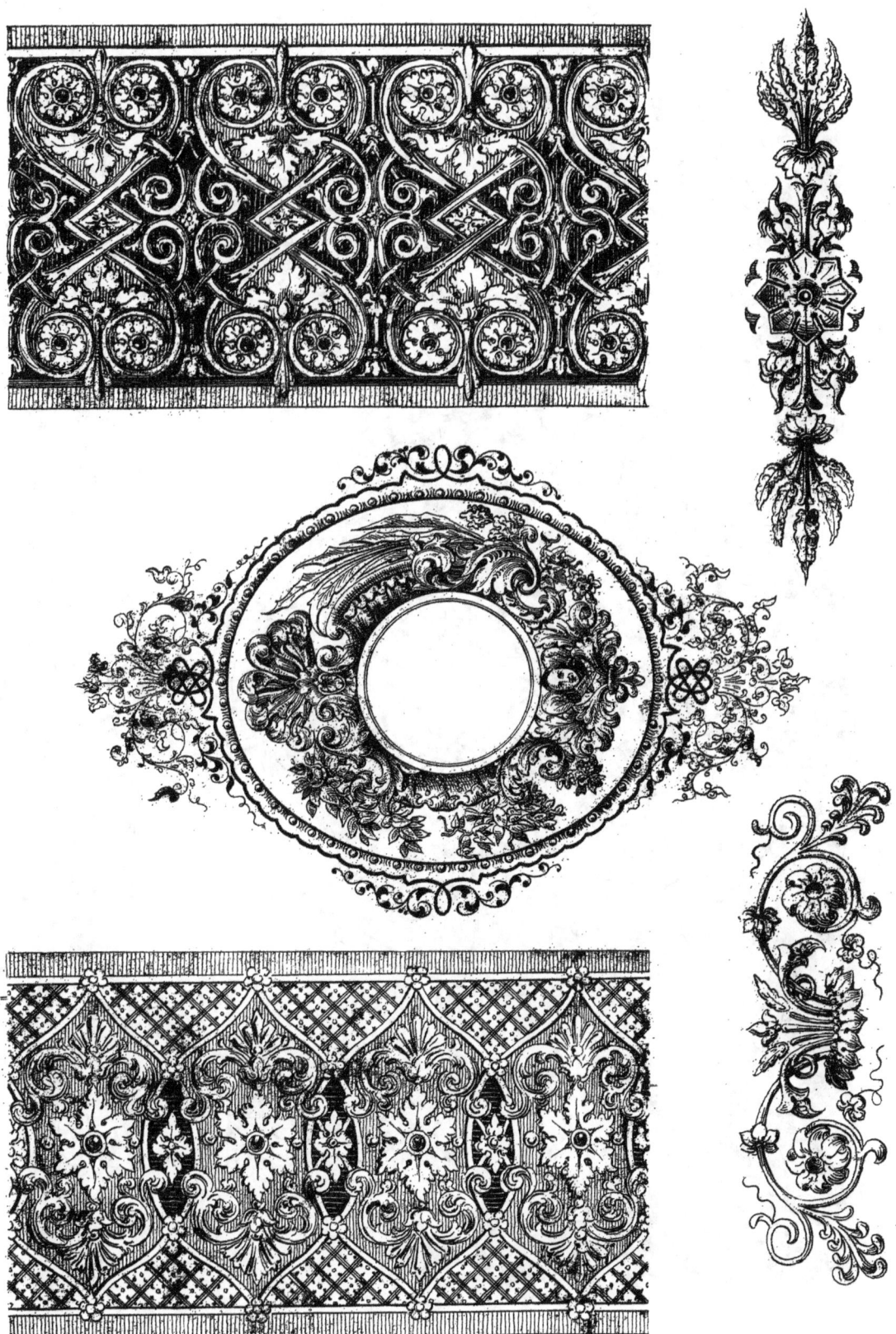

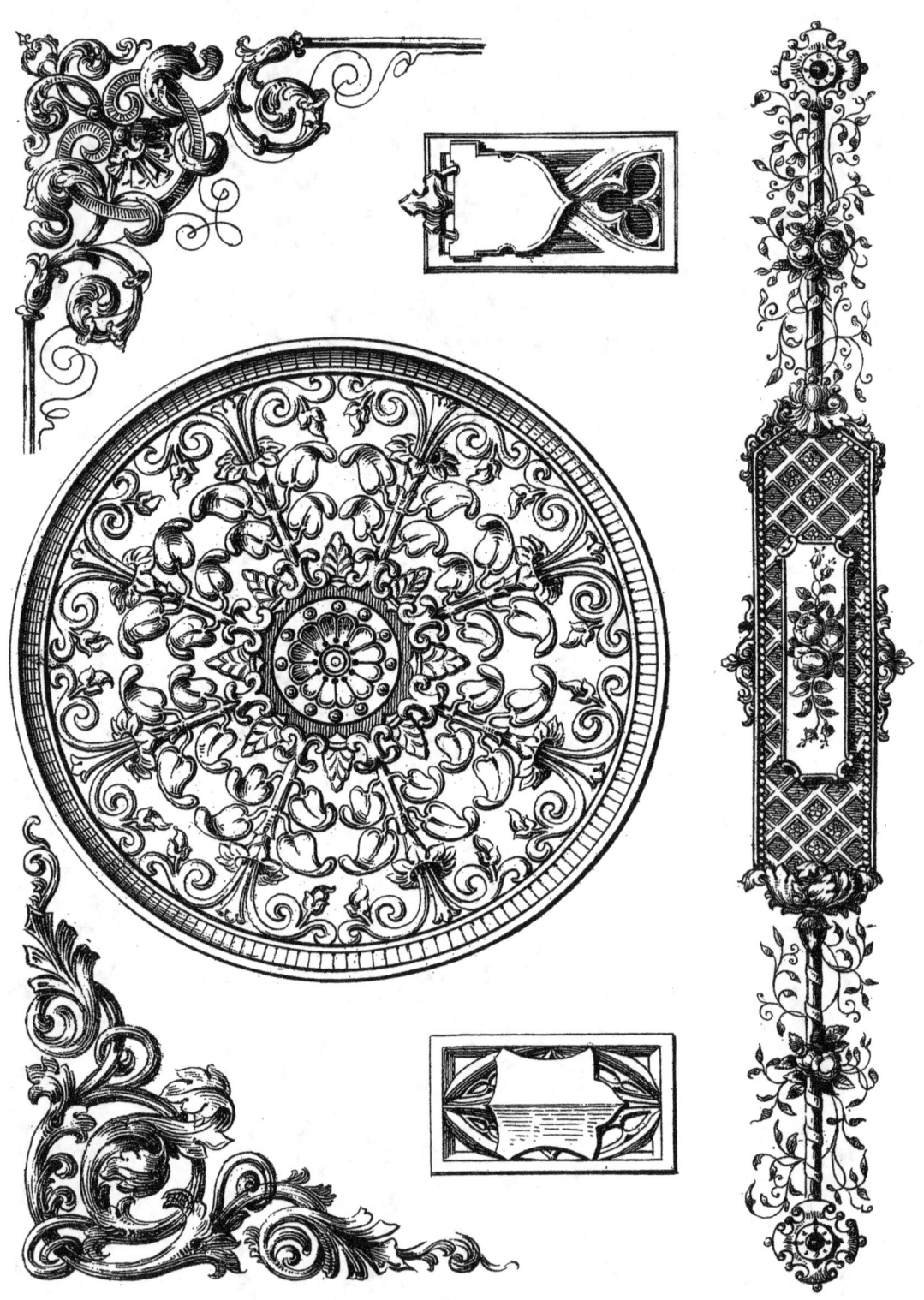

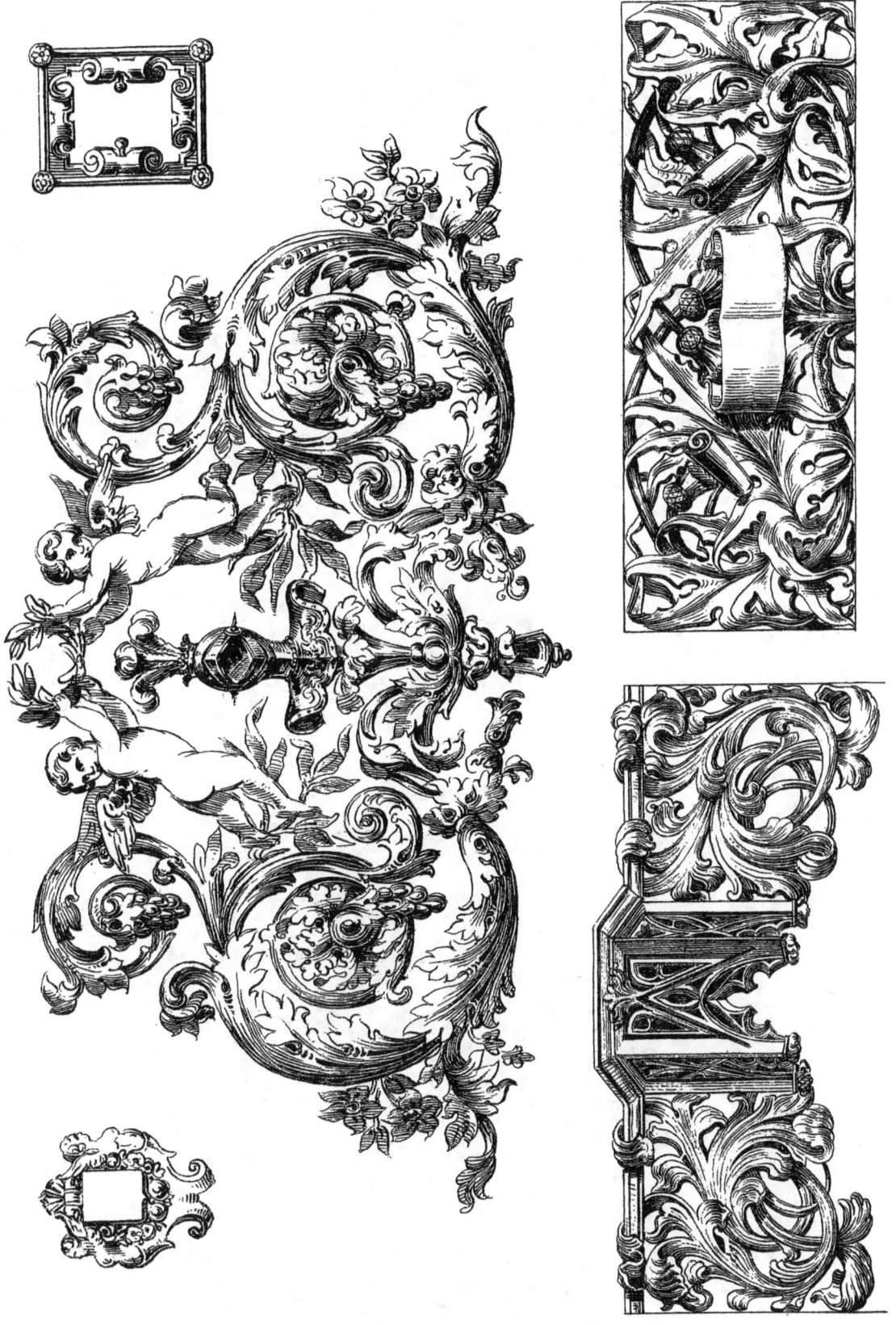

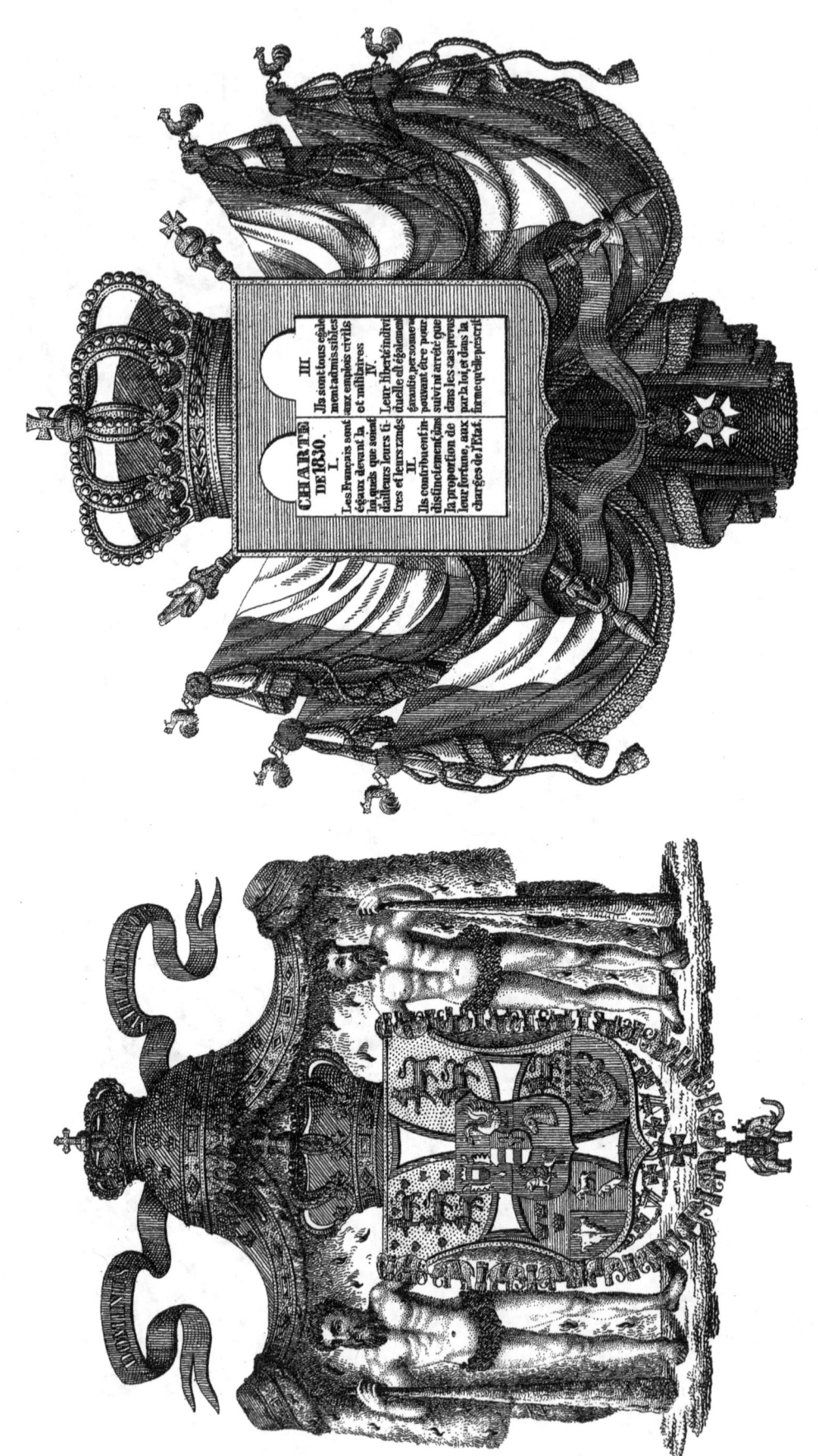

WAPPEN DES KÖNIGS VON DÄNEMARK.

WAPPEN DES KÖNIGS DER FRANZOSEN.

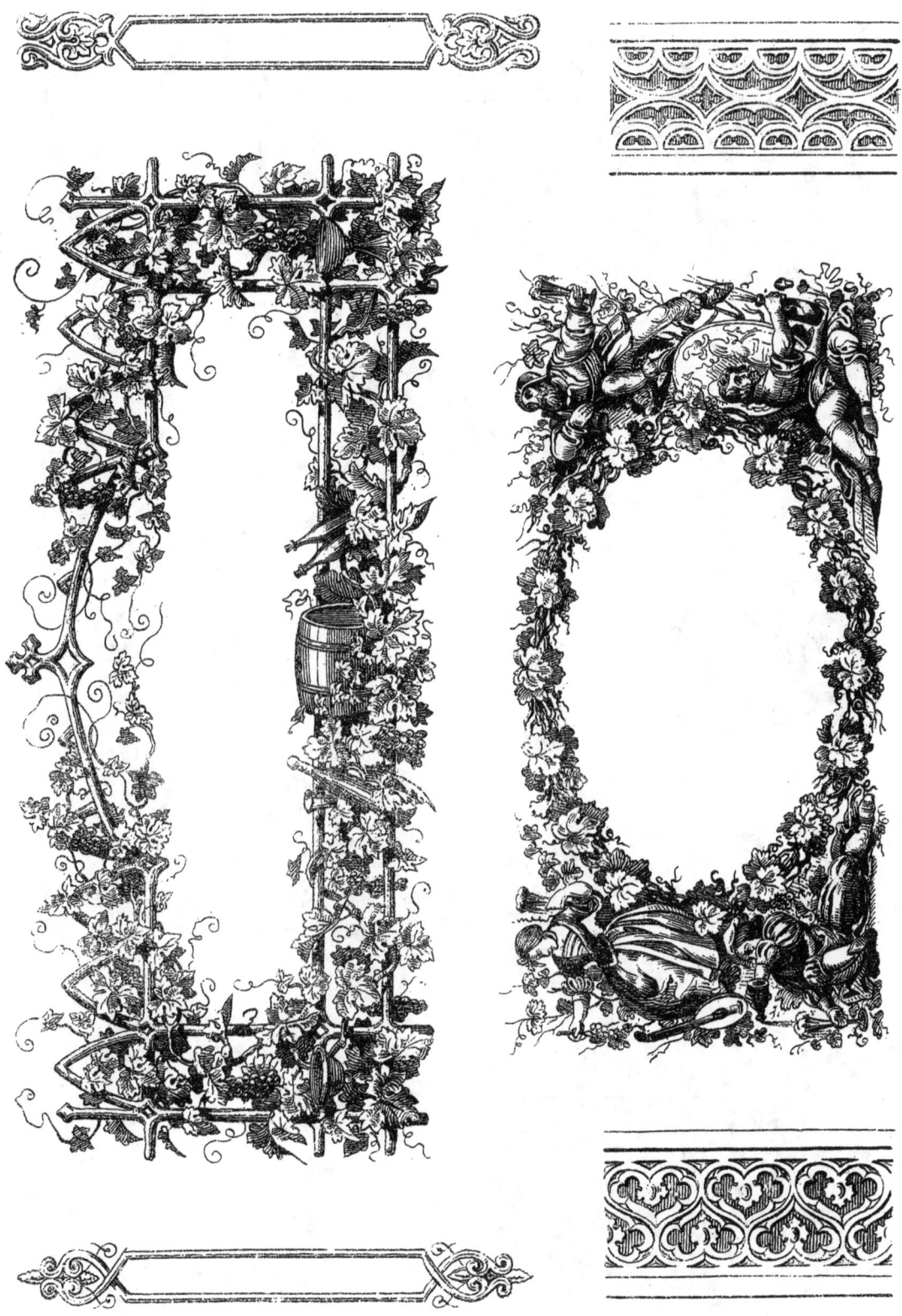

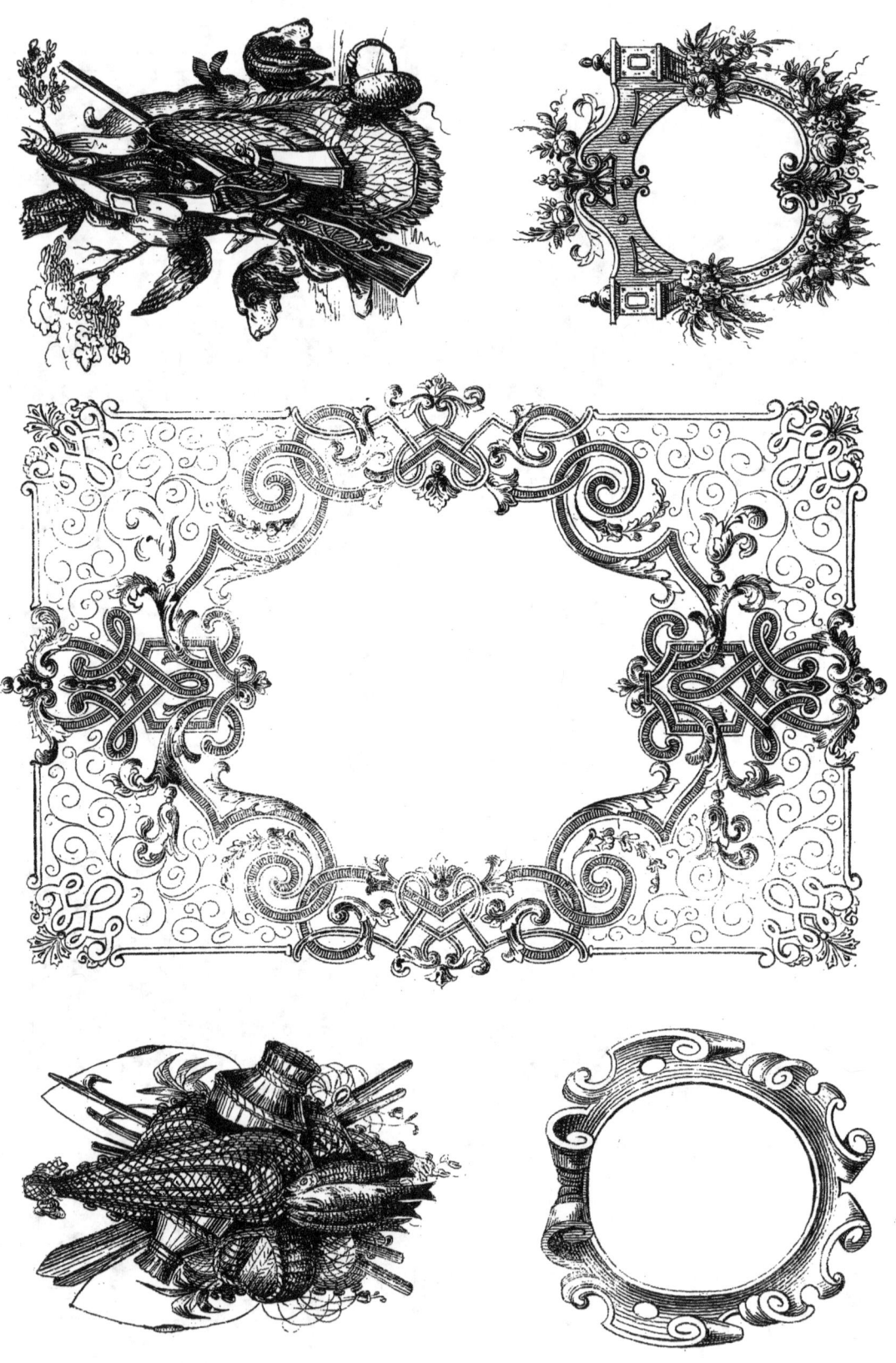

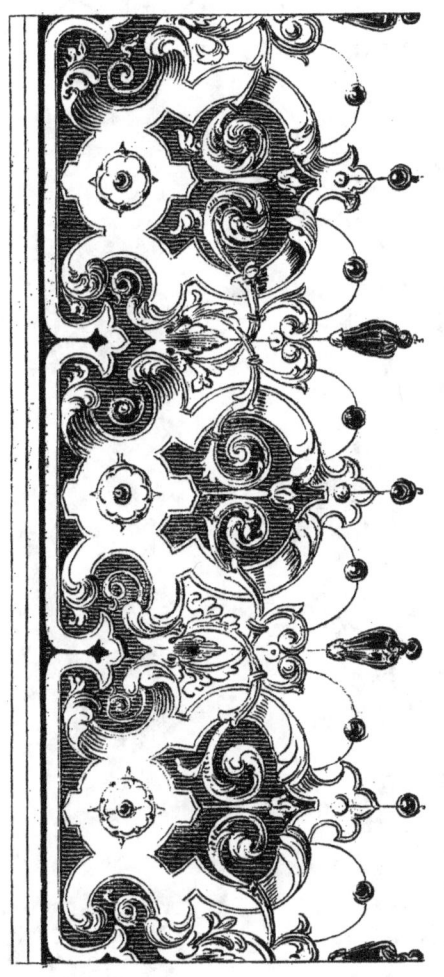
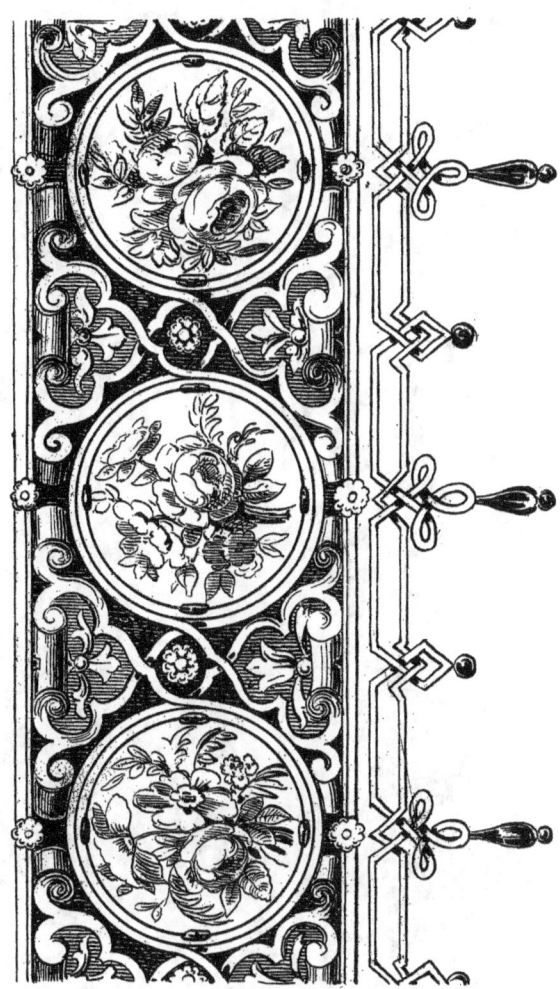
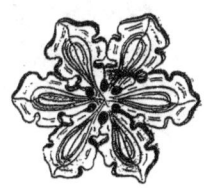

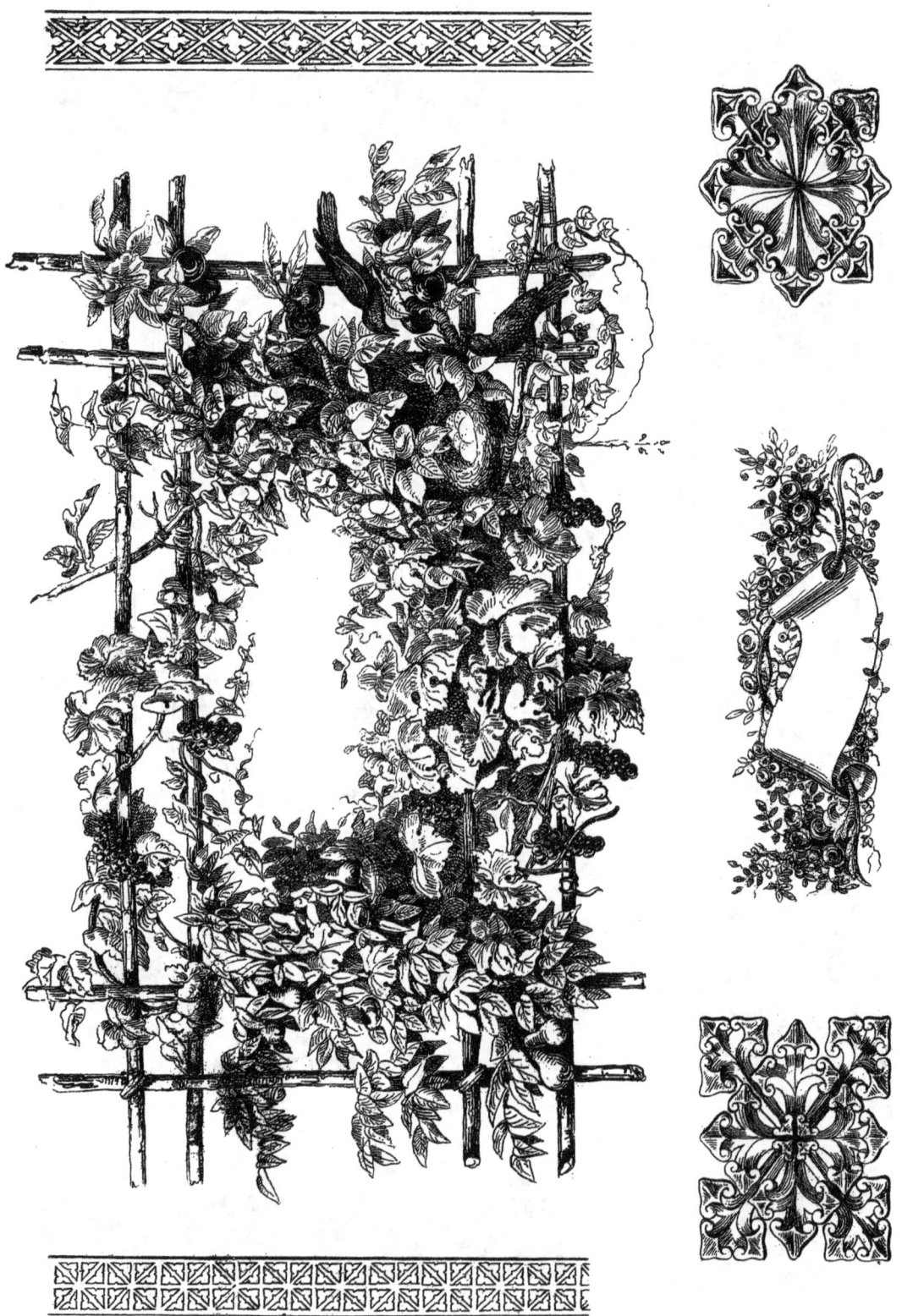

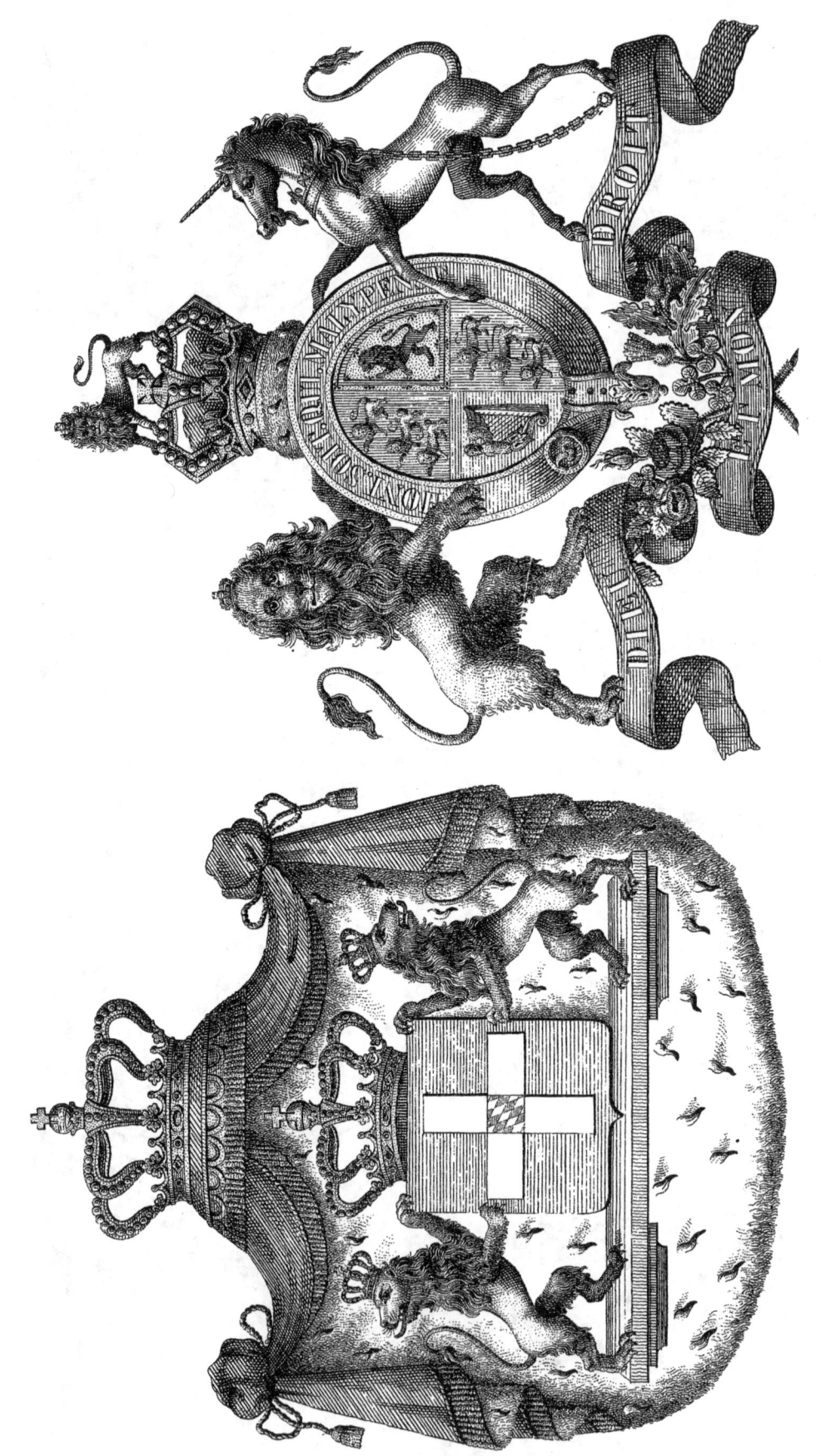

WAPPEN DES KÖNIGS VON GRIECHENLAND.   WAPPEN DER KÖNIGIN VON GROSSBRITANNIEN U. IRLAND.

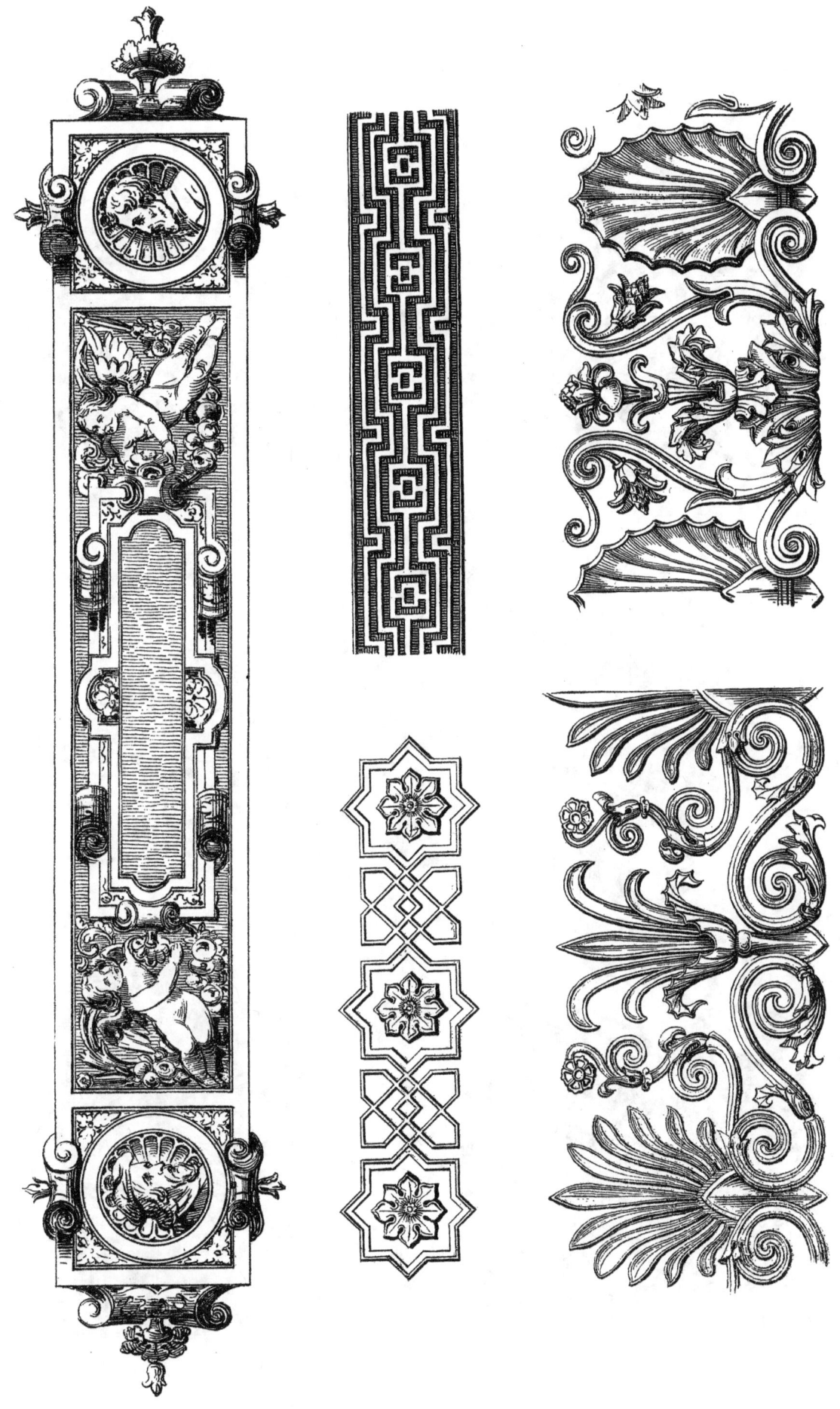

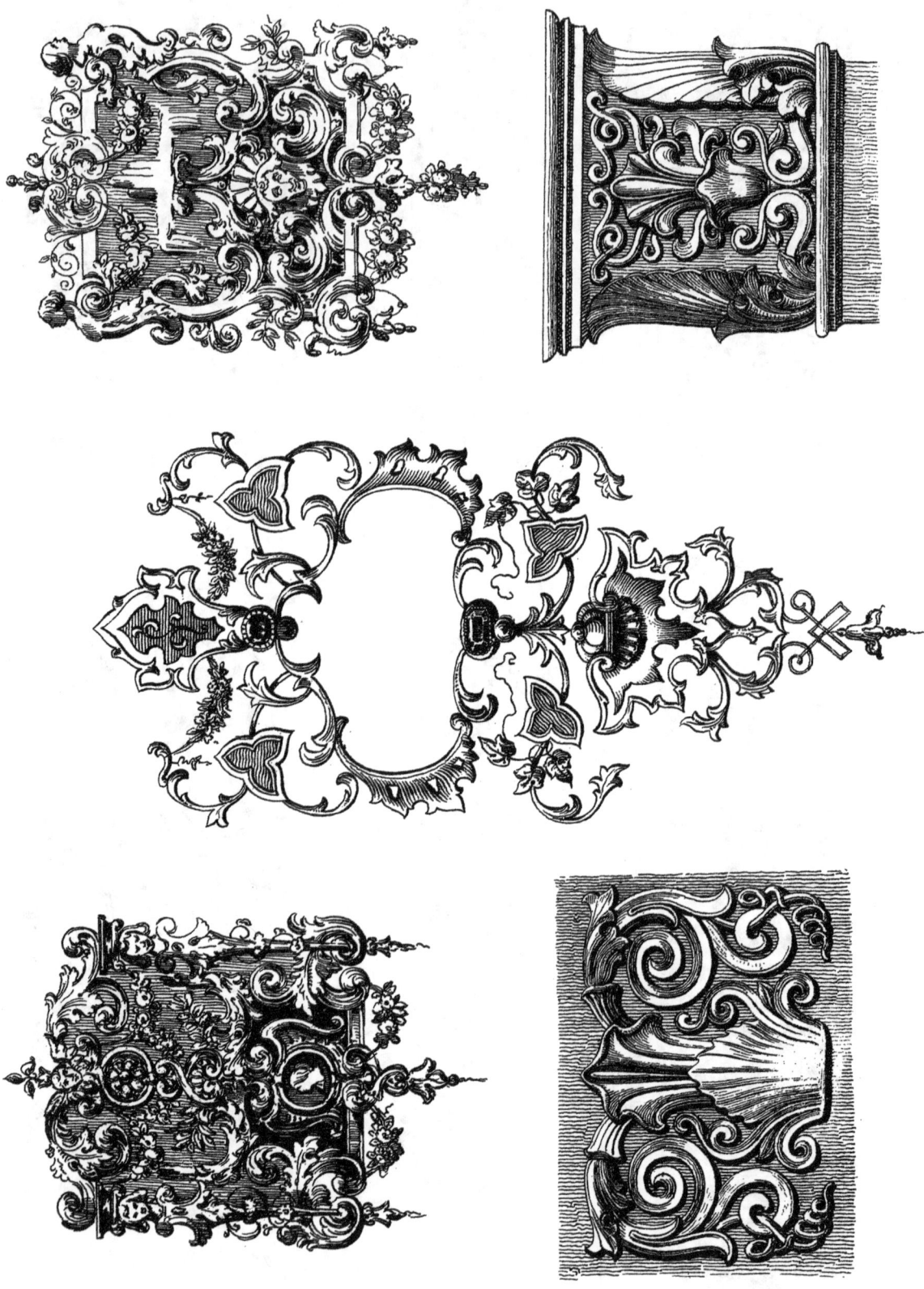

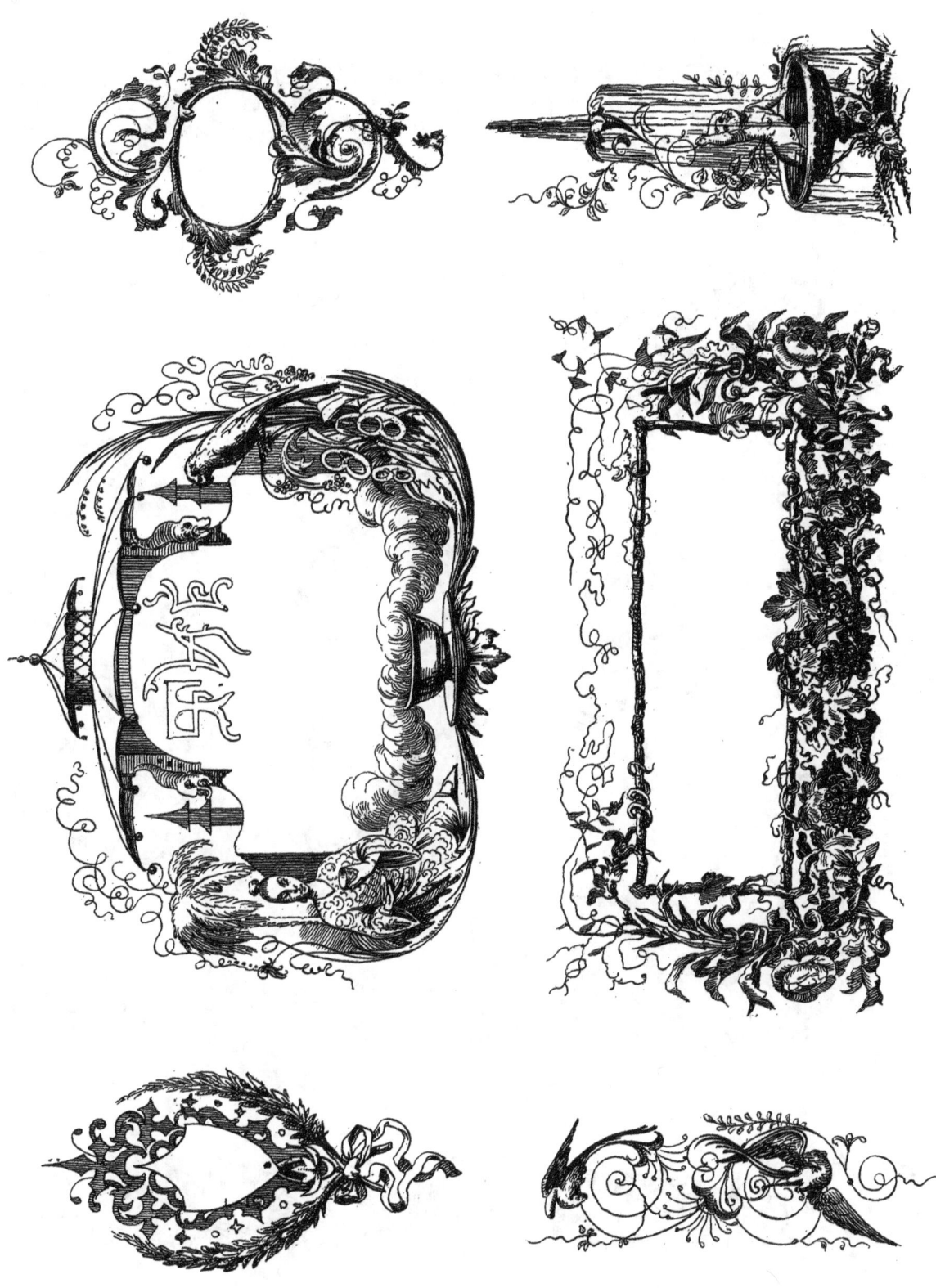

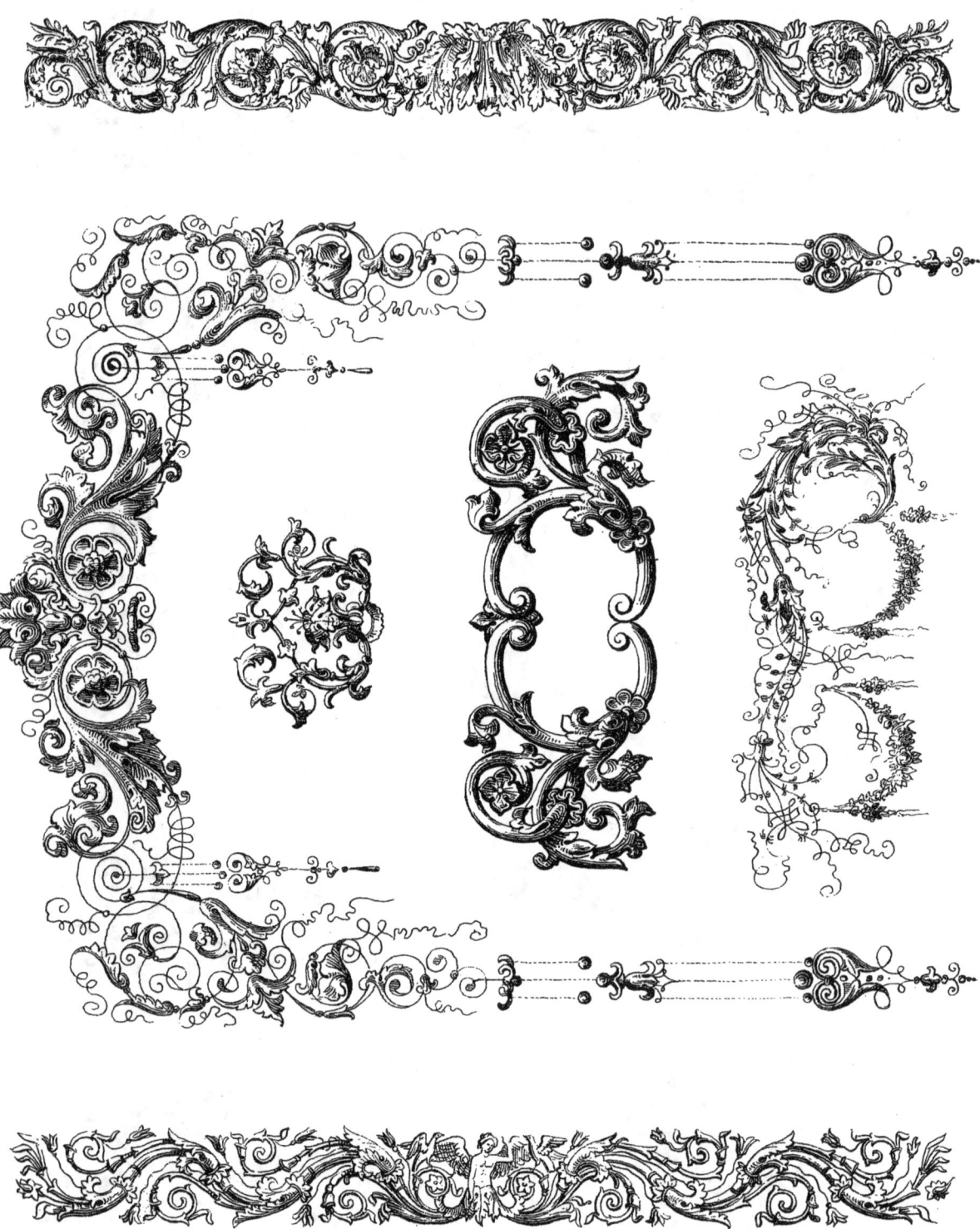

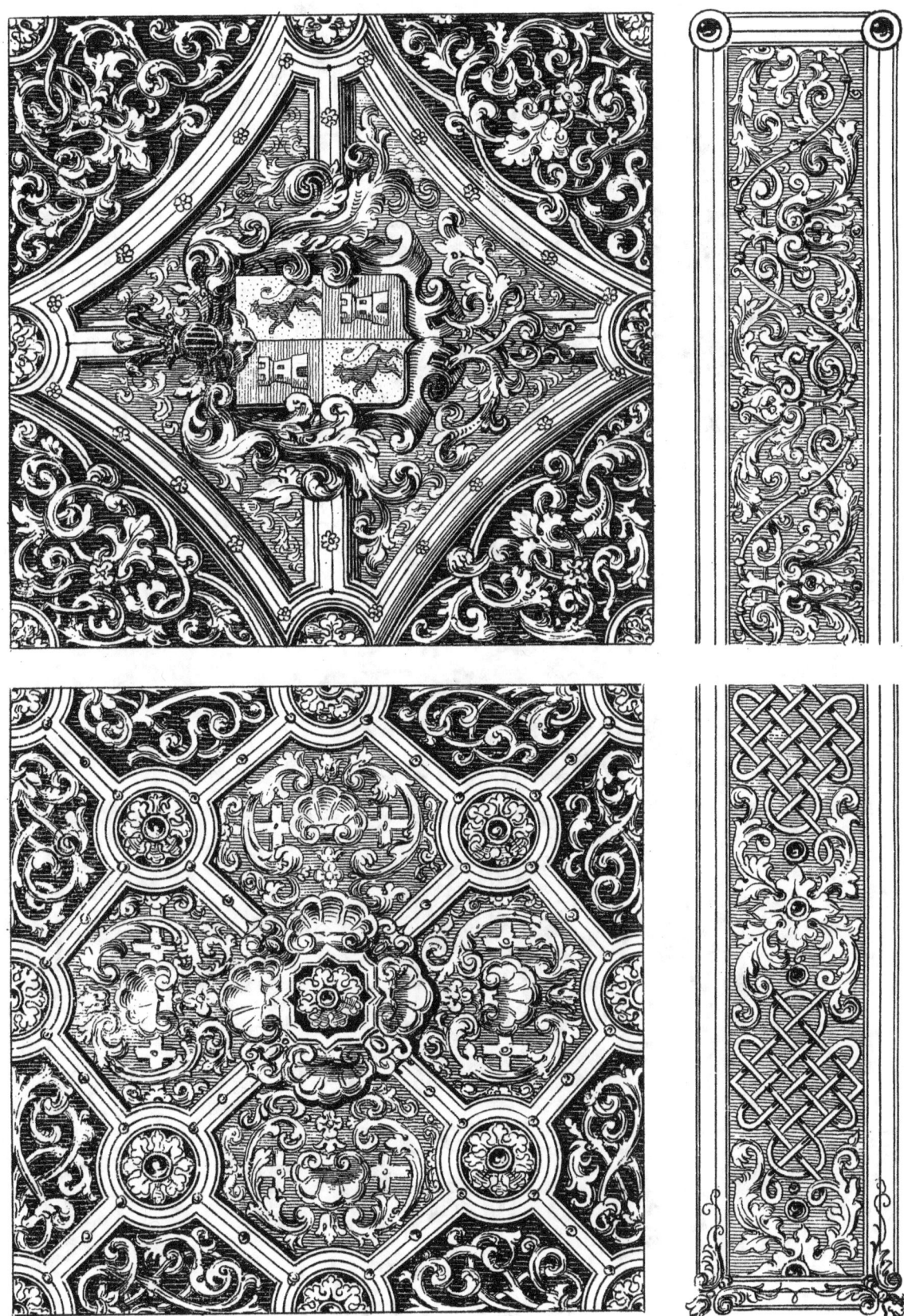

105

WAPPEN DES PABSTES.

WAPPEN DES KÖNIGS VON HANNOVER.

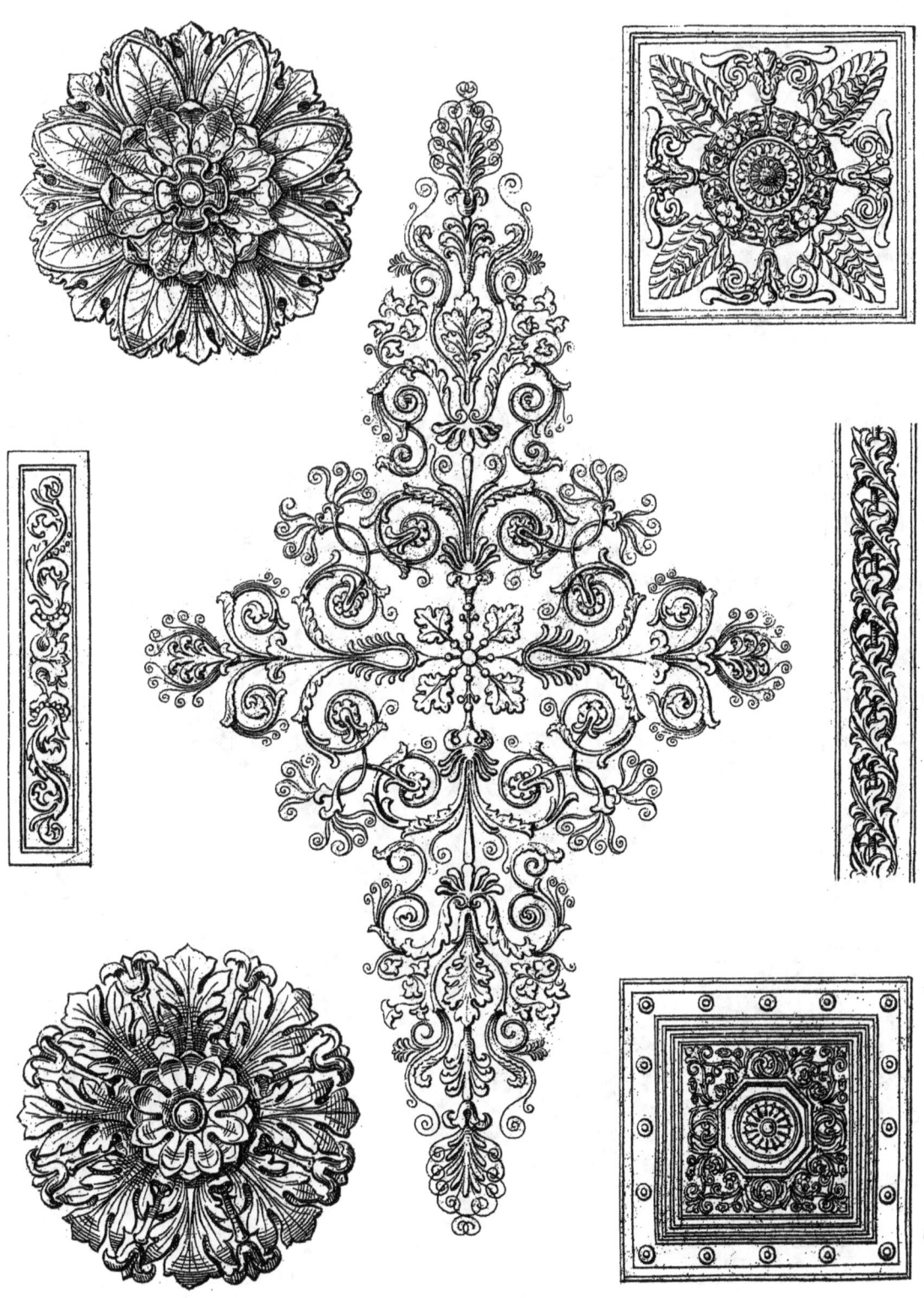

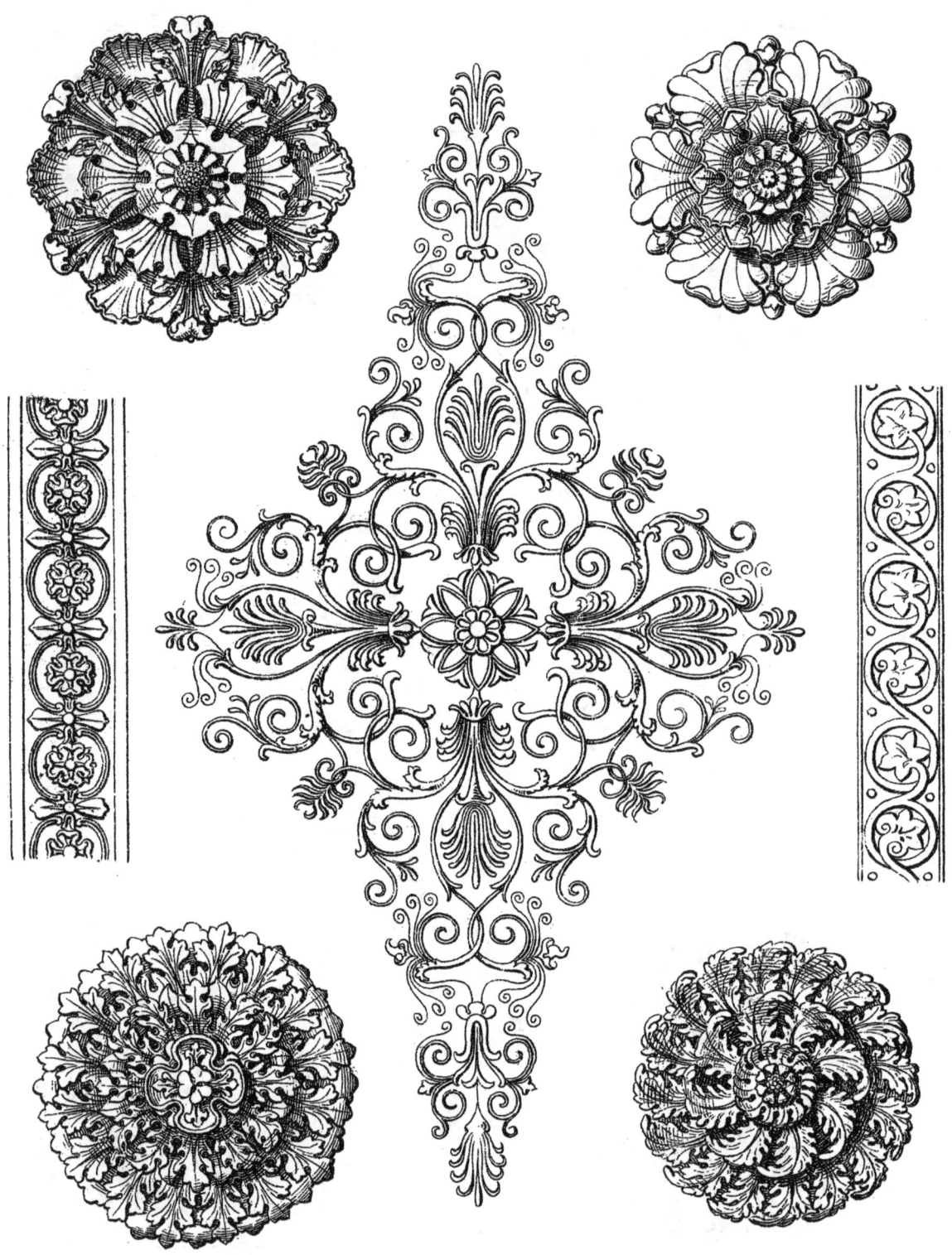

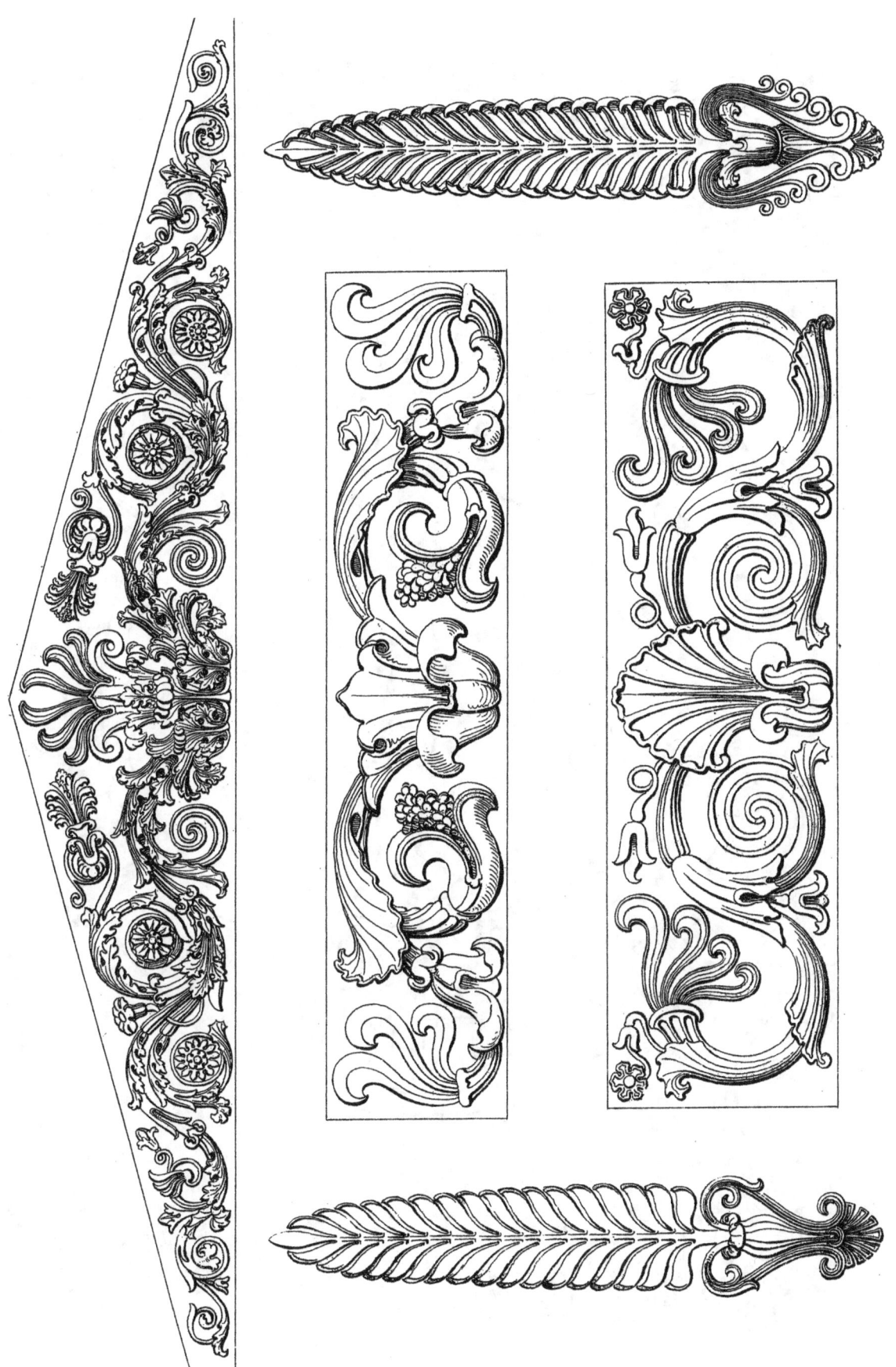

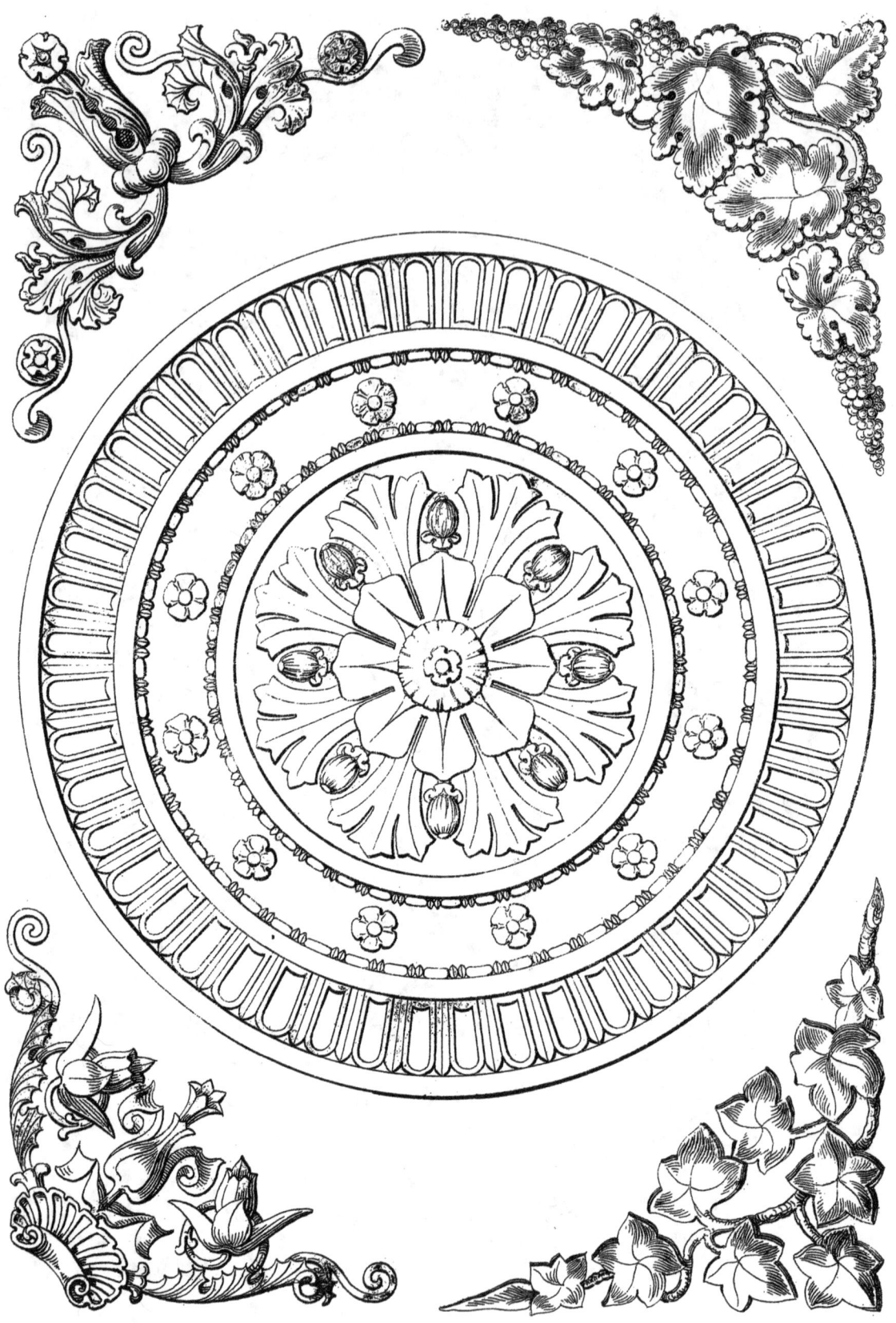

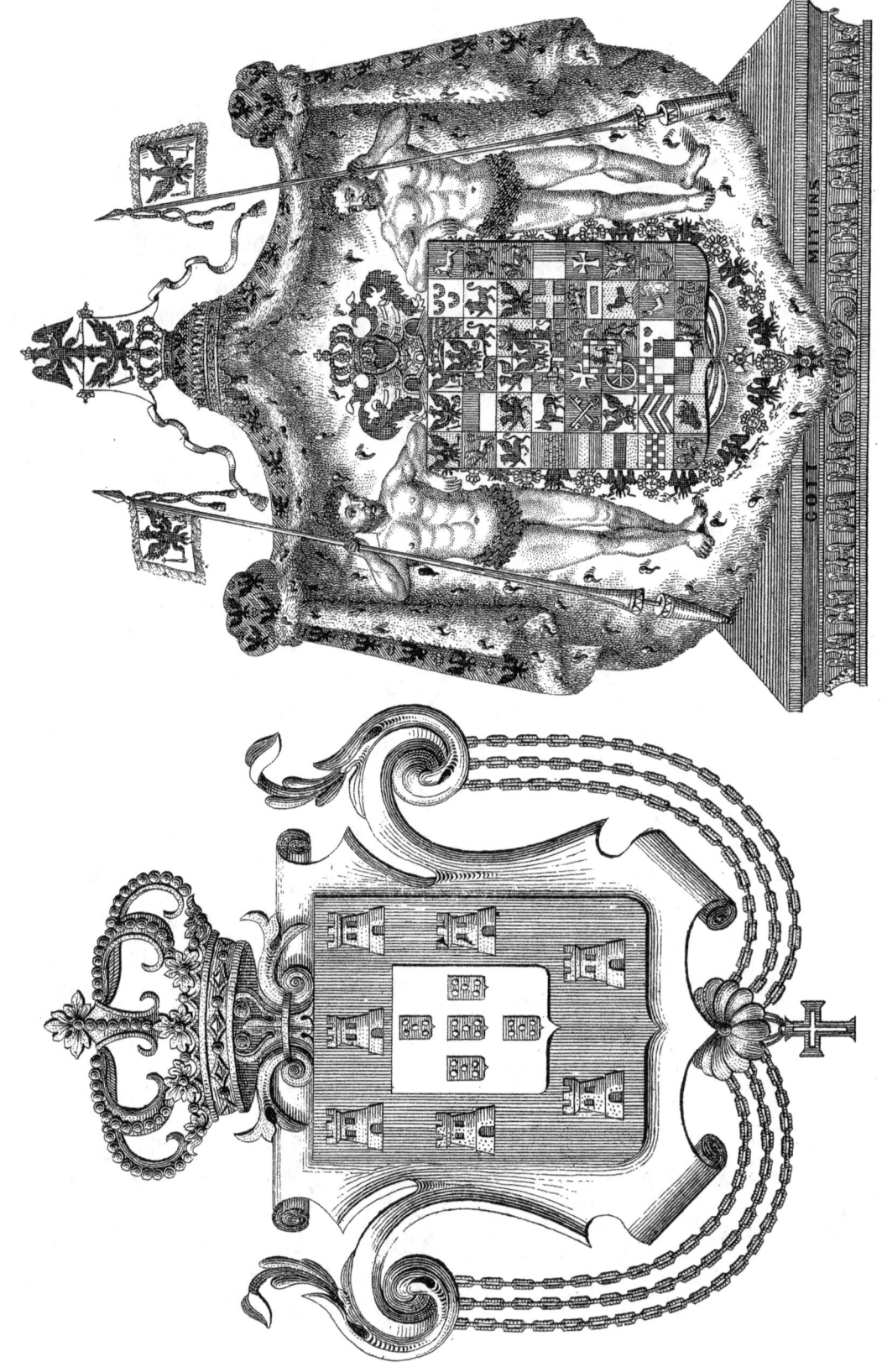

WAPPEN DES KÖNIGS VON PREUSSEN.

WAPPEN DES KÖNIGS VON PORTUGAL.

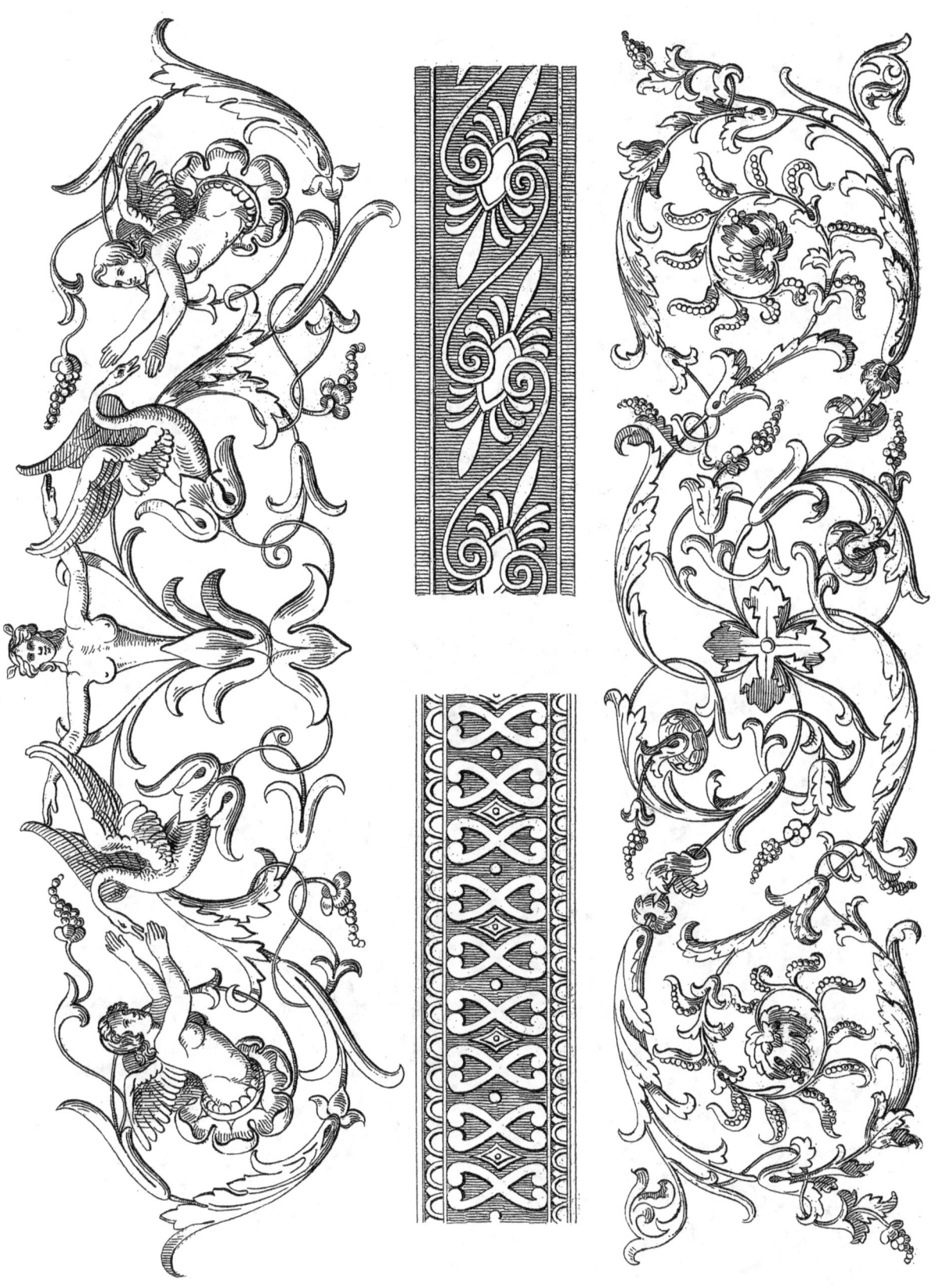

113

114

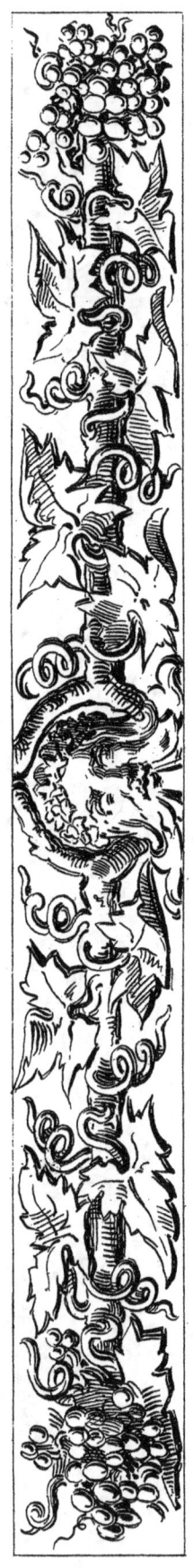
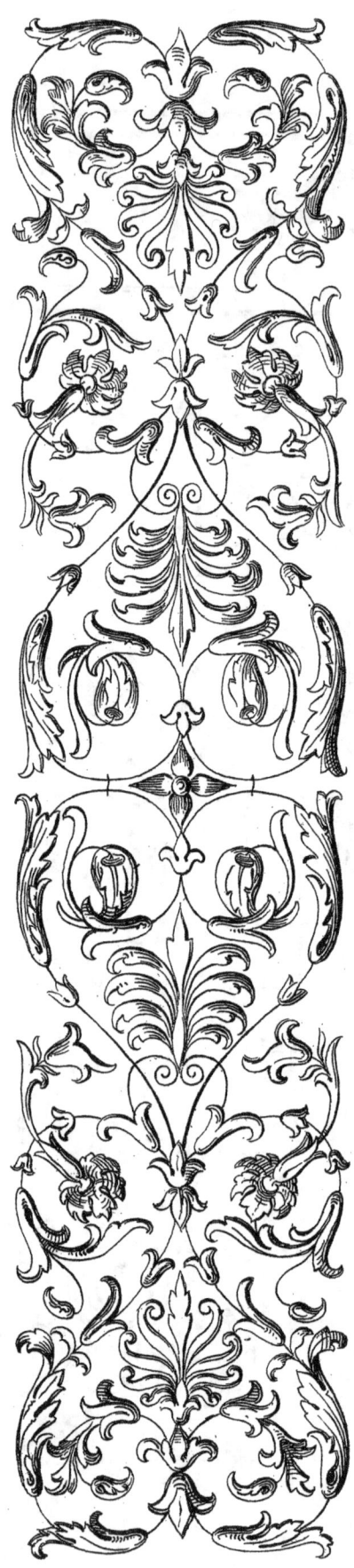
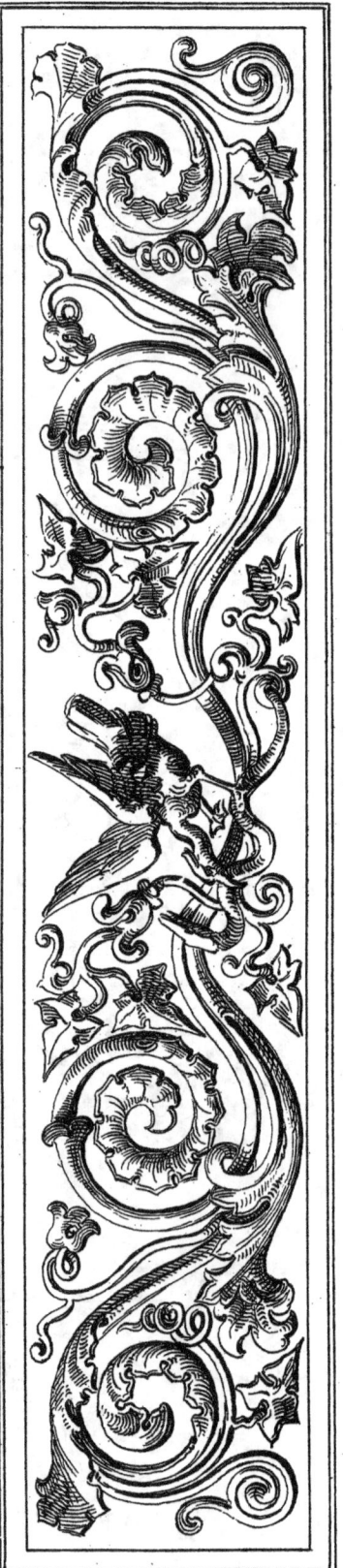

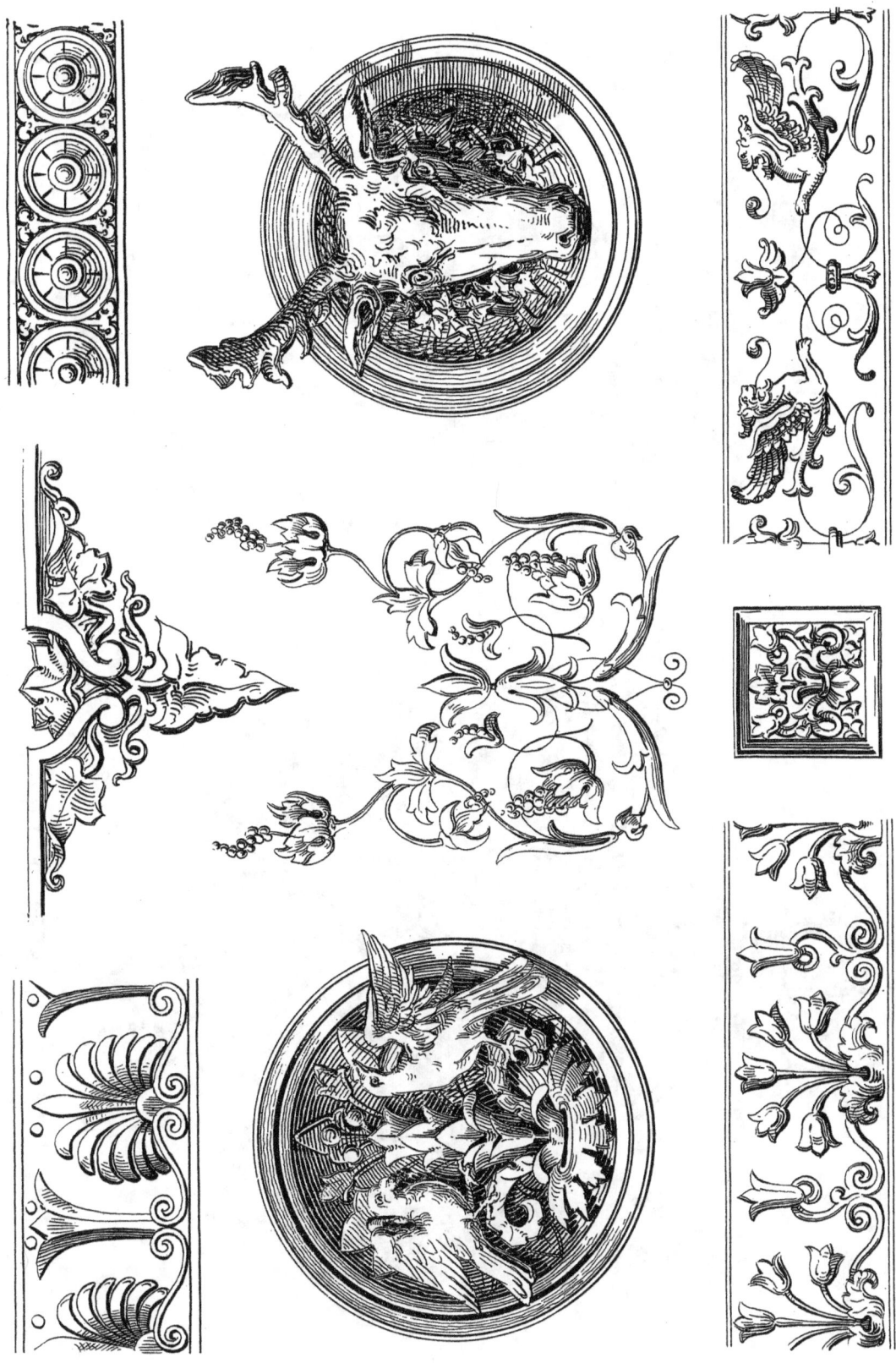

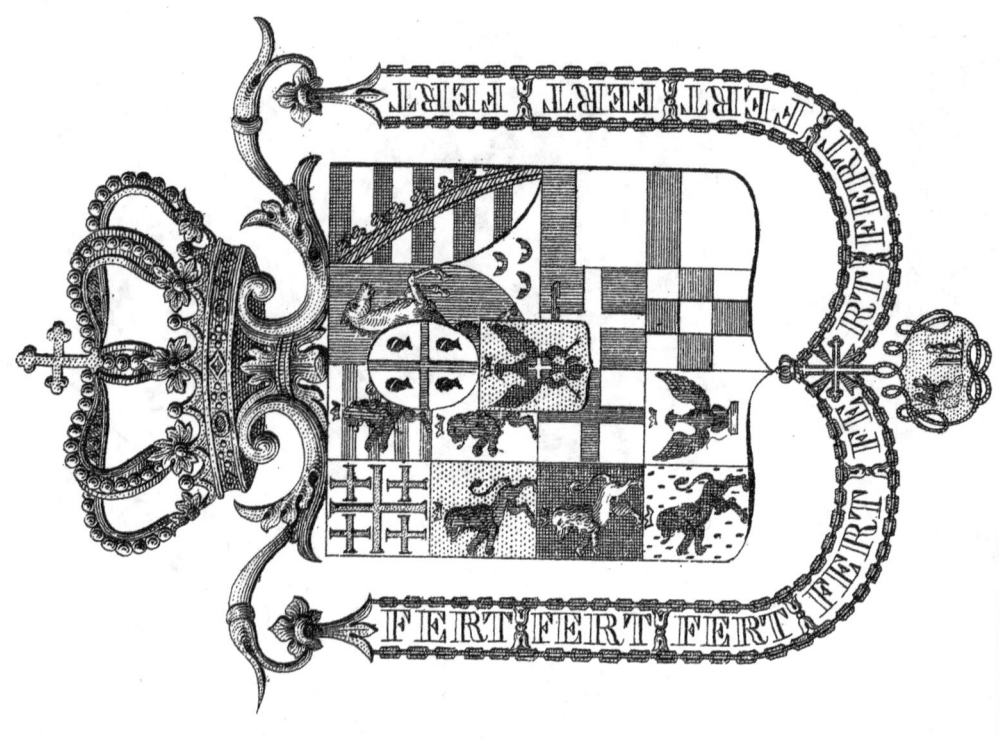

WAPPEN DES KÖNIGS VON SARDINIEN.

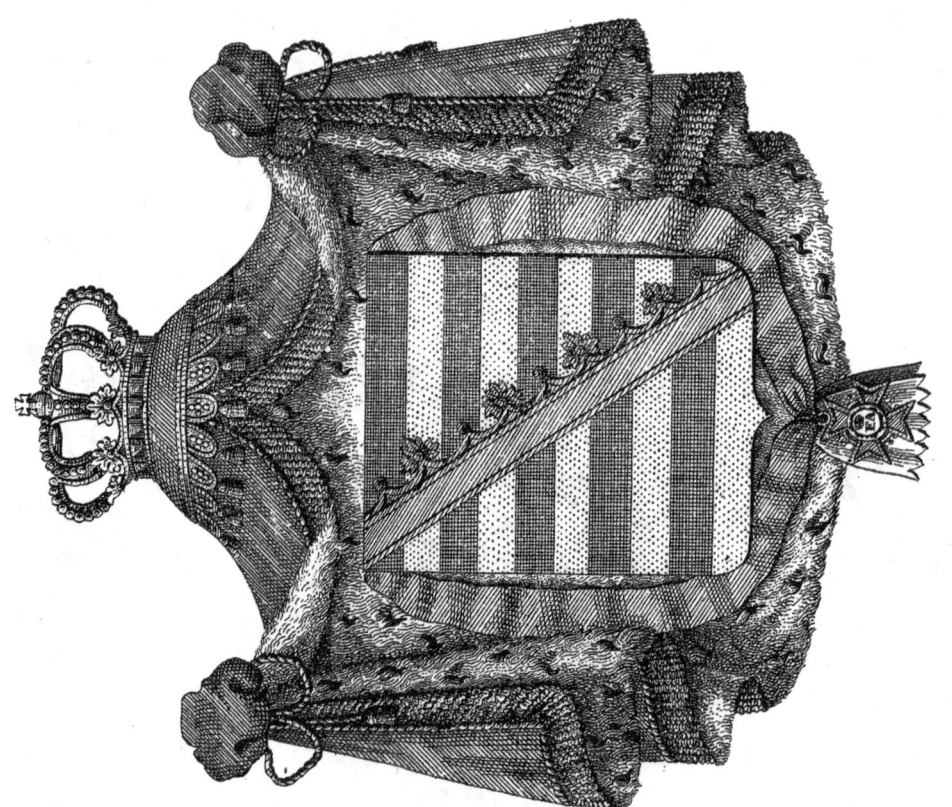

WAPPEN DES KÖNIGS VON SACHSEN.

118

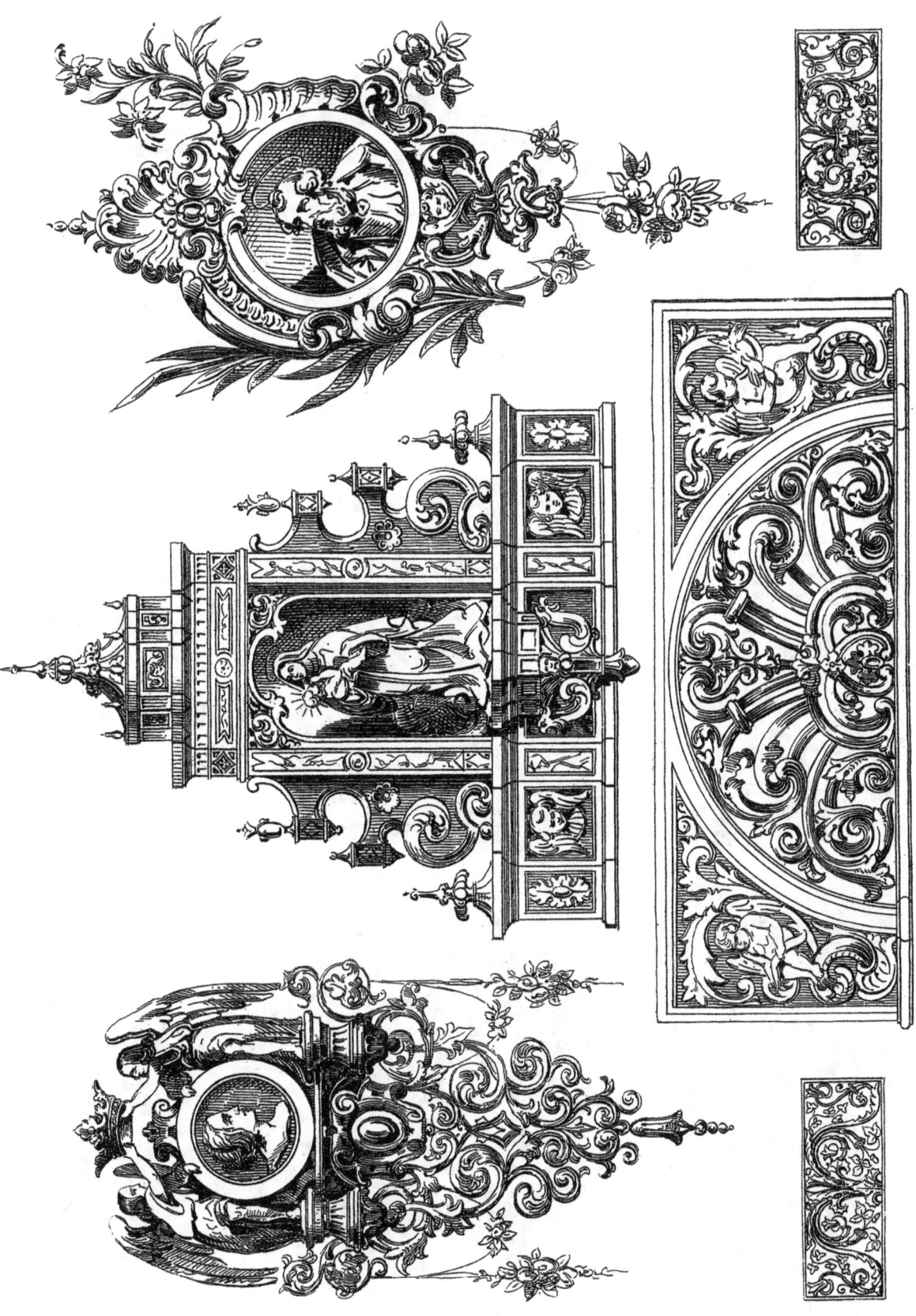

119

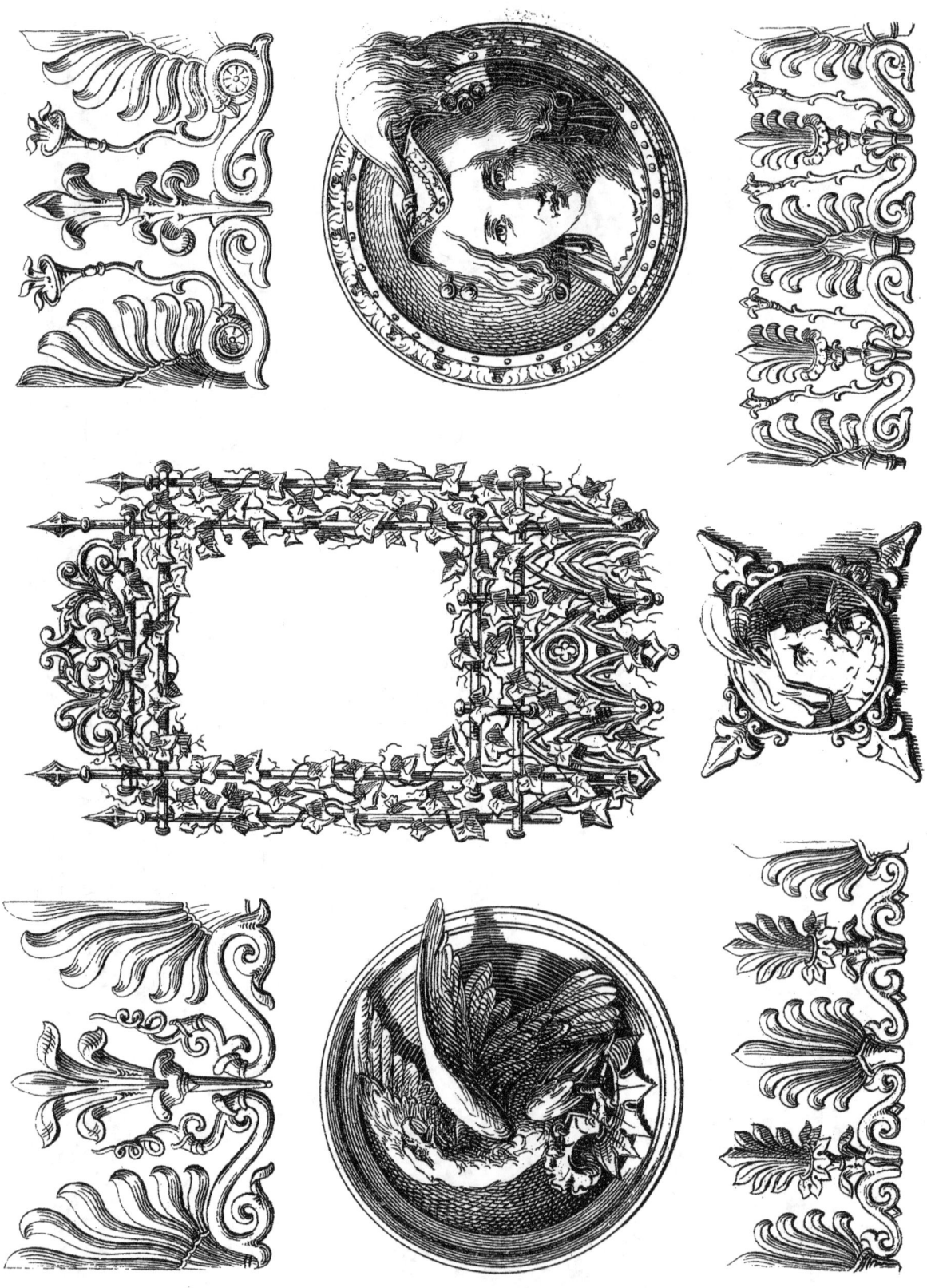

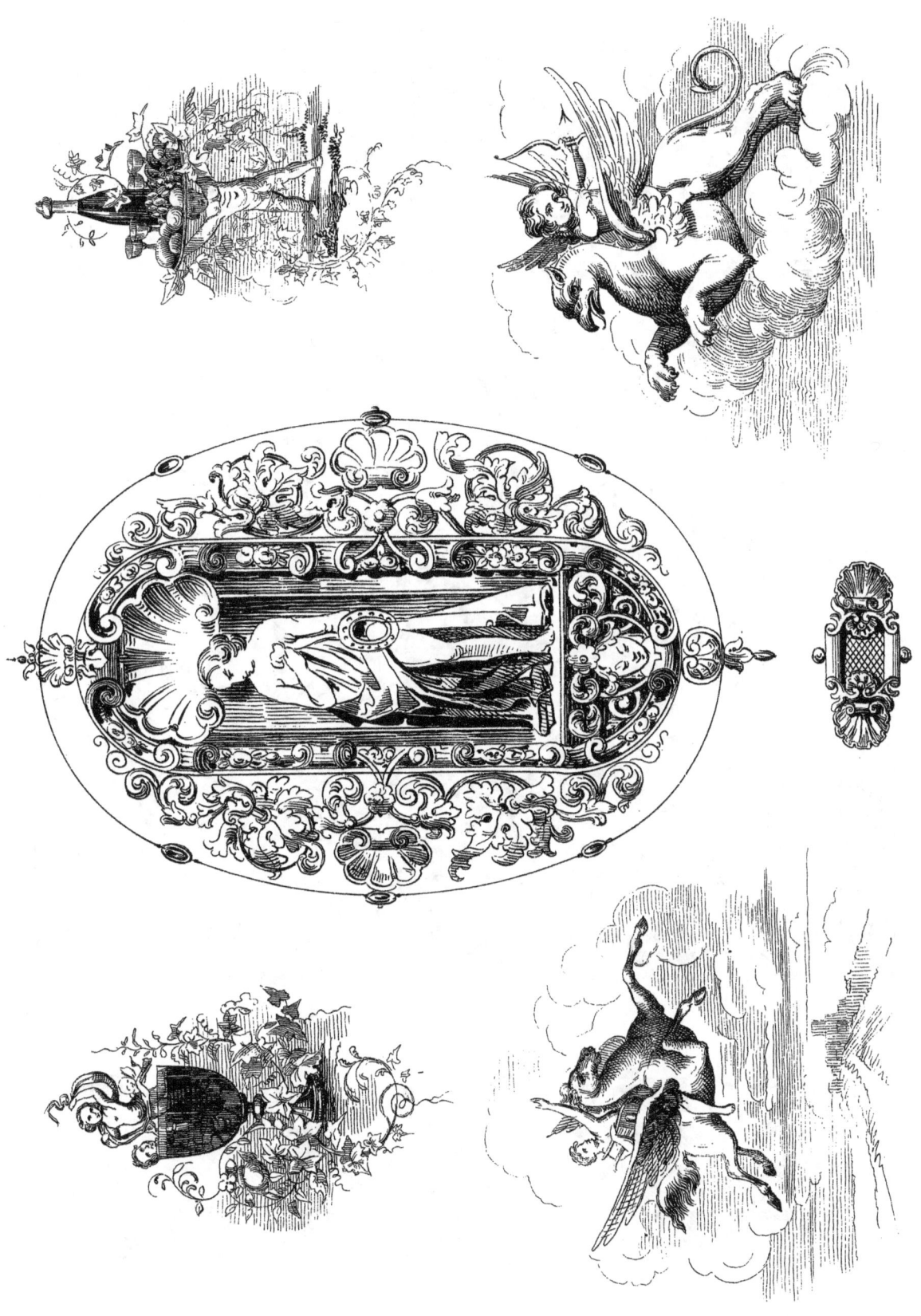

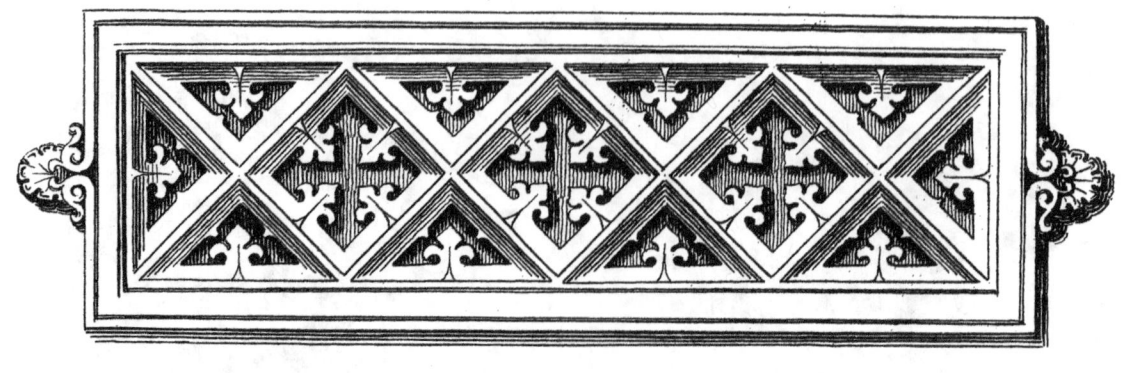

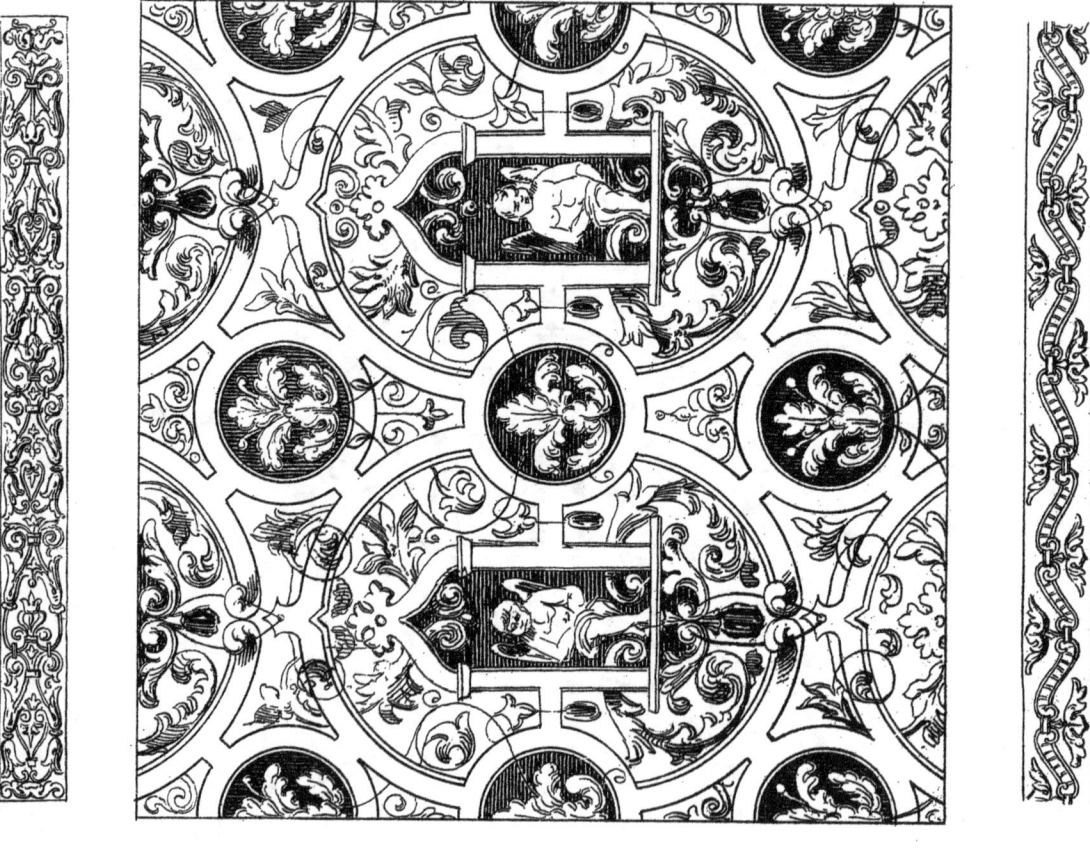

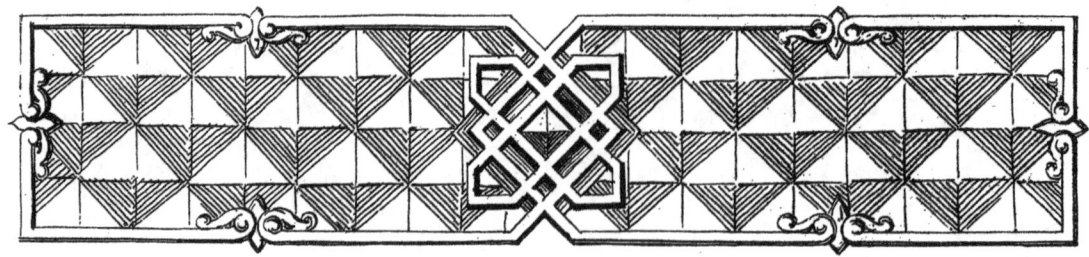

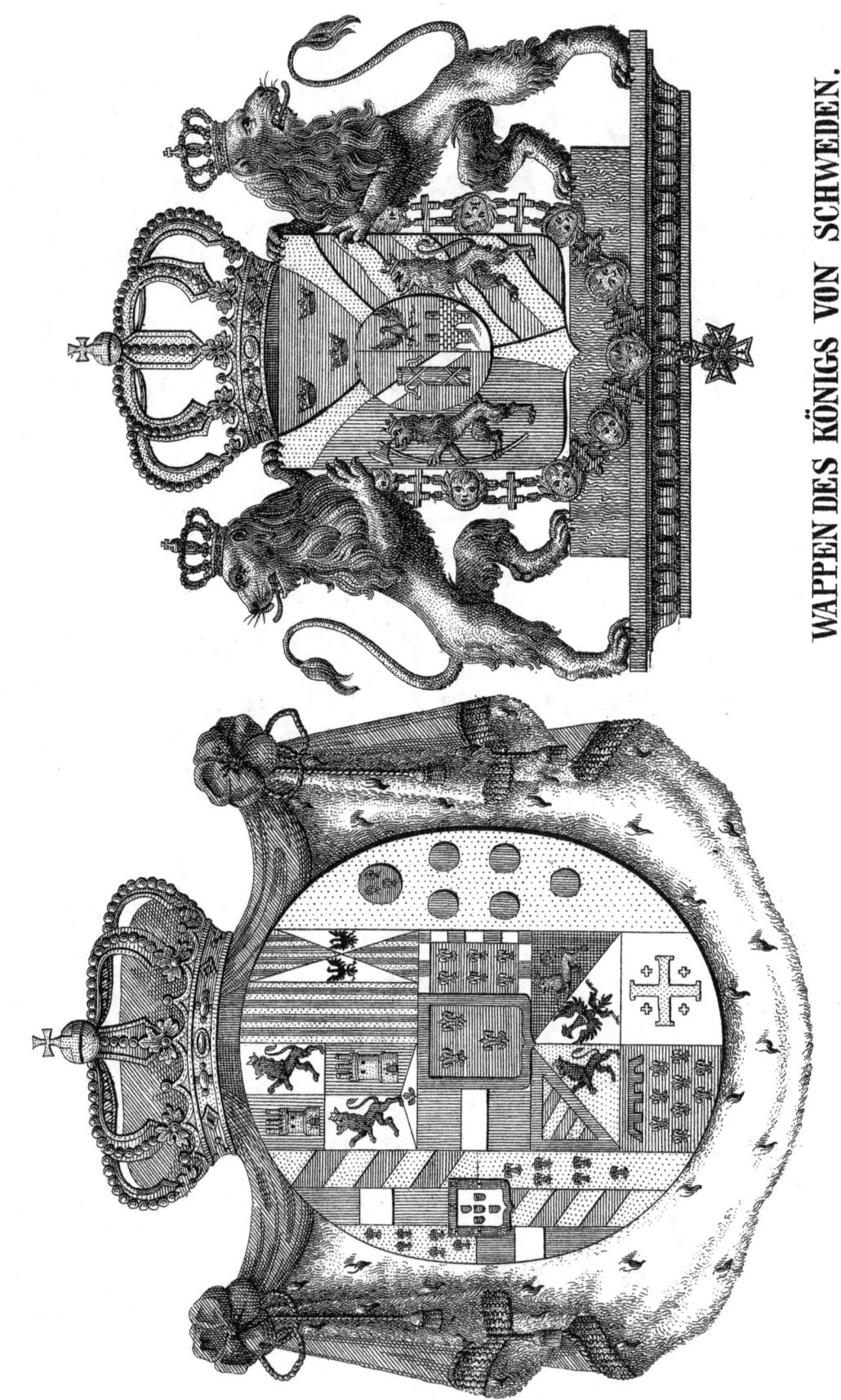

WAPPEN DES KÖNIGS VON SCHWEDEN.

WAPPEN DES KÖNIGS VON SICILIEN.

124

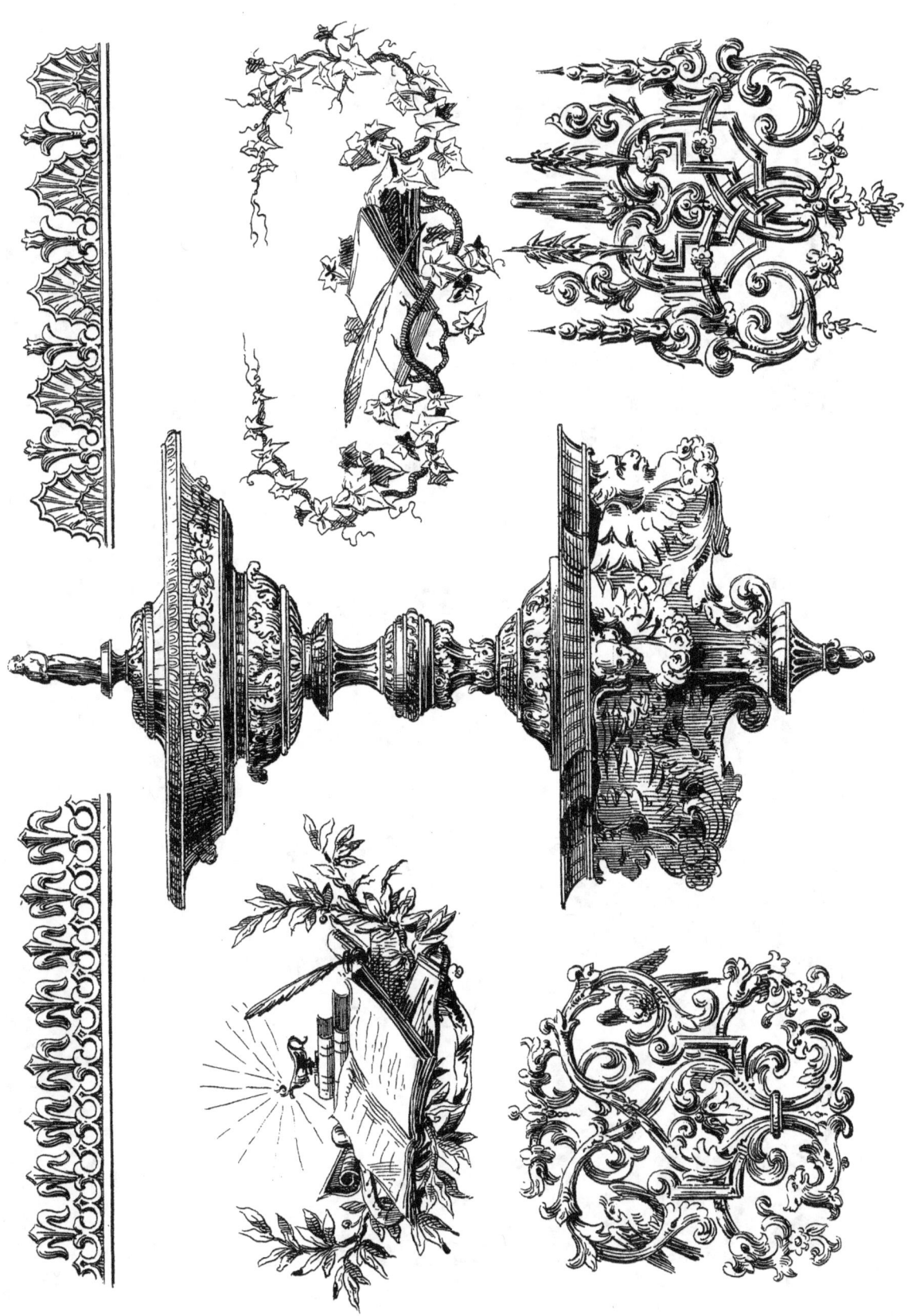

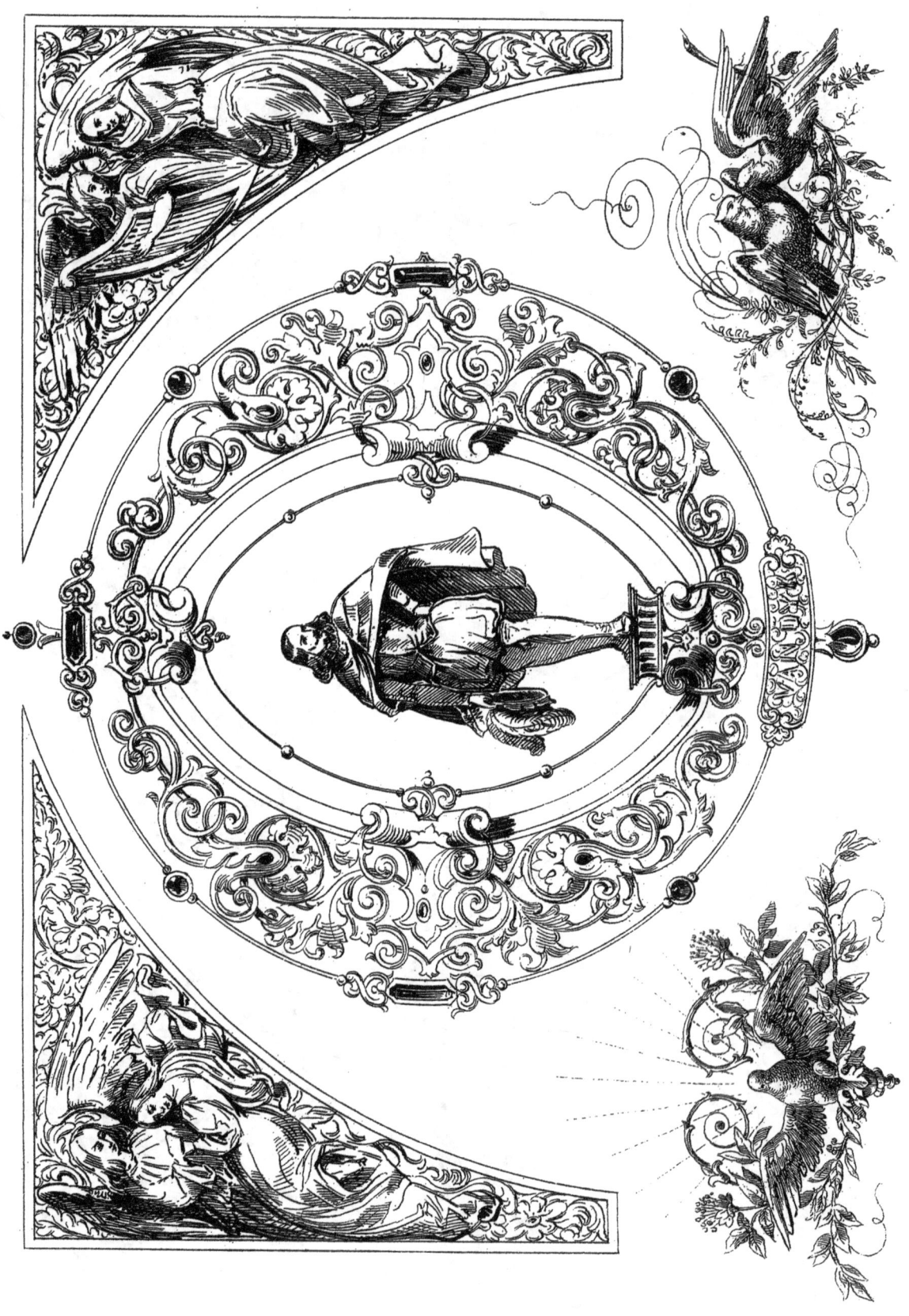

126

128

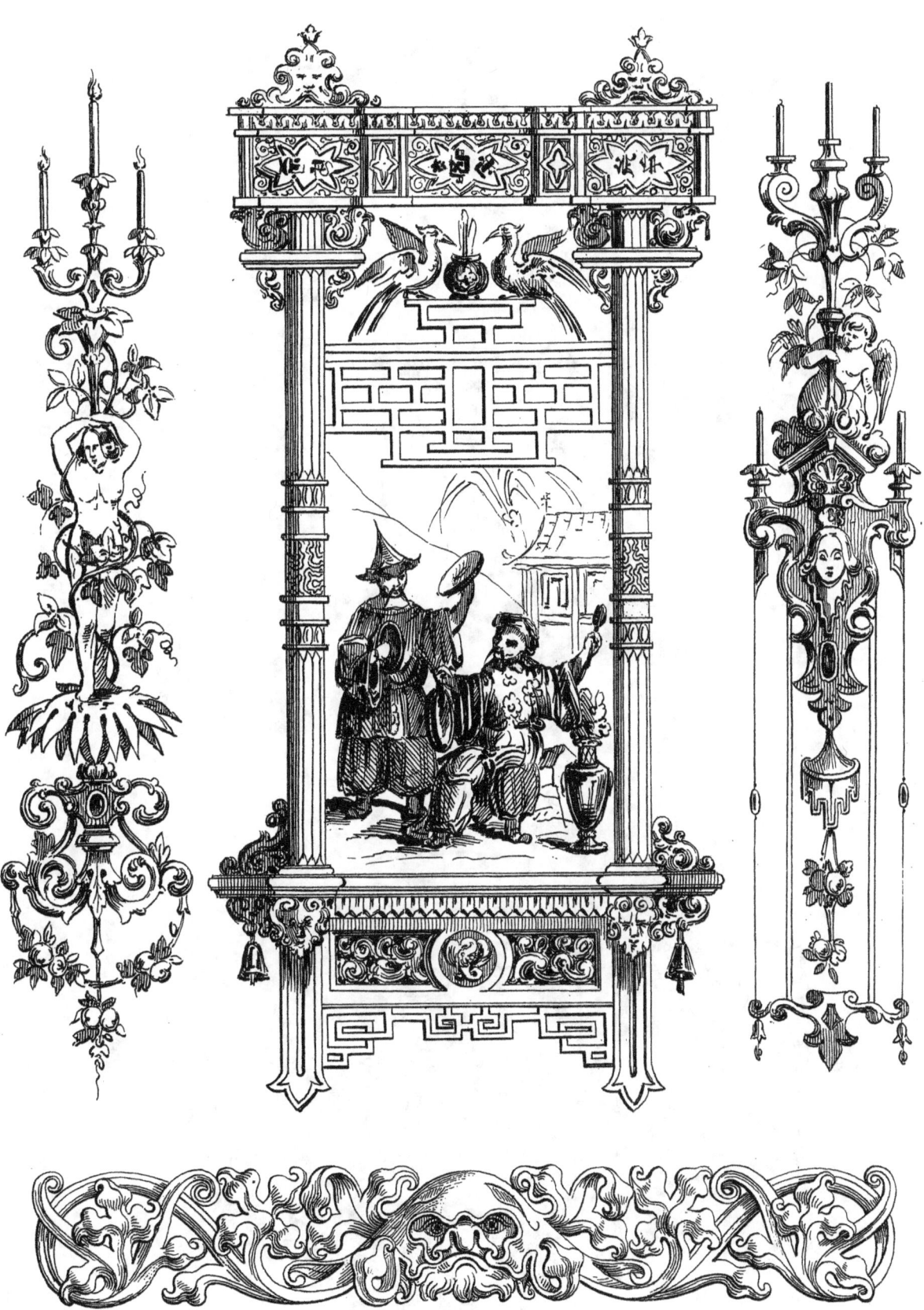

129

WAPPEN DES KÖNIGS VON WÜRTEMBERG

WAPPEN DES KÖNIGS VON SPANIEN.

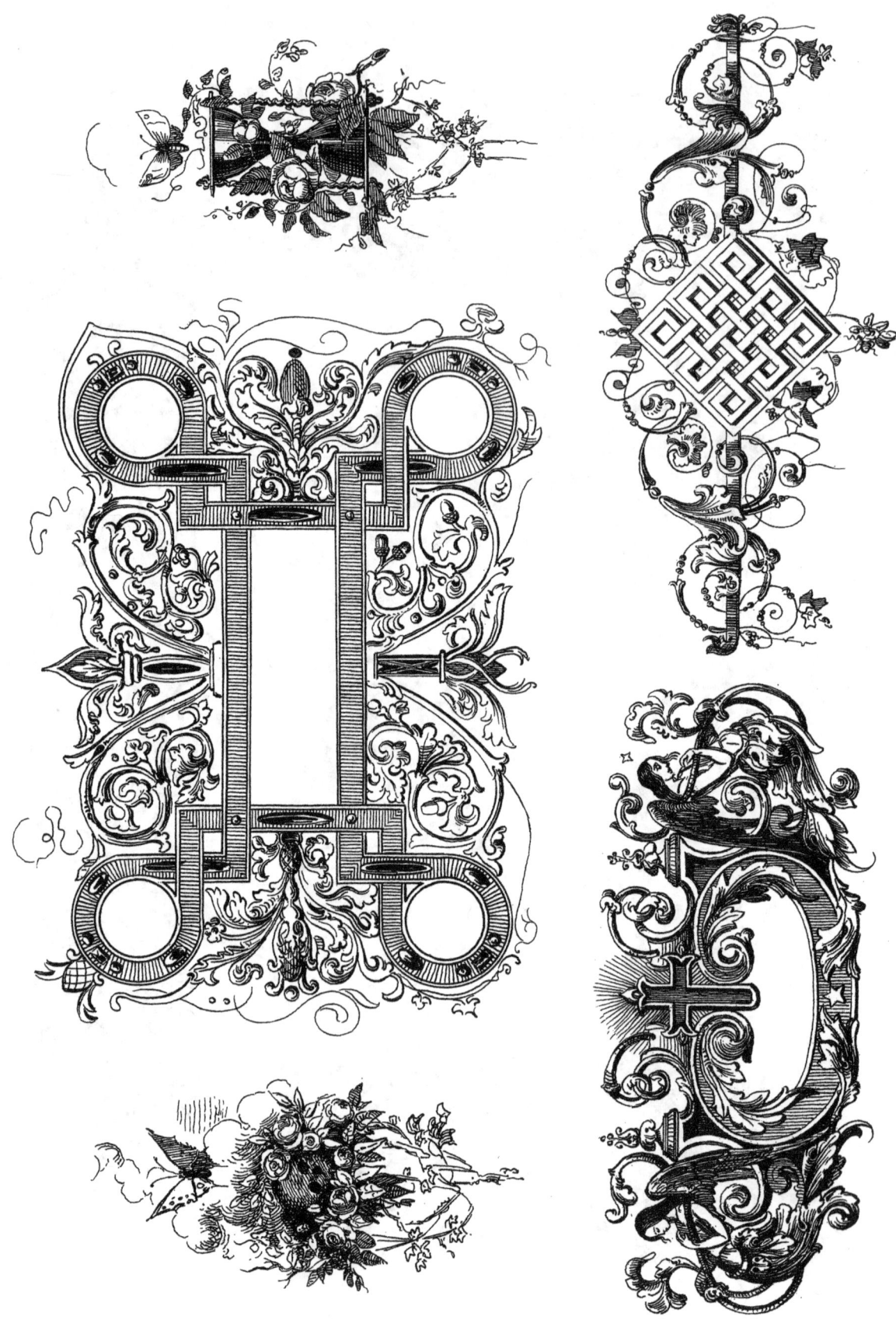

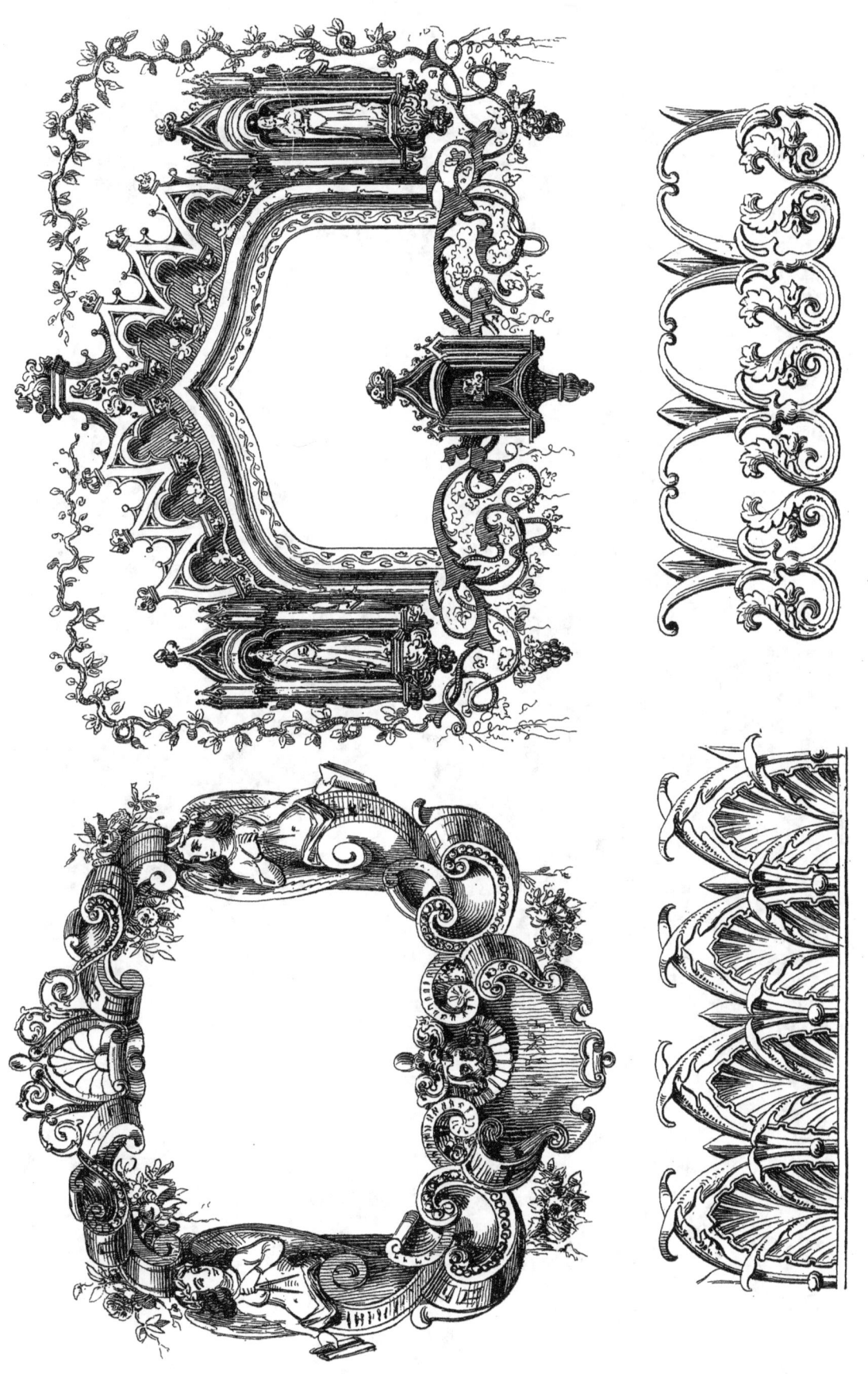

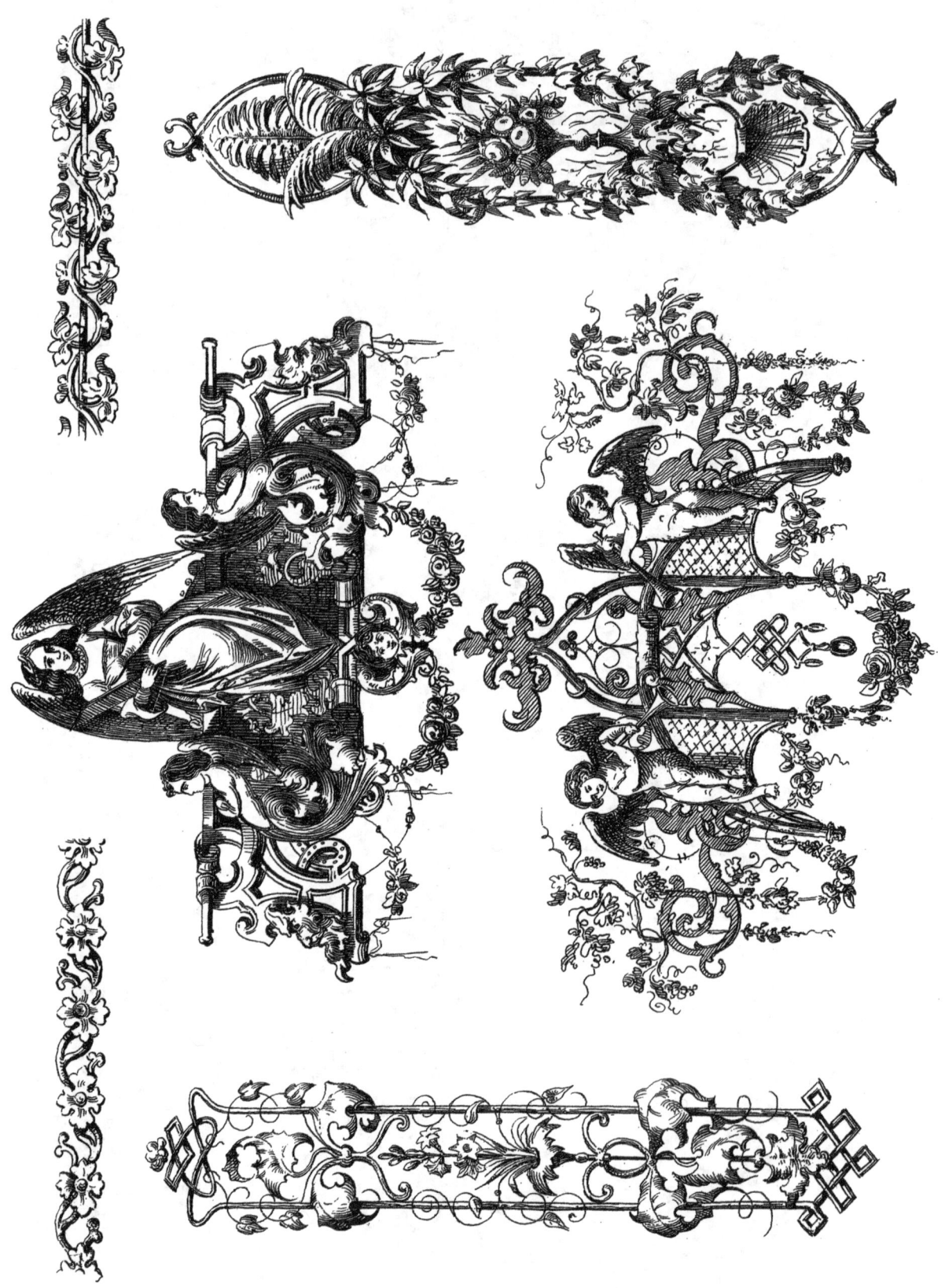

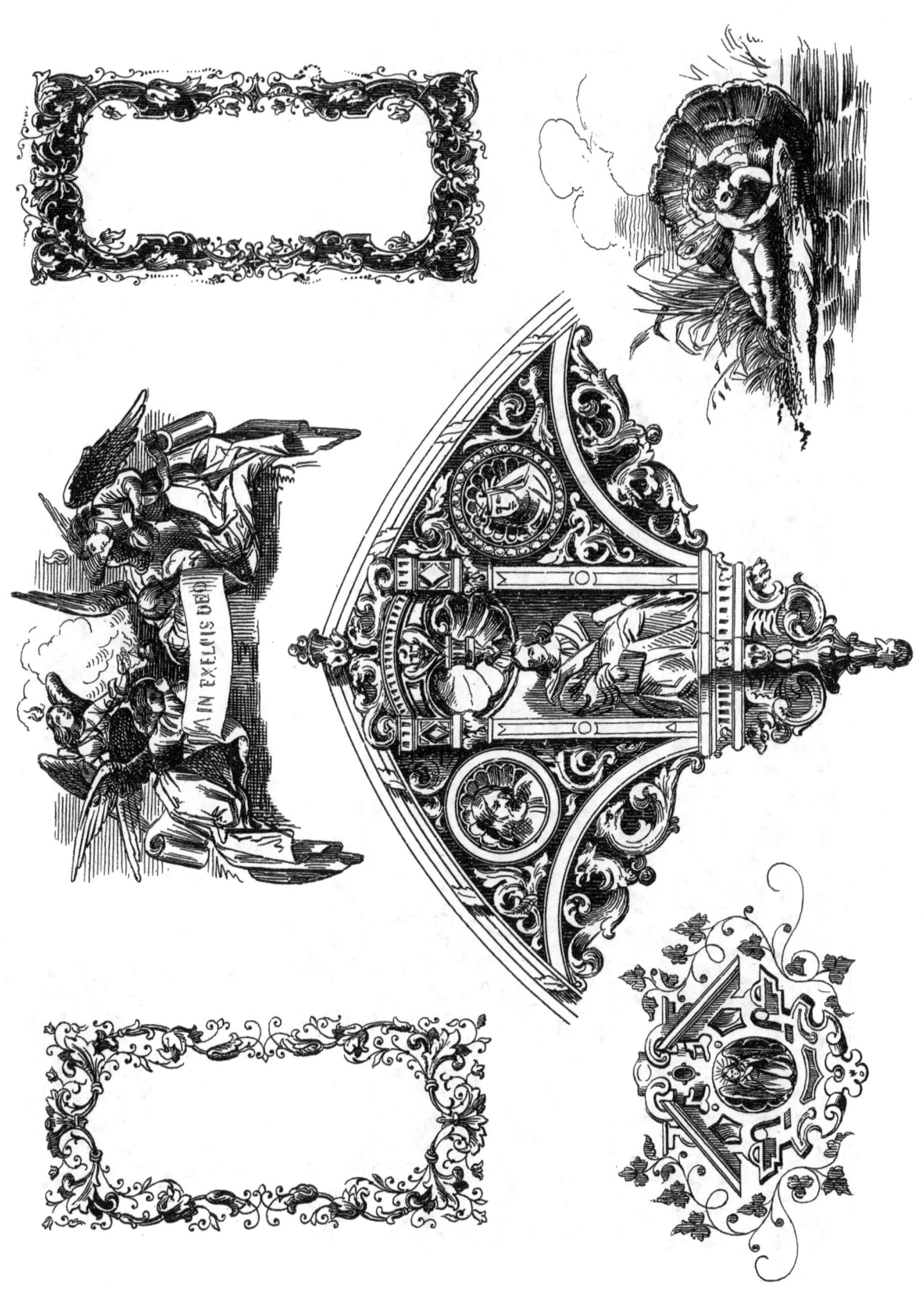

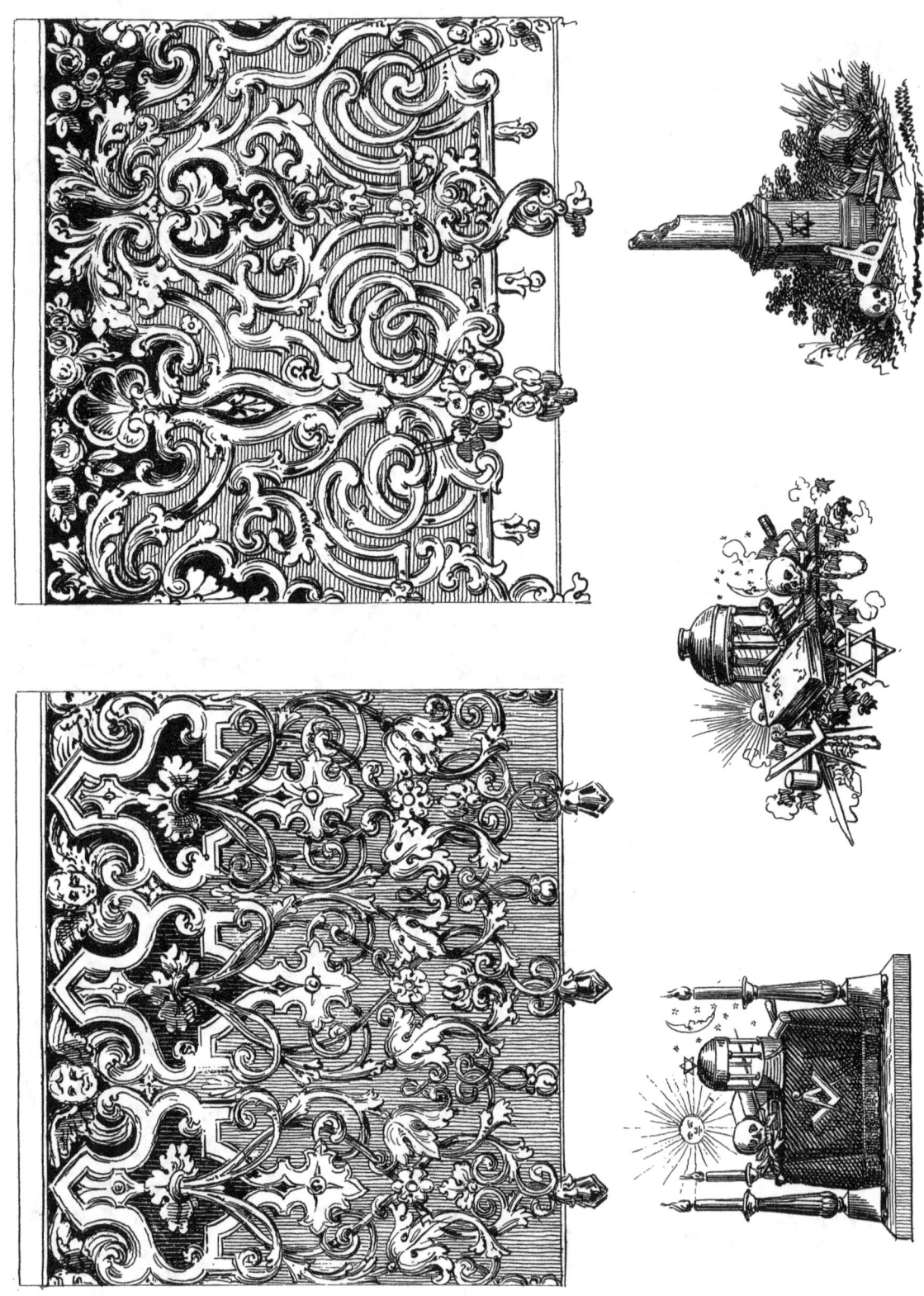

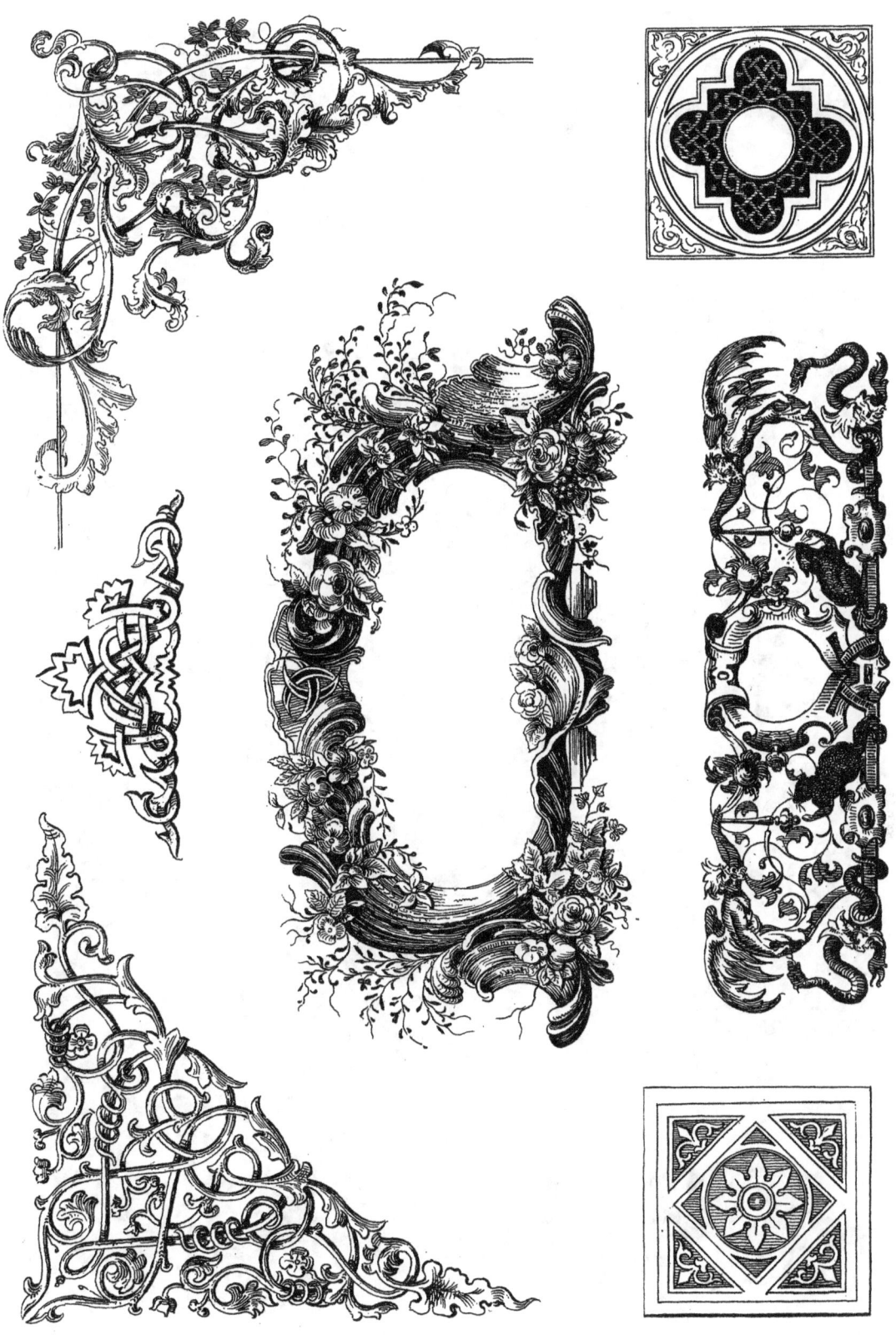

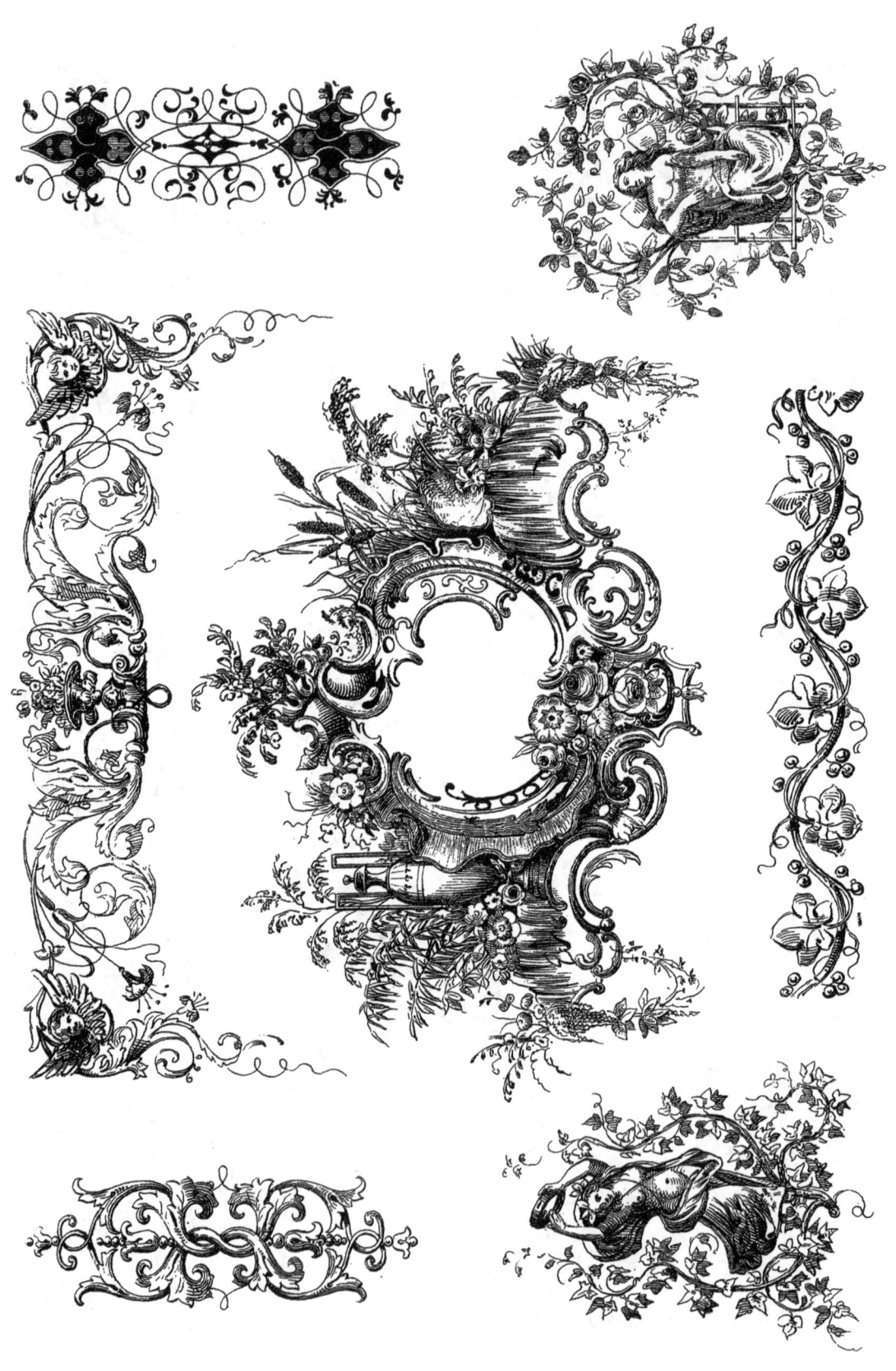

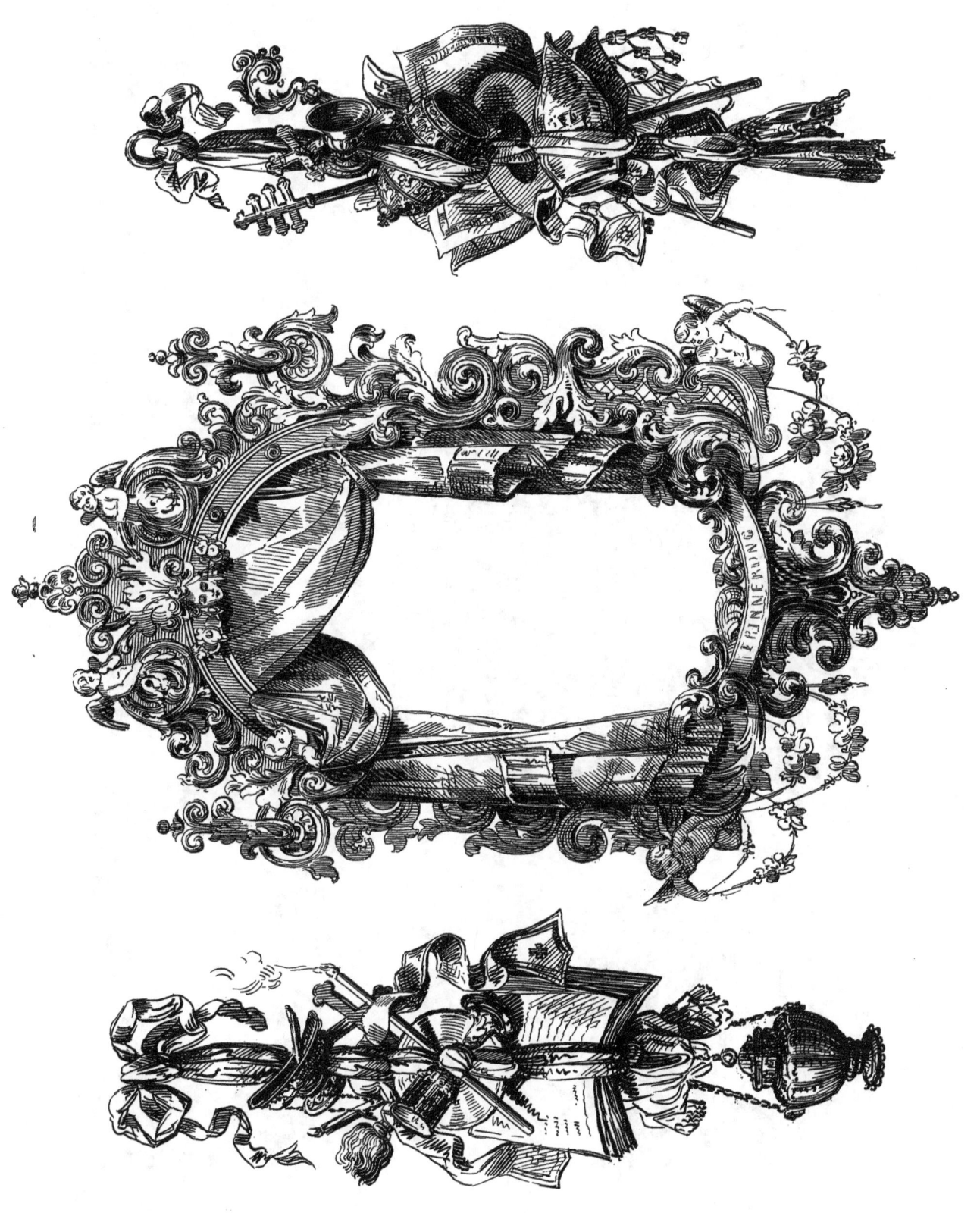

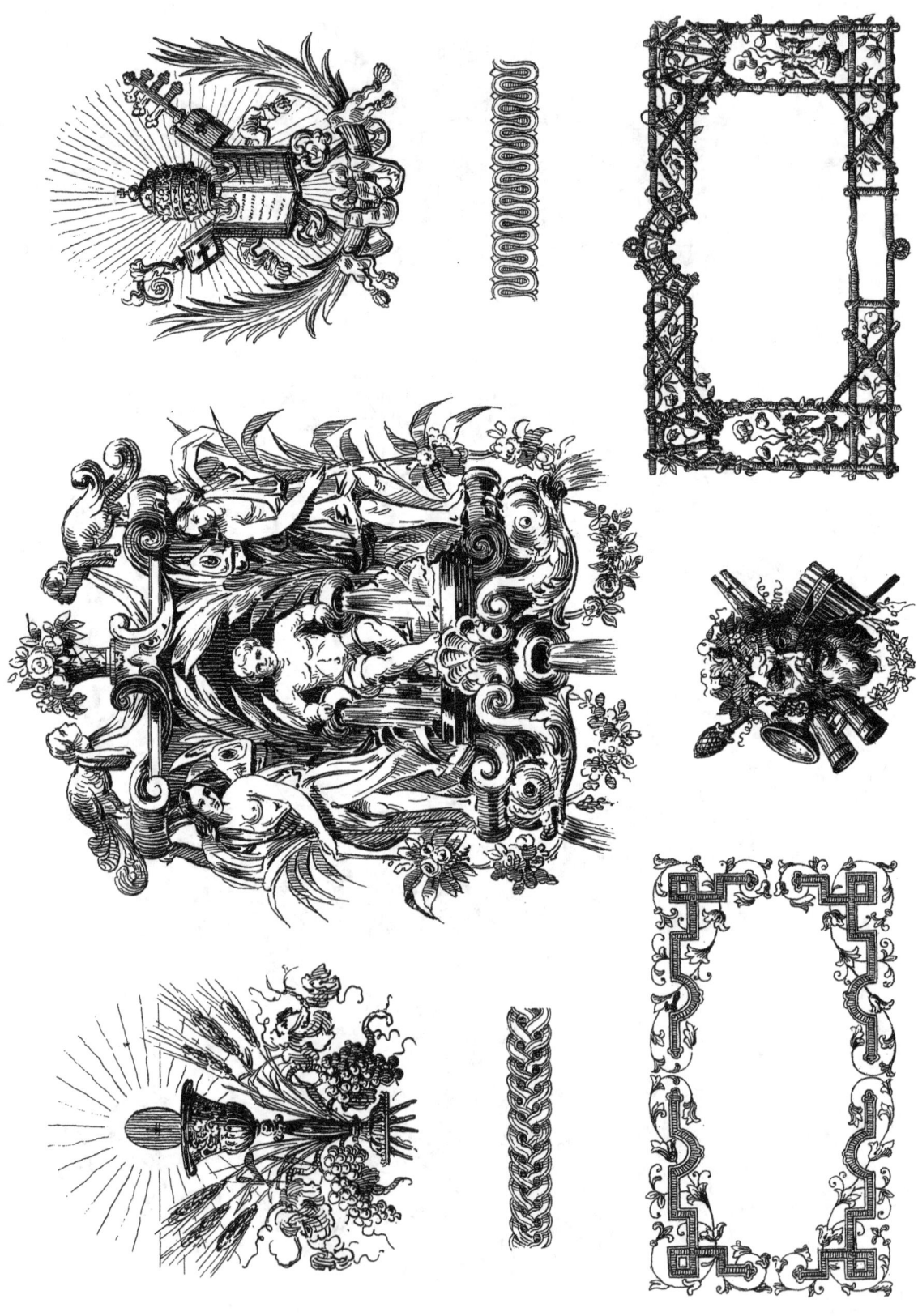

Die fünf Säulen nach ihrer Ordnung

Toscana. *Dorica.* *Jonica.*

zusammengestellt nach Vignola.

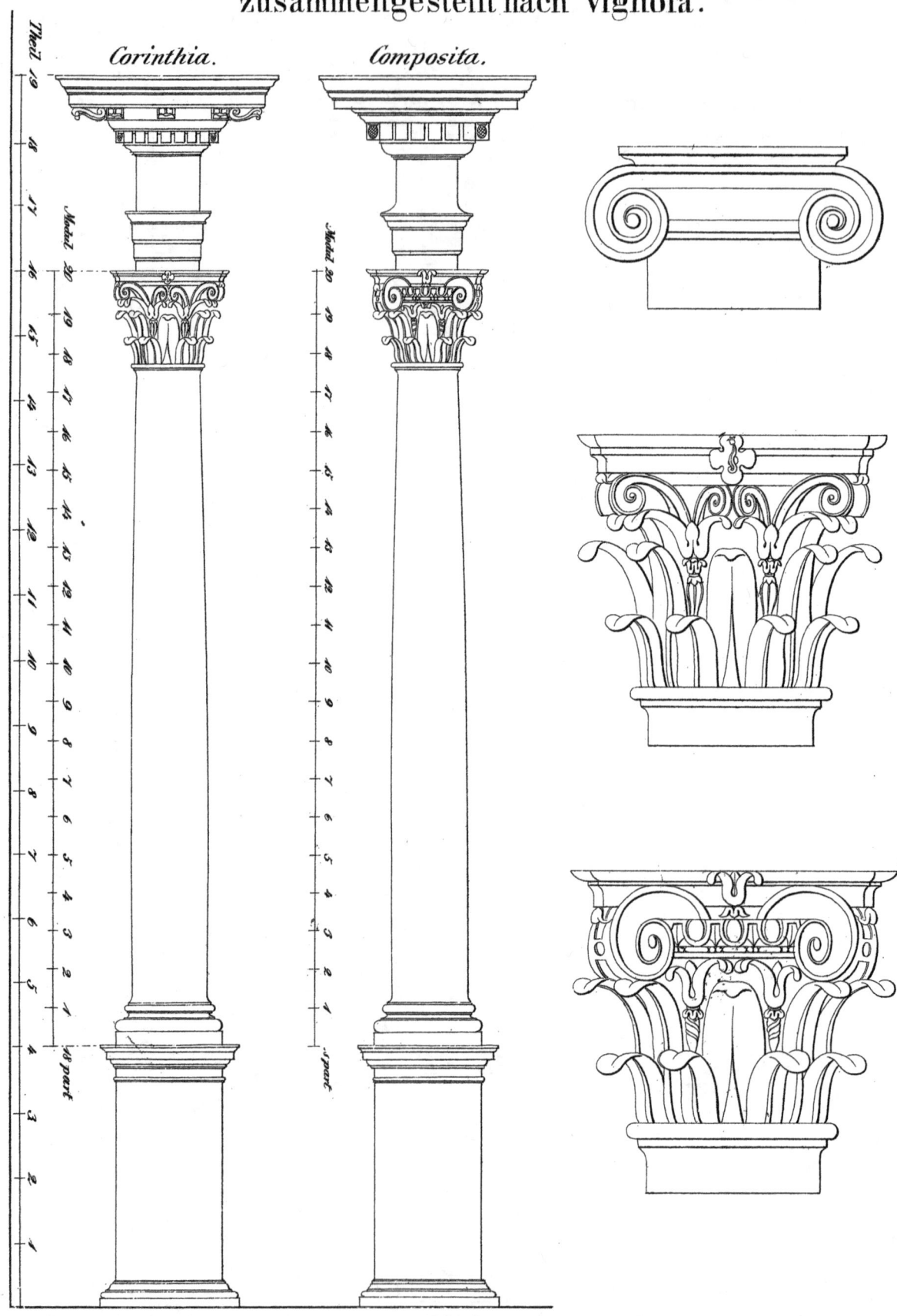

Corinthia.

Composita.